THE BON MARCHÉ

THE BON MARCHÉ

Bourgeois Culture and
the Department Store,
1869-1920

MICHAEL B. MILLER

PRINCETON UNIVERSITY PRESS
PRINCETON, NEW JERSEY

Copyright © 1981 by Princeton University Press

Published by Princeton University Press, Princeton, New Jersey
In the United Kingdom: Princeton University Press, Chichester, West Sussex

LIBRARY OF CONGRESS CATALOGING IN PUBLICATION DATA

Miller, Michael Barry, 1945-
The Bon Marché.

Bibliography: p.
Includes index.
1. Au Bon Marché, Paris—History.   2. France—
Social conditions.   I. Title.
HF5465. F835A95   381′.12′0944361   80-36797
ISBN 0-691-05321-9
ISBN 0-691-03494-X (pbk.)

First Princeton Paperback printing, 1994

Publication of this book has been aided by the
Paul Mellon Fund of Princeton University Press

This book has been composed in VIP Palatino

Princeton University Press books are printed on acid-free paper
and meet the guidelines for permanence and durability of the
Committee on Production Guidelines for Book Longevity of the
Council on Library Resources

Printed in the United States of America by Princeton Academic Press

3   5   7   9   10   8   6   4

Text designed by Laury A. Egan

TO MY MOTHER AND FATHER

Contents

List of Illustrations

1. The frontispiece of the 1911 *agenda*. At the top: Aristide and Marguerite Boucicaut. Below: views of the store in 1863, 1873 and 1910.

2. The monster exposition hall, dwarfing the city skyline. (From the frontispiece of the 1896 *agenda*.)

3. The colossus, wings outstretched, crowds crushing along the doors, a flurry of activity in the foreground. (From the frontispiece of the 1887 *agenda*.)

4. View of building with *gemeinschaftlich* foreground. (From the frontispiece of the 1888 *agenda*.)

5. The ribbons gallery (1886 *agenda*)

6. The rue de Sèvres entrance (1888 *agenda*)

7. The rue de Sèvres staircase during the *blanc* (1887 *agenda*)

8. The central staircase (1898 *agenda*)

9. The silk gallery (1879 *agenda*)

10. Winter concert in the store (1887 *agenda*)

11. Madame Boucicaut's funeral

12. The directors and council members posing for the *livre d'or*. Seated at the head of the table, from l. to r., are Ricois, Fillot, and Lucet.

13. *Demoiselles (livre d'or)*

14. Umbrella salesmen *(livre d'or)*

15. English lessons at night in the reading room (1887 *agenda*)

16. Fencing lessons (1887 *agenda*)

17. The reading room (1907 *agenda*)

18. Homage to Boucicaut (1900 fencing program)

19. The kitchen and main dining hall for employees (1901 *agenda*)

Acknowledgments

MANY PEOPLE have contributed in many ways to the writing of this book. First, I owe a special sense of gratitude to the *Direction* of the Bon Marché, and particularly to M. Alain Mathieu and M. Louis Mottin, for granting me access to store archives and for facilitating my research in countless other ways. Among the other members of the Bon Marché staff and personnel who dug up materials, answered my questions, and made my visit there a memorable one, I must single out M. Letourneur, M. Papon, M. Simonnot, Mlle. Leveque, Mlle. Parent, M. Poisson, M. Thomas, and Mlle. Fourgus.

Edward Selonick (of Shillito's), Michel Huber (of the University of Pennsylvania), and M. Levasseur (of the Associated Merchandising Corporation) all helped open doors for me in Paris. Special thanks in this regard must go to Derek Knee (of the International Association of Department Stores) and Mr. Daniel Roos.

François Gibault (great-grandson of Jules Plassard), Mme. Cotillon (daughter of Narcisse Fillot), M. and Mme. Philippe (granddaughter of Ernest Lucet), and M. Zédet (son of the administrator, Zédet) graciously answered questions about their parents or grandparents and made available several important documents. M. Pinet (former house archivist) was also kind enough to grant me an interview. M. Allégre (of Force Ouvrière) enabled me to review copies of employee newspapers not available in public archives. Mlle. Bonnard and M. Gombauty (of the Service des Recueils at the Bibliothèque Nationale) went out of their way to make available the publicity materials under their jurisdiction. Pierre Traissac (of the Louvre Department Store) allowed me to review what few store documents are available and willingly took time to answer my questions. I was equally well received by M. Naudet (of the Samaritaine) and by M. André Berthault and Mlle. Solange Dumuis (of the Printemps). Pierre Bizet is to be credited for his excellent photographs of Bon Marché materials, a number of which appear in this edition.

Finally I wish to thank those historians whose advice, patience, and goodwill have contributed to the completion of this book. Bob Rosen, Tom Cochran, Jim Davis, and especially Jack Reece were all helpful in the writing of the dissertation upon which this book is based. During my stay in Paris, Maurice Lévy-Leboyer offered me much assistance. My knowledge of business history, and of many other things, has been enriched by my association with Alfred D. Chandler, Jr. During a postdoctoral year (supported by the Harvard-Newcomen postdoctoral fellowship), Professor Chandler, Albro Martin, and Tom McCraw read parts of the manuscript. Their comments have been much appreciated. So too have been the comments of Richard Herr. Martin Wiener has read the entire manuscript. My debts to him are too numerous to mention. Other colleagues (and friends) who have read parts of the manuscript, and whose advice and support have been invaluable, are Richard Smith, Allen Matusow, Francis Loewenheim, and Charles Garside, Jr. A last set of special thanks must go to my typist, Linda Quaidy.

THE BON MARCHÉ

Introduction

THE PARISIAN DEPARTMENT STORE of the late nineteenth century stood as a monument to the bourgeois culture that built it, sustained it, marvelled at it, found its image in it. In its inspiration it captured that culture's entrepreneurial drive to master and organize the material world to its advantage. In its architecture it brought together the culture's commitment to functionalize its environment and the culture's irrepressible need to secure solidity and respectability for its works. In its values it flaunted the culture's identification with appearances and material possessions, reaffirmed the culture's dedication to productivity, personified the culture's pretensions to an egalitarian society. The department store was the bourgeoisie's world. It was the world of leisurely women celebrating a new rite of consumption. It was the world of clerks, civil in their manners, respectable in their dress, conscious of the service expected of them, laying claims to bourgeois status. It was the world of deliveries in an age when every bourgeois household maintained servants to receive them. It was the world of opulent displays that reminded the onlooker of all that bourgeois culture was capable of producing. It was, indeed, a world where bourgeois culture itself was on display. Bourgeois costumes, bourgeois occasions, bourgeois ambitions—the very range of bourgeois life style—were to be found on the store's shelves and counters and floors. The department store was, in short, a bourgeois celebration, an expression of what its culture stood for and where it had come over the past century.

But if the department store mirrored the style of a culture and the creations of an age, the reflection could be as disquieting as it was gratifying. More than a wondrous instrument of the culture it was designed to serve (and profit from), the department store was a commitment to certain paths that

culture was coming to follow. It was a commitment to assembling thousands of employees in a single work place. It
was a commitment to an organizing principle requiring a
meticulous division of labor, a super-imposition of several
hierarchical levels of command, and a systematization of the
entire work process. It was a commitment to a production
principle based on quantity and economy of costs and to a
consumption principle based on self-indulgence. It was a
commitment to making the accoutrements of bourgeois culture available to seemingly unlimited numbers of Frenchmen
and Frenchwomen. The department store was not only the
bourgeoisie's world; it was the most visible symbol of how
that world was changing. The store's bureaus reflected the
proliferation of offices that could be found in insurance companies, banks, railroad companies, and some industrial concerns. The store's clerks and managers reflected the expansion of the bourgeoisie into sizeable new groups and the
mushrooming of organizational positions that were coming
to characterize middle-class careers. The store's clientele reflected the throngs who were flocking to summer resorts, the
swarms who were packing the city mass transit, the crowds
who were reading the new mass press. The store's sales reflected the cluster of bourgeois uniforms to be seen in the
crush along city boulevards or on Sunday strolls through city
parks. Much of this the bourgeois could admire, much he
could see as the logical realization of his culture. But bourgeois culture in France had other roots, roots of thrift and
self-restraint, of a sense of community that stressed stability
and harmony and the natural exercise of authority that came
with familiarity in its relationships, roots that worshipped individual fulfillment and an independent place in society,
roots that longed for distinction from those on lower social
rungs, roots that believed in the family as the fundamental
and most reliable of organizing principles; and so, much of
this was troubling as well because it clashed with other values
and traditions the bourgeoisie held dear. How to reconcile
this world the bourgeoisie was bringing forth with the one it

had earlier come to form was a critical question bourgeois culture was to face by the latter part of the nineteenth century.

This study of the Bon Marché Department Store is about this search for reconciliation. It is an examination of how the institution that was so clearly the child of bourgeois culture, mirroring its triumphs and prodding its anxieties, served as an arena for the accommodation of that culture to the coming of a mass, bureaucratized age. By institution I have meant the department store, generically speaking, but I might just as well have meant the Bon Marché; for no Parisian *grand magasin** of the nineteenth century was so associated with the department store in the French mind as was the Bon Marché. In the years before the First World War the Bon Marché was the quintessential big store. It was the world's largest department store, and if its claim to being the world's first was somewhat askew, few people if any were willing to argue. When Emile Zola decided to write a novel about department stores (appropriately because "I wish, in *Au bonheur des dames*, to create the poetry of modern activity"),[1] he began his research at the Bon Marché. Certainly no other department store spawned so many namesakes around the world. If the department store, then, has struck me as a central reflection of the milieu and dilemma of bourgeois culture before the First World War, the Bon Marché has equally struck me as the proper vehicle for a case study of how bourgeois France sought to come to terms with an emerging mass, bureaucratic society.

More specifically, what I have chosen to focus on in this study is the process by which the individuals who built and ran the Bon Marché sought to create new sets of social relationships, perceptions, and roles that would permit the adaptation of themselves, their work force, their clientele, and the bourgeois public to the changing society that the department

* Department store.
[1] Emile Zola, Notes for *Au bonheur des dames*, Bibliothèque Nationale, NAF10277, p. 2. For the novel, Emile Zola, *Au bonheur des dames* (Paris: Charpentier, 1883). Page references are from the Livre de Poche édition, Paris, 1960.

store represented and was itself helping to bring about. In so doing I have attempted to bring to life the world of the Bon Marché which was so much a part of the bourgeoisie's culture and its historical flux. The term "bourgeois culture" I have chosen to define in an inclusive rather than exclusive sense. I have identified it, not by what was uniquely bourgeois, but by what characterized bourgeois values, behavior, life style, and relationships, and the institutional expressions in which these were embodied. My purpose has been to portray the diverse and dynamic sides of this culture—how it was composed of many elements and how its multiformity, molded by changes often of its own making, created fundamental conflicts in need of resolution.

A history of the Bon Marché is by definition a business history. But it is business history of a different sort. Traditionally, business historians, especially those engaged in writing the history of an individual firm, have looked upon themselves as economic historians analyzing the economic (or business) performance of the firm at hand. They have been concerned with questions of entrepreneurship, investment, growth, markets, private and public constraints, and the like. This has been characteristic of the business history of America, Great Britain, and the few excellent business histories that we possess on French firms.[2] It has also been the case where the genre of department store studies is concerned.[3]

[2] See for example Patrick Fridenson, *Histoire des usines Renault* (Paris: Editions du Seuil, 1972); François Caron, *Histoire de l'exploitation d'un grand réseau* (La Haye: Mouton, 1973).

[3] For professional studies on department stores, see Ralph Hower, *History of Macy's of New York 1858-1919* (Cambridge: Harvard University Press, 1976); Borris Emmet and John Jeuck, *Catalogues and Counters: A History of Sears, Roebuck and Company* (Chicago: University of Chicago Press, 1950); Hrant Pasdermadjian, *The Department Store* (London: Newman Books, 1954); Herbert Adams Gibbons, *John Wanamaker*, 2 vols. (New York: Harper and Brothers, 1926); Robert Twyman, *History of Marshall Field and Co. 1852-1906* (Philadelphia: University of Pennsylvania Press, 1954). The discussions of department stores in the works of C. Wright Mills and Daniel Boorstin are exceptions to this trend, but these are brief, impressionistic (although

In writing this history, I have taken another path. While I have tried to bring into account some of the more important interests of the traditional business historian, my primary concern has been the social history of a modern business firm. I have turned to sources that business historians in the past have been prone to overlook: pictures, public relations remnants, the historical paraphernalia of the firm's internal social life. My subject has been neither growth nor perform-ance, but the business enterprise as a reflection of its culture and as a factor in shaping the character and evolution of that culture in a time of social change.

Business history as social history has in turn meant a con-centration on certain themes that have largely been neglected in the histories of a particular business firm. One such theme centers on the role of paternalism, paternalism here referring not simply to employer-sponsored benefits for employees, but to the pervasive idea of an internal work community that accompanies these benefits and that informs all relationships within the enterprise. The subject is a complex one, although this complexity has rarely been dwelled on, or even consid-ered. Paternalism in business and industry generally has been seen as a manifestation of early attempts to recruit, stabilize, and discipline a work force and as a manifestation of the sentiments of early entrepreneurs whose unwilling-ness to relinquish a vestige of authority led them to organize the lives of their employees. Most historians have been con-tent to assign paternalism to the dust-bins of the early stages

stimulating), and part of more generalized essays. C. Wright Mills, *White Col-lar* (London: Oxford University Press, 1951); Daniel Boorstin, *The Americans: The Democratic Experience* (New York: Random House, 1973). French studies of department stores have been either company panegyrics or anecdotal ex-cursions. For examples of these see Marc Dasquet, *Le Bon Marché* (Paris: Edi-tions de Minuit, 1955); Charles D'Ydewalle, *Au Bon Marché* (Paris: Plon, 1965); Fernand Laudet, *La Samaritaine* (Paris: Dunod, 1933); Pierre MacOrlan, *Le Printemps* (Paris: Gallimard, 1930); Francis Ambrière, *La vie secrète des grands magasins* (Paris: Les Oeuvres Français, 1938); Paul Jarry, *Les magasins de nouveautés: histoire retrospective et anecdotique* (Paris: André Barry, 1948). Among centennial publications by French stores, the best is *Le Printemps, cent ans de jeunesse*, ed. Solange Dumuis (Paris: 1965).

of industrialization and to grant it little place in the workings of more mature industrial/bureaucratic economies.

But paternalism did not readily die out as Western economies became more advanced, nor was it simply a prolongation of labor policies determined in an earlier era, as one recent writer has proposed.[4] In France it could be found most prominently among some of the largest, the most dynamic, and the most innovative firms in the French economy well into the twentieth century, where it served purposes in accordance with its times. In the United States it flourished under the name of welfare capitalism, spreading most rapidly after the 1890s and reaching its peak in the 1920s. That is, paternalism became most entrenched in the United States —was viewed as most necessary by American businessmen—at precisely the moment when the modern corporation was being formed.[5]

The case of Japan provides still further complications. If paternalistic values and paternalistic modes of relationships bear little relation to the organization of modern economies, how, then, does one explain their persistence, indeed their pervasiveness, at the heart of the second strongest economy in the world today? There are those who argue that Japanese industrial growth represents a temporary cultural aberration, and that Japan in the long run will come to resemble the Western model. But others have presented equally persuasive arguments that convergence of this sort will not come about. One recent study has even suggested that if con-

[4] Peter Stearns, *Paths to Authority: The Middle Class and the Industrial Labor Force in France, 1820-1848* (Urbana: University of Illinois Press, 1978).

[5] This development has been most thoroughly traced in Stuart D. Brandes, *American Welfare Capitalism 1880-1940* (Chicago: University of Chicago Press, 1976) and Daniel Nelson, *Managers and Workers: Origins of the New Factory System in the United States, 1880-1920* (Madison: University of Wisconsin Press, 1975). See also Robert Ozanne, *A Century of Labor-Management Relations at McCormick and International Harvester* (Madison: University of Wisconsin Press, 1967); Stanley Buder, *Pullman* (New York: Oxford University Press, 1967); George Sweet Gibb and Evelyn Knowlton, *History of Standard Oil of New Jersey*, vol. 2: *The Resurgent Years 1911-1927* (New York: Harper Brothers, 1956).

vergence is occurring, it is most likely running in the direction of the Japanese model, not vice versa. More to the point, even if convergence along Western lines were to occur, there remains the question of why the Japanese economy grew so rapidly and so successfully without shedding its paternalistic skin. Better still, one needs to ask in what ways the Japanese paternalistic style—most rooted within the largest firms—contributed to this rapidity and success.[6]

The uses of paternalism can, therefore, be a very involved subject, and it has been my intention to treat them as such throughout this study. In my effort to reconstruct the social history of the Bon Marché, I have placed the store's very rich and deeply imbedded paternalistic relationships at the center of my analysis because I have come to believe that these relationships provide the key to understanding how the Bon Marché, as a bourgeois institution, approached the problem of adaptation to the basic changes of its age. In particular, I have pursued this thought along two levels. First, I have attempted to place the role of paternalism in a far more comprehensive context than has previously been the case. This has meant exploring not only how paternalism could be directed at forming and controlling a work force, but also how it could be used to build a work force of organization men and women integrated into a bureaucratic and dynamic work environment. It has also meant turning paternalism on its head, viewing paternalism not simply as an entrepreneurial strategy directed at workers, but as an entrepreneurial response to businessmen's own needs for socialization in a period of changing business roles. And it has further meant examining the public relations uses of paternalism as an instrument of

[6] For the convergence view along Western lines, see Robert M. Marsh and Hiroshi Mannari, *Modernization and the Japanese Factory* (Princeton University Press, 1976). For convergence in a contrary light, see Ronald Dore, *British Factory-Japanese Factory: The Origins of National Diversity in Industrial Relations* (Berkeley: University of California Press, 1973). On relationships between the Japanese paternalistic model and Japanese economic performance, see James G. Abegglen, *The Japanese Factory* (Glencoe: The Free Press, 1958); Ezra F. Vogel, *Japan as Number One: Lessons for America* (Cambridge: Harvard University Press, 1979), pp. 131-57.

cultural reconciliation in a time of fundamental shifts in the character of French society. In each instance—socialization of employee, owner, bourgeois public—the accent has been on the relevancy of paternalism to the emergence of the modern business firm. Second, I have stressed the special nature of paternalism at the Bon Marché, the way in which it was structured and oriented. The meaning of this perspective will become clearer as we consider the question of social change—which forms a second theme in the Bon Marché's history.

There is a tendency to see social change in modern times as representing a dramatic break with past traditions, values, ways of life. This is especially true in regard to those changes—bureaucratization, the emergence of a mass society—which have characterized Western culture since the latter part of the nineteenth century. Max Weber's perception of an unrelenting rationalizing process and his speculations on the disenchantment of the modern world have largely contributed to this frame of mind.[7] So, too, has the disposition to picture a society that has progressed through the obliteration of its earlier organic, or *gemeinschaftlich*, ties.[8] The image that has been drawn has been one of a century of sweeping shifts and upheavals, often painful and traumatic, and often leaving a residue of inner tensions and conflicts. It is a view that, to a point, intersects with the central problems contemplated in this study. Indeed, one of my contentions is that the coming of institutions like the department store—reflection as they were of the bourgeoisie's world—posed at the same time a fundamental dilemma for a culture that continued to value family ties and community relationships, and that remained

[7] H. H. Gerth and C. Wright Mills, ed., *From Max Weber: Essays in Sociology* (New York: Oxford University Press, paperback, 1958), pp. 51, 139, 155.

[8] For the original formulation of the concepts, see Ferdinand Tönnies, *Community and Society [Gemeinschaft und Gesellschaft]* (New York: Harper and Row, Harper Torchbooks, 1963). *Gemeinschaft*, according to Tönnies, finds its most characteristic expression in the family or in collectivities like the neighborhood where organic and personal social relationships based on common sentiments and traditions prevail. *Gesellschaft*, on the other hand, is the world of self-interest and atomized individuals, the world of calculation and rationalization where the relationships of contract prevail.

permeated, therefore, with traditional *gemeinschaftlich* elements.

Yet social change need not occur through a radical break with the past. There is an alternative pattern of change, one that proceeds through a restatement or restructuring of traditions and values to fit new needs, new ends. Traditional values and patterns of social organization can be far more flexible than is generally allowed. Once reoriented, they can lend themselves to the purposes of change and, even more, provide the social cohesion necessary for the successful and rapid realization of that change. Investigators of transitional developments in India have seen this occurring. They have, for example, pointed to how the cohesiveness of the caste structure, once adapted for new ends, can be effective in achieving political and social change.[9] Likewise, an observer of the Japanese factory system has suggested that the Japanese factory represents a "rephrasing" of "feudal loyalties, commitments, rewards, and methods of leadership" within the framework of modern industry, and he has gone on to remark that this rephrasing was critical to Japan's evolution into a modern industrialized economy.[10]

A similar approach to social change seems to me to have occurred at the Bon Marché. It is an approach that can be seen especially—to return to the previous theme—in the way that paternalism was structured at the firm; for paternalism at the Bon Marché was designed so that family relationships, a sense of community—in short *gemeinschaftlich* values persistent in bourgeois culture—were now identified with the workings of a mass, bureaucratic enterprise and were, in fact, made to work for the success of that enterprise. In this way, the Bon Marché was able to reconcile the dichotomous strains that it represented in French bourgeois culture, thus illustrating how that culture could accommodate to its new social setting.

A third theme—the role of the family firm in French economic development—follows directly from the preoccupation

[9] Lloyd I. Rudolph and Susanne Hoeber Rudolph, *The Modernity of Tradition* (Chicago: University of Chicago Press, 1967).

[10] Abegglen, *Japanese Factory*, pp. 131, 134.

with paternalism and social change at the Bon Marché. It is a theme that has not been neglected in earlier business history, largely because of the writings of David Landes. Landes is an historian who has constantly sought the answers to economic questions in the realm of social speculations. His influence has particularly been felt in his suggestion that entrepreneurial and attitudinal factors, not a supposed lack of resources and ready capital, were principally responsible for braking French economic growth once the race to industrialization had begun in the West. In making this argument, Landes has pointed to the prevalence of the family firm in France, where household and business have been inextricably mixed and where anti-business attitudes in society have been reflected in the firm's assumed *raison d'être* as a family fiefdom rather than as a business end in itself. Reluctant to dilute authority and control through expansion, preferring established security to the risks of dynamism, and emphasizing an entrepreneurial role predicated on traditional relationships rather than on drive and competitiveness, the French family firm, according to Landes, has been an inherently conservative business institution.[11]

Landes' ideas have not gone unchallenged. Some critics have argued that it is a mistake to view the problems of French economic growth through the prism of the family firm or of entrepreneurial values.[12] These sentiments have been

[11] David Landes, "French Entrepreneurship and Industrial Growth in the Nineteenth Century," *Journal of Economic History* (May 1949), pp. 45-61; David Landes, "French Business and the Businessman: A Social and Cultural Analysis," in *Modern France*, ed., Edward Mead Earle (Princeton: Princeton University Press, 1951), pp. 334-53. Landes has further claimed that social values in France have consistently stressed individualism and quality and thus have been inimical, on the side of demand, to the development of a marketplace based on large, dynamic units of mass production and mass distribution. A similar argument, including an analysis of the French family firm, can be found in an unpublished and highly impressionistic manuscript of Jesse Pitts. Jesse R. Pitts, "The Bourgeois Family and French Economic Retardation" (Ph.D. dissertation, Harvard University, 1957).

[12] Charles Kindleberger, *Economic Growth in France and Britain 1851-1950* (Cambridge: Harvard University Press, 1964). See also the series of debates between Landes and Alexander Gerschenkron in *Explorations in Entrepreneurial History* (October 1953, May 1954, December 1954).

echoed by others, who have further argued that the performance of the French economy and French businessmen over
the past 150 years has been far more creditable than has generally been allowed.[13] Still, Landes' interpretation of the
French family firm remains imbedded in the historiography
of modern France. Perhaps the substantial reason for this
tenacity is that none of Landes' critics has attempted to reverse him on his own terrain. They have questioned the concept of retarded economic growth in France; they have cast
doubts on the influence of the French family firm as the
primary obstacle to growth; and they have pointed to the
exceptions—the dynamic French companies that were also
family firms (Landes, himself, has not been afraid to call attention to such firms, although he has seen them primarily as
anomalies or as reinforcements of those values that hindered
dynamism elsewhere). But they have not asked why it is that
family firms can be dynamic as well as retardive, why those
values and relationships so readily seen as an impediment to
dynamic business performance tend to be repeated in some
of France's most successful firms, or how these values and relationships may have promoted rather than impeded that
success.

In looking at the social history of a specific family firm that
was also one of the most successful business endeavors in
France before the First World War, I have been drawn to precisely these sorts of questions. My concern has been to point
to the positive role that household values can play in the evolution of a modern business enterprise, such as bringing a
sense of loyalty and cohesiveness to a bureaucratized and
large-scale work environment. I have wished to show how,
in a culture that placed a premium on family relationships

[13] François Crouzet, "French Economic Growth in the Nineteenth Century
Reconsidered," *History* (June 1974), pp. 167-79; Maurice Lévy-Leboyer, "La
croissance économique en France au XIXe siècle. Résultats préliminaires,"
Annales E.S.C. (July-August 1968), pp. 788-801; Maurice Lévy-Leboyer, "In-
novation and Business Strategies in Nineteenth and Twentieth Century
France," in *Enterprise and Entrepreneurs in Nineteenth and Twentieth Century
France*, ed., Edward C. Carter (Baltimore: The Johns Hopkins University
Press, 1976), pp. 87-136.

and on family ownership, the persistence of household values and modes could simply represent a preference to pursue business change through a restructuring of these values and modes rather than through the more difficult path of abandoning them. No doubt at many French businesses household values could and did present the sort of obstacle to change that Landes has described. But, as my discussion of paternalism and social change suggests, this need not have been the case with all family firms. As we shall see, the Bon Marché was a firm not only permeated with household relationships, but a firm that relied upon these relationships for its transition into a modern business enterprise, a firm that utilized these relationships to secure its remarkable success, and, what is more, a firm that recognized the essential role that these relationships played in assuring the continuity of that success.

Lastly, the themes of paternalism, social change, and the family firm come together in some reflections on that elusive but inescapable subject for anyone writing on the transformations of modern times—the idea of a managerial revolution. That such a revolution has occurred within the business world over the past hundred years cannot be disputed.[14] But the degree of change implicit in the notion of revolution is debatable, and this too I have attempted to incorporate into my portrait of the Bon Marché. This has not meant simply presenting the history of a family firm that was capable of building a highly dynamic, highly rationalized enterprise with a substantial managerial hierarchy. More important, I have been concerned with questioning the effect that the managerial revolution has had on the internal social relationships of the modern business firm. I have attempted to show,

[14] For the best discussion of this to date, see Alfred D. Chandler, Jr., *The Visible Hand: The Managerial Revolution in American Business* (Cambridge: Harvard University Press, 1977). See also Adolph A. Berle and Gardiner C. Means, *The Modern Corporation and Private Property* (New York: Macmillan, 1932); Reinhard Bendix, *Work and Authority in Industry* (New York: Harper and Row, 1963); John Kenneth Galbraith, *The New Industrial State* (Boston: Houghton Mifflin, 1967).

again returning to the earlier themes of paternalism and of social change, that bureaucratization and rationalization in business, accompanied by a correspondingly growing role for managers, has not necessarily entailed a disappearance of household relationships within the enterprise. Impersonal, bureaucratized, managerially run firms, on the one hand, the household relationships of the family firm, on the other, have been a contrast too keenly drawn in the past. The managerial and family ethos are not mutually exclusive; they can in fact work together, the one complementing and completing the other. This, certainly, was the case with the Bon Marché.

The problem of imaginary lines in history brings me to a final remark. More than twenty years ago Reinhard Bendix pointed to the interdependence between entrepreneurial strategies and the shape of the working-class experience.[15] Yet few labor or business historians have given this much heed. The former, by and large, have been content to write their histories irrespective of the business context in which these have occurred. Labor history has told us much about working-class movements, working-class lives, the nature of working-class work. But it has told us little about how the history of the workers has been molded by the values and concerns of the men who employed them. Businessmen and their firms have been left to the business historians, as though neither were critical to the working-man's world.[16] For their part, most business historians have been content to see themselves as economic historians, and thus to ignore the questions that a social historian might ask. They have told us much about business firms, business structures, and business politics, but they have had little to say on the businessman as a contributor and participant in his wider social world, or on the intertwining of the growth and success of an enterprise with its employee relations. Thus, for both business and labor historians, the history of the businessman has been made to stand apart from the history of the worker.

[15] Bendix, *Work*.
[16] For two exceptions see, Rolande Trempé, *Les mineurs de Carmaux, 1848-1914* (Paris: Les Editions Ouvrières, 1971); Stearns, *Paths*.

This book will, I hope, suggest an alternative. It will remind the historian of modern society that his is the history of
both the middle and working classes, and that the history of
one has in fact been the history of the other. Business and
labor historians need to recognize that there is much to learn
from one another. Social historians need to realize that the
bourgeoisie as much as the working class gave shape to the
society that emerged with industrialization (and that labor
does not exclude the white-collar worker). Economic historians need to acknowledge the social context within which
economic changes take place. Only when we arrive at these
understandings will we truly begin to see how our culture
has evolved.

PART ONE

Revolution in Retailing

☐ NEW STORES

IN THE LATE PARISIAN SUMMER of 1869 several men, and one woman, gathered near the junction of the sixth and seventh arrondissements to witness the laying of a cornerstone. It is unlikely they had come a great distance that particularly warm day, since many Parisians, including the well-to-do, still lived in or near their shops, workshops, or offices. Yet if some had come a certain distance, even from the opposite right bank, their journey could not have been a difficult one. No longer was Paris an impassable maze of streets and alleyways, too narrow to accommodate the traffic of a mid-century capital, too haphazard in design to permit cross-town circulation. Now the broad boulevards that Baron Haussmann had built cut through Paris along a rational plan that effectively removed those barriers to intra-city travel that for centuries had confined Parisians to their immediate quarter or that rendered unpleasant any effort to shuttle about. Indeed if our travellers had desired, they might have come in one of the carriages of the Compagnie Générale des Omnibus that now moved through the city streets with relative ease. In the meantime, those who came on foot might have walked to the ceremony along the new Rue de Rennes or on the path of the soon to be built Boulevard Raspail which would pass near the new building's site.

Their presence was not noticed by the press that day. More important matters—the emperor's health, the constitutional reforms just recently granted, the meeting of the International Association of Workingmen at Basel—were the stories that preoccupied the public mind on September 9 and 10. Little attention could be devoted to the erection of a new build-

ing at a time when fundamental transitions seemed both possible and immediate.

Yet in their own way our little group had gathered together
precisely to commemorate such a transition. Certainly they
were aware of the events about them, and perhaps they felt it
fitting that at a time of change for the French polity they too
were engaged in changes of a fundamental nature. Unquestionably they were aware as well of the changes in the Parisian landscape, and, as they journeyed to their ceremony,
either in carriages or afoot, they could not but have reflected
on how well Haussmann's new boulevards would serve the
purpose for which they were assembling.

In such a setting and such a mood we might well imagine
the scene as Aristide Boucicaut, his wife, and his principal associates laid the cornerstone for the first department store in
France. To be sure, the old Bon Marché that the new building
was replacing already covered a substantial floor-space and
supported a substantial sales volume of more than twenty
million francs a year.[1] Nor was the Bon Marché the only Parisian store in 1869 that could boast of generous dimensions
and bountiful sales. Yet what was significant about this particular moment in September was that for the first time a
store was being constructed that was formally conceived and
systematically designed to house a *grand magasin*. Prone at
times to exaggerate, Boucicaut would be nothing less than
candid when a few years later he would distinguish the first
completed section of the new building from its rivals and the
Bon Marché's own past with the proclamation that his was
now "the only [store] specifically constructed and entirely intended for a great trade in *nouveautés*."[2]

The story behind the emergence of this new building and
its basic concept is not an especially dramatic one, in large
part because we simply lack the materials to reconstruct
the personal struggles, dreams, and gambles that underlay
Boucicaut's vision or the fortunes of his predecessors and

[1] The exchange rate throughout the nineteenth century was approximately
five francs to the dollar.
[2] *Le Siècle*, 30 March 1872.

contemporaries. Undoubtedly much of the romance and grandeur that Zola conveyed to us in the character of Mouret was indeed part of the unfolding of the moment, but Mouret is too much a hodgepodge of varied observations and literary imagination, and too lacking in historical roots, to provide us with more than a feel for the developments with which we are concerned.[3] Still, if it is a story that necessarily lacks the passion we might wish to attribute to it, it is one nevertheless that derives from, and forms part of, the basic business and economic transformations that so significantly marked the nineteenth century in France and elsewhere. Essentially it is a story that follows two paths of change.

The first of these was a revolution in retailing that can be traced to the appearance of new kinds of stores—dry goods firms known as *magasins de nouveautés*—in the 1830s and 1840s. After a period of testing and growth, these firms, with their accent on turnover, were to lead to the formation of the department store. The period of transition was not a lengthy one, only a few decades at most, and when the final stages came they changed in spurts. Still, the fundamental fact that must be recognized is that department stores, in France as elsewhere, did not spring up overnight. All the great emporia of the prewar era—the Bon Marché, the Louvre, the Printemps, and others—had either modest or intermediate origins, all passed through a *magasin de nouveautés* phase, and all were predicated upon new commercial practices and upon new commercial frames of mind that had developed in the decades immediately preceding their founding.

To appreciate the degree to which the *magasins de nouveautés* departed from traditional merchandising practices in France, it is necessary to recall the conditions of retailing bequeathed by the ancien régime and still predominant at the time of the creation of the July Monarchy. Before the Revolution, most retailing in France was governed by a guild system concerned primarily with maintaining established levels of craftsmanship and with assuring that no merchant or small

[3] The owner of Zola's Au Bonheur des Dames was Octave Mouret.

producer (and most often these were one and the same) encroached on the trade of his neighbor. The guilds regulated and limited entry into the various trades. They insisted that each seller be confined to a single specialty and to a single shop; they set standards of work; and they set conditions for procuring supplies. At times they set a minimum selling price to prevent "unfair" competition. Advertising was effectively restricted to street signs and street cries, listings in almanacs, and, apparently more exceptional than the rule, almanacs by individual proprietors that might also serve as a store prospectus. Thus little leeway was left to entrepreneurial innovation.

This picture is, to some extent, an incomplete one. There were certain "privileged places" of commerce in each major town that were outside the guilds' jurisdiction, as were the *colporteurs* or peddlers that thronged the city streets. There were also the great fairs and the *merciers*, the one group of merchants who were permitted to sell all varieties of merchandise (although they were prohibited from all forms of manufacture). Yet none of these represented much of a break with the prevailing traditions of the period. The "privileged places" tended to establish their own guild-like regulations, while *colporteurs*, who might engage in more competitive trading, were by their very nature anything but the vanguard of a commercial revolution. Fairs were but seasonal events among individual sellers, and in no way may these be seen as predecessors to department stores. As for the *merciers*, their shops were at best early models of general stores, while their merchandising habits, covered by guild restrictions, remained the same as those of their less diverse colleagues.

This does not mean that we should discount all possibility of changing attitudes beneath a more visible guild screen. The constant accusations and litigations within the guild communities point to the restlessness of a number of their members. Nor should we doubt that the advances in window display and store décor that were common in London in the eighteenth century were unknown to the Parisians. But if we truly wish to cite examples of a shift from the governing norms of the times, we must wait until the end of the eight-eenth century, when new stores calling themselves *magasins de modes* appeared on the Parisian scene. One of these, the Petit Dunkerque, is known to have sold at fixed prices rather than abiding by the customary ritual of bargaining over each item. Characteristic of the period, however, these stores did not make much immediate headway, nor did they differ sig-nificantly from the *merciers* out of which they had evolved.[4]

It might be expected that some greater change would have occurred with the suppression of the guilds, but few shop-keepers were prepared to abandon either the traditions or the mentality of the past. Again there were exceptions, enterpris-ing merchants like Balzac's perfumer, César Birotteau, who did not shrink from pursuing greater sales or from employing ambitious publicity schemes to achieve these ends. Yet it was in the proprietor of the Maison du Chat-qui-pelote that re-tailers during the opening decades of the new century would undoubtedly have recognized their portrait, and to glimpse behind the centuries-old facades that housed the boutiques of Paris in these years would be to find a way of business that differed little from its pre-Revolutionary predecessors. If stripped of its legal sanctions, the guiding principle for the community of shopkeepers remained the right of each hon-orable merchant to a set share of the trade, and there was no need of a French Malthus to justify in prose what all shop-keepers already were certain of—that any increase in sales on the part of one of their number would result in a correspond-ing decrease for the others. Consequently, the *boutiquiers* per-

[4] Alfred Franklin, *La vie privée d'autrefois*, vol. 15 (Paris: E. Plon, Nourrit, 1894), pp. 2-43; Etienne Martin Saint-Léon, *Histoire des corporations de métiers* (Paris: 1922; reprint ed., Geneva: Slatkine-Megariotis Reprints, 1976); Emile Coornaert, *Les corporations en France avant 1789* (Paris: Les Editions Ouvrières, 1968); Maurice de Gailhard-Bancel, *Les anciennes corporations de métiers et la lutte contre la fraude dans le commerce et la petite industrie* (Paris: Bloud et Cie., 1912), pp. 37-90; Jarry, *Les magasins*, pp. 18-19, 24. On England, see Dorothy Davis, *A History of Shopping* (London: Routledge and Kegan Paul, 1966), pp. 181-211. Davis and Hower also point out that the Quakers in England adopted a fixed price policy as early as the seventeenth century. Davis, *Shopping*, pp. 152-53; Hower, *Macy's*, p. 89.

sisted in their confinement to traditional specialties and bitterly resented any move toward merchandise diversification
by competitors.

Malthusianism of this sort equally stunted the development of an aggressive sales policy. Advertising, aside from
traditionally acceptable methods, was rejected almost out of
hand, and apparently the idea that consumption could be encouraged through price or service innovations never occurred
to these merchants. If it did, it too was evidently dismissed as
beyond the pale of respectable practice. Hence turnover was
simply not a marketing concept, and profits were sought
strictly through the medium of high prices on individual
sales. Nor was any attempt made to turn buying into a pleasant or convenient experience. The idea of "shopping" was,
for all practical purposes, non-existent, as entry into a shop
entailed an obligation to make a purchase. Returns or even
exchanges were unheard of. Indeed *caveat emptor* was the rul-
ing doctrine of the day. Consumers were offered neither fixed
nor marked prices to guide their way, and the common practice was to sell only after a long period of bargaining—and
probably haggling—over the price.[5] Undoubtedly some
shopkeepers were scrupulous, but the image handed down
to us is that many others were not, and most likely one entered a shop prepared for deception rather than service.

Why, with this lack of merchandising finesse, the shopkeepers of Paris should have nevertheless embellished their
boutiques with lavish trappings is uncertain. Perhaps it was
simply a matter of personal pride. Perhaps as well it was simply another example of their rudimentary understanding of
marketing, since most shopkeepers—for the most part dependent upon credit sales and hence frequently lacking sufficient working capital—could ill afford to squander their initial
investment on outlays that accorded so little with their merchandising philosophy.[6]

[5] Bargaining also meant a long, drawn-out selling process, another factor
that limited turnover and contributed to high prices.

[6] Honoré de Balzac, *La comédie humaine*, vol. 10: *Histoire de la grandeur et de
la décadence de César Birotteau* (Paris: Furne, J. J. Dubochet, J. Hetzel, 1844);

Just when the critical shift began to occur in this pattern is questionable. Some of the most successful of the *magasins de nouveautés*—the Coin de Rue, the Petit Saint-Thomas, the Deux Magots—could trace their origins as far back as the Restoration. But ownership in these early years was not always the same as later on, and it is unlikely that there was much difference at the beginning between these stores and the other small shops of the period. By the 1830s, however, there were definite signs of change—advertisements from the late 1830s called attention to fixed and marked prices—and with the 1840s one could truly begin to speak of *magasins de nouveautés* which had broken radically with the commercial traditions of the past.

The term *magasins de nouveautés*, or drapery and fancy goods store, may not in itself seem indicative of great change, and indeed these stores dealt almost exclusively in dry goods—silks, woolens, cloths, shawls, lingerie, hosiery, gloves, ready-to-wear, and the like, plus occasionally items like furs, umbrellas, and sewing goods.[7] Yet for the times this constituted a revolutionary grouping of what were still regarded as diverse sets of specialties, and almost immediately there were complaints from the tradition-minded small merchants.[8] The new stores were revolutionary as well in their organization along departmental rather than general merchandising lines and especially in their pioneering use of new merchandising techniques. The Ville de Paris, by far the largest *magasin de nouveautés* in the 1840s (it claimed a workforce of 150 employees and a yearly sales volume of 10-12 million francs in 1844), was now selling at low prices for high turnover. It also used fixed and marked prices, permitted free entry, and was willing to exchange or reimburse "purchases

---

Honoré de Balzac, *La maison du chat-qui-pelote* (Paris: Garniers Frères, 1963); Zola, *Au bonheur*; Adeline Daumard, *La Bourgeoisie parisienne de 1815 à 1848* (Paris: S.E.V.P.E.N., 1963), pp. 446-52.

[7] *Annuaire-Almanach du commerce*, 1845. It is not known whether these stores had wholesale operations like a number of their American counterparts.

[8] See Chapter VI.

that are not entirely satisfactory." Advertising, no longer suspect, was welcomed as a valuable sales tool.[9] Likewise, if the dating of an 1844 catalogue from the Petit Saint-Thomas is correct, this left-bank firm had learned the value of buying in bulk quantities at discount prices from suppliers in order to pass the merchandise on at low retail prices to its clientele. The catalogue referred to a mail-order service that the store had recently organized, and it added that "knowing very well that low prices do not entirely suffice to satisfy the consumer, we see to it that he finds in our store the complaisance and politeness that he has the right to expect, as well as the freedom to view the merchandise without being harassed to buy it." In addition, by at least the end of the decade the Petit Saint-Thomas was offering annual special sales.[10] No wonder, then, that the public in the 1840s began to look to extraordinary images to express their amazement with the commercial changes occurring about them. One account spoke of "monster stores" (and already was complaining of their bureaucratic character).[11] Another, the 1847 *Almanach Prophétique*, perhaps only half in jest, painted scenes of a future of *magasins* so vast that omnibuses would be required to transport customers from one department to another.[12]

If there was an unmistakably fantastic side to the *Almanach Prophétique*'s vision, there was an equally unmistakable realization that what had occurred in the 1840s was only the beginning of a far greater commercial revolution, as the succeeding two decades were to prove. In the 1840s the Ville de Paris had been an anomaly. In the 1860s the average large store had a sales volume of 10-12 million francs a year. By the end of the decade there were stores with annual sales volumes twice as

[9] *Le Siècle*, 8 October 1843: *L'Illustration*, 11 May 1844; H.-L. Delloye, ed., *Album revue de l'industrie parisienne* (Paris: Garnier Frères, 1844).

[10] Catalogue, Petit Saint-Thomas, 1844, Bibliothèque Nationale, 4 WZ3230. There is no printed date on this catalogue—the dating of 1844 has been marked on its cover by the staff of the Bibliothèque Nationale. *La Presse*, 28 October 1850.

[11] *Paris comique, revue amusante* (Paris: Chez Aubert, 1844), pp. 10-11.

[12] Dasquet, *Bon Marché*, p. 55.

large and with staffs of perhaps as many as 500 employees.
Advertising was now common and extensive, including the
use of full-page ads that frequently announced enormous lots
for sale. In February 1853 the Coin de Rue had 3,000 rolls of
Madapolam cloth and 1,500 *robes albanaises* for sale. In 1862
the Ville de Paris advertised a lot of 3,000 dozen cloth nap-
kins. In April of the same year the Bon Marché was announcing a sale of 1,500 parasols.[13] Perhaps even more telling of the
period than numbers was a sense of the maturing of the
magasins de nouveautés, of the standardization and more assured exploitation of the new merchandising practices. The
average *magasin de nouveautés* now sold only for high turnover
at low and fixed prices, offered exchanges, permitted free entry, and generally stressed an ambiance agreeable to the consumer. Expositions or sales were becoming a semi-regular
feature. The principle of organization by departments had
become fundamental. Hierarchical chains of command were
developing.[14]

Among the *magasins de nouveautés* established in these decades could be found nearly all of the future leading department stores of Paris. In addition to the Bon Marché, whose
story we shall explore shortly,[15] there were the beginnings of
the Louvre and the Bazar de l'Hôtel de Ville in the mid-1850s,
and the Printemps in 1865. The early years of the Louvre,
which was to be the Bon Marché's principal competitor in the
prewar era, reveal both the difficulties that many of these
stores faced at their start and the rapid growth that could
come with perseverance.

The store's beginnings can be traced to the decision to build

---

[13] *La Presse*, 13 February 1853; 23 February 1862; 8 April 1862.

[14] Paul Avenel, *Les calicots* (Paris: Albert Delveau, 1866); F. Devinck,
*Pratique commerciale et recherches historiques sur la marche du commerce et de l'in-
dustrie* (Paris: Hachette, 1867), p. 91; A. Lescure, "Naissance et développement des grands magasins parisiens de 1852 à 1882" (Masters thesis, Faculté
des Lettres et Sciences Humaines de Nanterre, 1970), p. 28. See also advertisements for the period in *La Presse* and *Le Siècle*.

[15] Although the Bon Marché dates from at least the 1830s, a second founding may be said to have occurred when Aristide Boucicaut became a partner
there in 1852.

a grand hotel—to be situated between the newly constructed rue de Rivoli and the Palais Royal and hence to be called the Hôtel du Louvre—in preparation for the exposition of 1855. The original project, supported by Louis Napoleon and promoted by Emile Pereire, the Saint-Simonian who was to become one of the leading financiers of the Second Empire, called for a series of arcade shops along a part of the new hotel's exterior. But when Pereire found few merchants willing to lease the shops, he agreed to a proposal of Alfred Chauchard and Auguste Hériot to lease the ensemble as a *magasin de nouveautés*. As is often the case with the founders of these stores, the backgrounds of Chauchard and Hériot remain obscure, although we do know that the former had been a clerk at another *magasin de nouveautés*, the Pauvre Diable. This too forms part of a familiar pattern—that of ambitious men with training at one store seeking the financial support of another party (Chauchard and Hériot turned to a certain Faré) and then launching their own enterprise or buying into partnership.

The opening, in 1855, was less than grand. Management was poor, employees were not paid with regularity, and one of the cashiers made off with part of his receipts. Partly because of this, partly because Chauchard and Hériot wisely chose to plow their profits back into the operation, Faré withdrew. A new organization, backed by Pereire and several other investors and capitalized at 1,100,000 francs, was then formed, with Chauchard and Hériot in full command of the enterprise. Several more years of struggle and discouragement followed, but in 1861 sales volume finally advanced from a steady 5,000,000 francs to more than 7,000,000 francs, and five years later it totaled 13,000,000 francs. By the end of the following decade the Louvre was to be the first store to reach the then fabulous turnover of 100,000,000 francs in one year. By that time as well, the now Grands Magasins du Louvre had acquired ownership of the hotel and occupied a fair portion of the original building.[16]

[16] Georges d'Avenel, "Le mécanisme de la vie moderne: les grands maga-

France was not alone in such developments. Indeed if the Ville de Paris caused something of a sensation in Paris in the 1840s, A. T. Stewart's "Marble Palace" must have created an even greater stir among New Yorkers. Stewart was one of those enterprising young men who were quick to profit from New York's growing hold over the nation's trade in the second and third decades of the nineteenth century. Buying his goods at auction and then selling wholesale to outlying New York merchants or to country merchants who came to the city to order their own goods, Stewart was able to amass, alongside his retailing profits, a sufficient fortune to build in 1846 what was probably the first multi-story building expressly designed to handle a large volume of trade—the first of "The Marble Palaces" built by comparable enterprises. Like his Parisian confreres, Stewart's business was predicated upon the new merchandising practices of low markup and low and fixed prices, bulk buying, free entry, and returns. In 1862 he built still another building—this time a "Cast Iron Palace"— and by mid-decade he had an annual sales volume of perhaps as much as 50,000,000 dollars (although the bulk of this trade—42,000,000 dollars—was in wholesale).

An unparalleled success for his day, Stewart nevertheless had his limitations. Rather than seeking further growth by diversifying his lines, he remained confined to the basic dry-goods trade and instead chose to expand through backward integration. There was some merit in this strategy. But Stewart's grasp exceeded his organizational means. At the time of his death, in 1876, store sales had begun to decline, and gross mismanagement by Judge Henry Hilton, who came into possession of the firm following Stewart's death, turned

---

sins," *Revue des Deux Mondes* (15 July 1894), pp. 340-41; Zola, NAF10278, pp. 68, 204-05; Lescure, "Naissance," p. 28; *Le Louvre: grand hôtel et grands magasins*, 1880 Louvre Archives. While Zola and others place Chauchard at the Pauvre Diable, d'Avenel places him at the Ville de Paris. There is also a somewhat alternative version that suggests that the capitalization of 1,110,000 francs occurred during Faré's partnership and the Louvre occupied the entire building by 1878. See André Miramas, "Une entreprise séculaire: le Louvre," *Transmondia*, 1962.

decline into decay. In 1896, little more than an architectural carcass, A. T. Stewart's passed into the hands of John Wanamaker of Philadelphia.[17]

Stewart's was by far the largest store in mid-century America, but in many ways it was simply the most prominent example of a trend towards innovative retailing throughout the country. Other innovative and growing stores in New York in the 1850s and 1860s included Lord and Taylor; Arnold, Constable and Co.; and Macy's. The latter's sales volume was not yet impressive—only 1,024,621 dollars in 1870—but it was far more diverse than either Stewart's or the Parisian stores at this time, selling house furnishings, toys, stationery, and books in addition to dry goods. In Philadelphia John Wanamaker was beginning his pioneering work in advertising and publicity. In Chicago, Marshall Field's had by 1870 amassed a sales volume of 2,000,000 dollars in retailing and 13,000,000 dollars overall, if wholesale trade is included. Meanwhile, if British retailers were somewhat more sluggish than either their French or American counterparts, there were several notable exceptions, such as Whitely's of London. Opened only in 1863, Whitely's over the next ten years brought together in one enterprise ten neighboring shops that employed, altogether, 622 individuals. In 1872 Whitely took for himself the name of the "Universal Provider," although at the time this represented more pretensions than reality.[18]

The simultaneous occurrence of a retail revolution in France, America, and, to some extent, England in the mid-nineteenth century has led to something of a mini-debate over which country produced the first genuine department store. Largely because most accounts have tended (and still tend) to credit the Parisians with this invention, Ralph Hower

[17] Harry E. Resseguie, "Alexander Turney Stewart and the Development of the Department Store 1823-1876," *Business History Review* (Autumn 1965); Harry E. Resseguie, "The Decline and Fall of the Commercial Empire of A. T. Stewart," *Business History Review* (Autumn 1962).

[18] Hower, *Macy's*, p. 189; Twyman, *Marshall Field*, p. 177; Gibbon, *John Wanamaker*; Richard S. Lambert, *The Universal Provider* (London: George G. Harrap, 1938), pp. 64-73. All of Macy's sales were retail.

devoted a fair portion of his study of Macy's to demonstrating that American retail developments paralleled rather than imitated those in France. Not surprisingly, Hower stressed diversification of merchandise lines as the key element in the development of the department store, thus placing Macy's well near the head of the pack. Whether such debates are fruitful, let alone resolvable, is, at best, questionable. Perhaps more useful purposes can be served—as in a sense Hower was attempting to point out—by stressing the commonness of the phenomenon rather than by seeking out honors among individual stores. From the above account it should be clear that between 1840 and 1870 a significant change in retailing took place on both sides of the Atlantic and that by the 1870s this had led to the emergence of commercial enterprises which roughly were approximating—in their size, their organization and practices, and especially their unity of conception—what we have come to know as the modern department store. Whether the first of these was the Bon Marché of 1869, the later but more diverse Macy's of the 1870s and 1880s, John Wanamaker's "New Kind of Store" of 1877, or perhaps even the Stewart's of the 1840s may be left to the individual reader to decide. What *is* important is the fact that one is faced with a common big-city phenomenon of the period, and thus our attention might be better focused on the underlying social and economic developments that made such stores possible at this particular time. This, then, is the second path of change with which this chapter is concerned.

In France, as elsewhere,[19] the transition from small shop to department store took shape at roughly the same time as more fundamental transformations were occurring in the country's economic structure. Most notably, the middle decades of the century produced a rate of growth greater than at any other time between the Congress of Vienna and the First World War. One historian, François Crouzet, has suggested

[19] The following account will concentrate on the changes in France alone, although these developments, in their broadest outlines, differed little from what was occurring in America and Britain during roughly the same period.

that between 1840 and 1860 the mean annual growth rate for industry was half again as much as the rate for the century as a whole, and has added that if we wish to speak of a take-off phase in the French industrial revolution we would do well to situate it during these years. Even when the growth rate slowed after 1860, it did so gradually, according to Crouzet, so that in the 1860s and for most of the 1870s the rate remained above the century-long average.[20]

The impact a rate of growth accelerating at this pace could have on retailers is not difficult to estimate. In one sense the sheer force of a boom period, and the wave of confidence accompanying it, could only spill over into a dynamic and innovative frame of mind within the commercial world. As capital and markets expanded, so too did the opportunities to create new kinds of stores. The precise ties among promoters, financiers, merely wealthy individuals, and the founders of the *magasins de nouveautés* is a story that demands greater definition. Yet as has been seen in the case of the Louvre, and as shall be seen in regard to the Bon Marché, support of this kind was forthcoming.

Encouragement of another sort was also forthcoming, from the growing productive capacity of the nation. If by 1870 France was still in a fairly early stage of industrialization, there were nevertheless industries that had matured to the point where they could provide an abundant and steady flow of goods to the market at relatively low cost. This was especially true of the textile industry, the one sector upon which the new dry-goods stores were most dependent for their stocks. In the north and northeast, particularly in Alsace, competitive and technologically advanced firms had made

[20] Crouzet, "French Economic Growth," pp. 170-71. Crouzet suggests a 2.4% mean rate of growth for 1850-1860 as opposed to a 1.62% rate for the 1815-1913 period. National income is also estimated to have climbed from 9.1 billion francs in 1825 to 13.6 billion in 1847 and then to 19.4 billion by 1859. See François Perroux, "Prises de vues sur la croissance de l'économie française, 1780-1950," in *Income and Wealth*, vol. 5, ed., Simon Kuznets (London: Bowes & Bowes, 1955), p. 61.

France the largest producer of cotton goods on the continent. By the sixties these regions possessed over 3,500,000 spindles combined. To this must be added another 3,000,000 spindles in the less sophisticated industry of Normandy, although even here there were advances in mechanization and productivity—in the cotton tulle industry, for example, centered in Calais.[21]

Mass production of this kind required a retail system far more efficient and far more expansive than anything small shopkeepers might be able to offer. Consequently, incentives on the part of producers or jobbers to stimulate buying in large lots, and initiatives on the part of new merchants to purchase such batches at low prices, became a growing practice, from at least the mid-1840s on, as advertisements of the time attest.[22] With the 1850s came the advent of special great sales, another consequence of increasing productive capacity in an era when the market was still largely unregulated and subject to fluctuations. How much these sales contributed to the success of individual *magasins de nouveautés* can only be surmised. Yet we do know from Zola's portrait of Mouret that it was not uncommon to stake everything on one great sale; and it may be supposed that the ability to buy from a manufacturer or wholesaler at a moment of oversupply, and to unload at favorable prices to the consumer, provided not a few of the new stores with the impetus to further growth.

Meanwhile, the surge of productivity meant not only a greater abundance of goods sent to market, but a basic recasting of the nature of trades or crafts, and in turn a recasting of the kinds of goods that were now available. Accustomed as we are to looking upon the Industrial Revolution as a factory-oriented system, we would do well to remember that for

[21] David Landes, *The Unbound Prometheus* (Cambridge: Cambridge University Press, 1969), pp. 159-65; Georges Duveau, *La vie ouvrière en France sous le second empire* (Paris: Gallimard, 1946), pp. 162-67, 183-84.

[22] The role of wholesalers in stimulating change in this period unfortunately is far less defined than it is for America. For further remarks on wholesalers and the new stores, see Chapter II.

much of the century economic change was to be found as well in the back rooms and attics of the sweatshops. Here the stimulus to greater production came less from concentration or technology (although the sewing machine was to prove an invaluable aide to the clothing industry) than from combining a simplification of the manufacturing process with the employment of semi-skilled labor. For many, especially old craftsmen, the result was a debasement of their trades. For others, the entrepreneurs and the consumers who bought their goods, it was simply a matter of developing a market of more convenient, and less expensive, products. This was the case of ready-to-wear, which by the 1840s was threatening the master tailors and shoemakers, while at the same time providing the *magasins de nouveautés* with a product that particularly suited their needs.

Ready-to-wear became an increasingly acceptable alternative to tailor-made clothing or the markets in secondhand clothes over the course of the first half of the nineteenth century. Initially the changeover was gradual; there was resistance on the part of consumers and there were limitations on the areas to which the trade might spread. Women's fashions, for instance, were an especially difficult market to penetrate. Well into the century, ready-to-wear for women remained confined primarily to less fashion-sensitive items like coats, dressing gowns, and dress accessories. But there were too many advantages to ready-to-wear to keep it in check for long. Because it required less time and less skill to produce, and because the sale of ready-to-wear was nearly always for cash, in contrast to the credit policies of tailors, its price could be considerably lower than clothes made to order. There was also considerable attraction in the speed with which ready-to-wear could be purchased. Concomitantly, each of these factors—low prices and speed of purchase—made ready-to-wear precisely the sort of product that new stores concerned with turnover would wish to promote. Thus the spread of ready-to-wear tended to parallel the spread of the *magasins de nouveautés*, and by mid-century it had become not only a significant part of the clothing, shoe, and lingerie

trade, but also a common feature in the new emporia of
Paris.[23]

Supply and demand had, of course, another side. If new
and increased goods, low prices, and special sales might increase the market, so too might an expanding market encour-
age production and innovative retailing; and this was precisely what was happening in mid-century France. Although
purchasing power was by no means as diffuse as it would
later become, the wealth of the country was growing, and
growing fairly rapidly. Between 1840 and 1870 France maintained a per-capita rate of growth of 1.84, which, if not spectacular, was nevertheless relatively high for the period.[24] At
the same time, savings deposits climbed from 62,000,000
francs in 1835 to 358,000,000 in 1847 and then to 632,000,000
in 1870. By that year as well there were over 2,000,000 separate accounts in the country.[25] But even more important for
the retailers of Paris was the growing concentration of the
market. During the first half of the century the population of
Paris practically doubled, from 547,000 to a little more than a
million. Over the next twenty years an additional 600,000 in-
habitants joined the census rolls.[26] And this was simply the
resident Parisian market. The figures do not include the
thousands of provincial and foreign visitors who might arrive
in the capital weekly, or the millions who poured into Paris
for the expositions of 1855 and 1867.

It was, furthermore, an increasingly accessible market.
When Louis Napoleon and Baron Haussmann planned the

[23] Chambre de Commerce de Paris, *Statistique de l'industrie à Paris résultant
de l'enquête faite par la Chambre de Commerce pour les années 1847-48* (Paris: Guillaumin et Cie., 1851), pp. 109-12, 297-98; Office du Travail, *La petite industrie
(salaires et durée du travail): le vêtement à Paris* (Paris: 1896), pp. 15-17, 298-99,
395-96, 573-98.

[24] Simon Kuznets, "Notes on the Pattern of U.S. Economic Growth," in
The Reinterpretation of American Economic History, ed., Robert Fogel (New
York: Harper and Row, 1971), pp. 17-19.

[25] A. de Lavergne and L. Paul Henry, *La richesse de la France* (Paris: Marcel
Rivière, 1908), pp. 170-72.

[26] Louis Chevalier, *La formation de la population parisienne* (Paris: Presses
Universitaires de France, 1950), p. 284.

rebuilding of Paris, they may not have thought much about the Ville de Paris or the Coin de Rue, and certainly they knew nothing of Aristide Boucicaut or his recent move to the Bon Marché. Their concerns were elsewhere, with alleviating a nearly unbearable traffic situation, with providing work for potentially troublesome construction workers, and above all with making Paris the brilliant capital of Europe. But as they cut through the tortuous back alleys of the city, laying down long, wide boulevards ideal for cross-city travel—and mass public transit—they created the very conditions by which the new stores could tap the vast Parisian market. Concurrently, the rationalization of the city's layout was accompanied by a reorganization of the more than seventeen omnibus companies that had sprung up since the first concession had been established in 1828. In 1855 a single service, the Compagnie Générale des Omnibus, was formed. Five years later it was transporting more than 70,000,000 passengers annually, still another advantage to enterprising merchants who no longer looked to the immediate neighborhood, or to chance passers-by, for their clientele.[27]

On the sides of both supply and demand, then, there were forces conducive to retail change in France. Mediating between the two, and absolutely critical to the development of either, was the coming of the railroad. Once again the middle decades of the nineteenth century were the crucial years. At the beginning of the 1840s, when the French government was at last prepared to mandate a plan for a national network of trunk lines radiating out of Paris, there were less than a thousand kilometers of track throughout the entire country. Eight years later, Thiers' "toy"[28] was operating across 1,830 kilometers of new track, and within another twelve years

[27] Louis Lagarrigue, *Cent ans de transports en commun dans la région parisienne* (Paris: 1956), pp. 25-31, 38-43. For further omnibus figures see Maxime du Camp, *Paris, ses organes, ses fonctions et sa vie*, vol. 1, 2d ed. (Paris: Hachette, 1873), p. 259.

[28] Thiers is reputed to have greeted the concession of a line from Paris to St. Germain in 1835 with the remark, "We must give that to Paris, as a toy; but it will never carry a single passenger or package." Quoted in J. H. Clapham, *The Economic Development of France and Germany 1851-1914* (Cambridge: Cambridge University Press, 1936), p. 144.

there were more than 7,000 kilometers of operative track in the country, including practically all of the trackage envisioned in the original plan of 1842. By 1870 the trunk lines of the system were essentially completed.[29]

It would be difficult to exaggerate the importance of this construction. If the railroad did not, in a sense, *make* the Industrial Revolution, one simply cannot imagine the fruition of this Revolution without it. It is common to point to the stimulus that railroad building gave to the development of heavy industry, and this should not be minimized (although in France, as in the United States, a fair proportion of rails in the early years of construction were imported from Britain). Far more important, however, were the opportunities that a national transportation and communications network (the railroad was almost universally accompanied by the erection of telegraph lines) opened to the world of business. It was the railroad, increasing the regularity, volume, and speed of the flow of goods and materials first into the factories and then out of the factories and into the city markets, that made possible the coming of big business in both production and distribution. The effects of this process in France were perhaps slower and less extensive than those described by Alfred Chandler for the United States.[30] But the simultaneous growth in productive capacity and retail operations was as inextricably linked to the creation of a national railroad system as the latter had inextricably linked factory to market, city to city. Moreover, railroads did not simply bring finished goods to the new stores in unprecedented numbers. They brought passengers too, from the suburbs and outlying towns, and at the same time readily transported purchases back into the hinterlands. That a number of emerging department stores were to find their fortunes partly in their proximity to major commuter stations, partly in the expanse of their mail-order trade, was also a consequence of locomotive power.

[29] Ibid., pp. 145-49; Paul Boiteau, *Fortune publique et finances de la France*, vol. 1 (Paris: Guillaumin, 1866), pp. 180-222.
[30] Chandler, *Visible Hand*.

There was one other tie between the railroads and the rise of the big-business enterprise. From nearly the beginning of the century, the business world had become increasingly complex and increasingly sophisticated in its organizational and operational forms. One might even wish, as one historian has done for America, to speak of a general business revolution that made possible the exploitation of the more familiar technological or industrial revolutions.[31] In part this may be seen in an ever greater specialization of business roles or functions over the first half of the century; indeed both small shopkeepers who were now exclusively retailers and the *magasins de nouveautés* formed part of this process. It may also be seen in the appearance of subsidiary business activities that greatly facilitated other forms of business. For example, the establishment of a cheap, advertisement-oriented press in the 1830s at last made newspaper publicity a truly available means of expanding one's trade.[32] But the development of large-scale business also required the ability to manage, coordinate, and control one's operations, and this came only with the first big business itself—the railroad. Once a railroad company was operating over 500 or more kilometers of track—and this was the case with a number of companies by the 1860s—it was necessary to devise an efficient organizational structure and communications system if for no other reason than to keep the trains from running into each other. It was also necessary to see that track and equipment on all sections of the system were properly maintained, that sales agencies were available along the entire system, that thousands of employees and perhaps dozens of managers performed their duties effectively, and that operations in one sector were coordinated with those in another. To run such a system further required the collection of data on all phases of operations and an adequate understanding of the road's costs. In a variety of ways, then, the railroads were forced to

[31] Thomas C. Cochran, "The Business Revolution," *American Historical Review* (December 1974), pp. 1449-66.

[32] Marcel Galliot, *La publicité à travers les âges* (Paris: Editions Hommes et Techniques, 1955), pp. 86-100.

pioneer in running and controlling a large bureaucratic enterprise. All of which is not to say that either the new manufacturing or new retail establishments drew directly from
the railroad experience. But the model—along with a trans-
ferable body of knowledge—was there.[33]

Thus by 1869, when Boucicaut and his associates laid the
cornerstone for a new Bon Marché, the way had been paved
for the emergence of the department store. In a sense, construction began not only at the junction of two city arrondissements, but at the convergence of two revolutions—in retailing and the national economy—which had produced an
environment ripe for still further change and still further
growth. One might even be led to remark that it was the
forces and not the individuals that mattered; so that if
Boucicaut had not existed, one might just as easily follow the
course of the Louvre, or perhaps even the Printemps, without losing the thread of the *grand magasin's* subsequent evolution in France. But personalities and the fates of individual
enterprises do count for something in history, and if the
house Boucicaut built was to become not only the first but
also the leading department store in France for over half a
century, certainly we would do well to inquire why this was
so. For the remainder of this chapter, then, we must shift our
attention to the Bon Marché, looking first at the endowments
(and limitations) of the Boucicaut family and then briefly at
the store's later growth as the necessary backdrop for the rest
of the story.

Boucicaut, unfortunately, is a figure of whom we know far
too little, although certain facts are apparently clear. He was
born in Bellême in 1810, the son of a Norman hatter. He was
Catholic. At the age of eighteen he left home and took to
the road as the "associate" of an itinerant peddler. By 1835
he had arrived in the capital, where he met Marguerite
Guérin—the offspring of a seduction in the Saône-et-Loire
nineteen years earlier—and in the same year they were mar-

---

[33] Alfred D. Chandler, Jr., ed., *The Railroads* (New York: Harcourt, Brace
and World, 1965); Caron, *Histoire*.

ried. Soon after, or concurrently, he was engaged as an employee at the Petit Saint-Thomas, where he taught himself English and eventually rose to the position of department head. In 1839 he fathered a son, Aristide Jr., his only child. In 1852, managing to set aside (or borrow) 50,000 francs, he left the Petit Saint-Thomas and joined Paul Videau as co-proprietor of the Bon Marché, a left-bank store which at the time had twelve employees, four *rayons* or departments, and a sales volume of approximately 450,000 francs. In 1863, staked by the Frenchman Maillard, who had made his fortune as a confectioner in New York, Boucicaut bought out Videau and became sole owner of the store.[34] In 1869 he laid the cornerstone for France's first department store; and in 1877, when he died, he was proprietor of what was then probably the largest retail enterprise in the world.[35] From his portrait we know that he was of substantial build, that his beard was full, that his eyes were striking, and that his forehead was graced with a true *bosse normande*, the presumed sign of commercial talent.[36]

But facts of this sort do not reveal much about the inner man, or about Boucicaut the innovator or Boucicaut the "Bon Marché King," as one epitaphial review was wont to call him.[37] There are, of course, the usual anecdotes, but these are likely to be apocryphal and in any case do not bear repeating. Indeed the one unavoidable legend passed down to us by contemporaries and subsequent historians—that Boucicaut was the father of modern merchandising—simply will not hold in light of the above account.

What, therefore, should we make of Boucicaut, and how might we explain his accomplishments? In one respect he might be seen as the consummate student of the new merchandising, a man who had learned his lessons well during

[34] Boucicaut made semi-annual payments to Videau that eventually totaled 1,948,000 francs when completed in 1871. Bon Marché Archives (hereafter referred to as B.M.), *Achat du Bon Marché* documents.

[35] B.M., Notes of Jean Theodore Karcher, secretary to Madame Boucicaut.

[36] In more mundane terms, a *bosse normande* is a bump on the forehead.

[37] "Fortunes Made in Business: Aristide Boucicaut, the Bon Marché King," *London Society*, April 1879.

his tenure at the Petit Saint-Thomas and who then applied the knowledge he had acquired to his own enterprise with more skill and more success than his competitors. Low prices, trustworthiness, and an emphasis on service appear to have been trademarks of the Bon Marché from the early days of Boucicaut's arrival there. Yet a view of this sort fails to capture the entrepreneurial side of a man who chose to shape his own destiny with his own store at precisely the moment when the great boom period of the Second Empire was beginning. Nor does it explain why Boucicaut's Bon Marché was to outstrip the Petit Saint-Thomas to the point that differences between the two were to become as great as their resemblances. Imitation and adaptation alone are not sufficient to account for Boucicaut's success. Indeed, most of the earlier innovators were never able to establish a *grand magasin*, and those who did never created one of the first rank. Much in fact of the Bon Marché's later competition was to come from entrepreneurs who had received *their* training as department heads at the Bon Marché.[38] Evidently, then, there were other sides to the man, sides of conceptual genius that grasped far better than his predecessors the ultimate possibilities proffered by the revolution in merchandising and, equally important, sides of organizational genius that knew how to bridge dream with reality. In later chapters we shall see how this genius was translated into the formation of a remarkably effective work force and an equally effective public relations program. For our purposes here, however, such sides eventually lead back to the design for the 1869 building, and it is perhaps wise to return to this structure for a moment and to explore in what ways it delineates Boucicaut's talent for innovation, systematic unity, and organization.

Whether the plans for the new building were in gestation as early as Boucicaut's arrival at the Bon Marché in 1852, or whether they came only with the huge increase in sales in the 1860s, is, like so many other things about the man, simply unknown. Following the pattern of the other *magasins de*

---

[38] Both Jules Jaluzot, founder of the Printemps, and Louise Jay, cofounder of the Samaritaine, worked at the Bon Marché.

nouveautés, the Bon Marché expanded haphazardly during the middle decades of the century, either by adding to existing structures or by acquiring adjoining ones. In any event, it was not until the neighboring Hospice des Petits-Ménages was finally torn down in 1868 that Boucicaut was able to obtain control of the remainder of the block and truly contemplate a wholesale reconstruction of the Bon Marché. Once he embarked on this project, however, he did so with the bent of mind of a man who fully comprehended the novelty of his undertaking.

For his architect Boucicaut chose L. A. Boileau and for his engineer Gustave Eiffel, two men who were pioneers in the functional architectural uses that could be made of iron and glass. Together they devised a plan that would employ a framework of thin iron columns and a roofing of glass skylights to work to the best advantage of a giant retail operation. The role of the iron was to provide for open, spacious bays in which large quantities of goods could readily be displayed and through which vast crowds could move with ease. The skylights, capping what in effect was a series of interior courts, were to permit a maximum influx of natural light, which was deemed necessary for display purposes. At the same time, the functional and systematic character of the plan was made complete by the provision for central offices on the top floors and a depot that could send and receive packages and store merchandise in a first-level basement. A second-level basement was also built to house the heavy machinery for heating (and later for lighting). Altogether the project was, in its very scope, breathtaking for its day. When construction finally came to a halt in 1887, the building occupied the entire square bordered by the rues Babylone, Sèvres, Bac, and Velpeau, and covered 52,800 square meters of surface space. In its final form it represented a notable step in the history of iron and glass architecture, a "model of elegance," and an indication of what a *grand magasin* might truly be like.[39]

[39] Sigfried Giedion, *Space, Time and Architecture* (Cambridge: Harvard University Press, 1959), pp. 236-41; Cucheval-Clarigny and Flavien, *Etude sur le*

Boucicaut did not live to see his new building completed. Construction proceeded slowly, perhaps for reasons of finance, perhaps because Boucicaut preferred to build one section at a time so as not to disrupt his trade of the moment.[40] Yet by the time of his death Boucicaut had, in effect, established the Bon Marché Department Store. Between 1869 and 1877 the merchandising ideas of the 1840s, the 1850s, and the 1860s were transformed into the maxims by which business was now routinely conducted. Merchandise selection slowly, yet inexorably, began to diversify. Organizational unity between merchandising sectors (departments) and bureaucratic sectors (offices and services) was carefully coordinated.

In sheer size alone the Bon Marché far surpassed the *magasins de nouveautés* of the late 1860s. Sales volume in 1877 was 73,000,000 francs, more than three times what it had been when the new building was begun. Employees now numbered 1,788, an astounding figure for the period. Only the Louvre could be seen to be competing on similar terms at this time.[41]

Following Boucicaut's death, the Bon Marché passed into the hands of his son, whose impact upon the store was minimal. A sickly young man with a somewhat besmirched reputation,[42] Aristide Jr. had never taken an active interest in the house. Preferring agriculture, the arts, and travel to the commercial life—not altogether unusual for the scion of a successful merchant—he remained removed from the daily affairs of the business. Not even the formation of a co-partnership between father and son in 1871 could alter the younger Boucicaut's predisposition for more gentlemanly pursuits, although presumably he kept one eye on the firm's annual balance sheet. Perhaps characteristically, perhaps with insight, he did not choose to take the reins of the house once

Bon Marché, Les Grandes Usines de Turgan (Paris: Librairie des Dictionnaires, approx. 1890).

[40] Cucheval-Clarigny, *Etude*, p. 52.

[41] Lescure, "Naissance," p. 28.

[42] See reports on Boucicaut, *fils* in Préfecture de Police, Ba 967.

it became his own. Instead he appointed two designated directors from among his father's closest associates to manage the Bon Marché. Meanwhile his own health was steadily failing, and within two years after his father's death he too was in his grave, passing the store on to his mother.

With Madame Boucicaut we come upon another legendary figure in French commerce. Born of peasant origins and out of wedlock, she had come to Paris in the 1830s as an apprentice in a laundry. Later she was to find work in a small restaurant, and it was here that she met Aristide Boucicaut. At this point the record becomes lost, and the next forty years of her life are not even obscure—they simply are unknown. It would be tempting to suggest that the time was spent working alongside her husband in the making of the Bon Marché. After her death it indeed became fashionable to assume that she had personally taken over the direction of the house during the remaining eight years of her life (she died in 1887). Yet store archives reveal that she was frequently absent from Paris during these years, and that, although she retained an interest in the daily affairs of the firm, she too preferred to remain in the background and to entrust the matter of management to associates.[43]

It is unlikely, therefore, that Marguerite Boucicaut had much, if anything, to do in a business way with the success of the Bon Marché. A simple and uneducated woman, she was not cut of the same pattern as a Louise Jay, who alongside her husband truly shared in the founding and making of the Samaritaine. But she did have her own gifts—those of compassion and concern for the individuals in her charge—and, mixed with a sensibility for the practical concerns of the firm, she was to use these talents in remarkable ways that counted for as much as business acumen in the subsequent fortunes of the store. She was also concerned with the Bon Marché itself, and its status after her death, to the point that she brought a number of her closest associates into partnership with the

[43] See especially B.M., Letters of Jean Theodore Karcher to Madame Boucicaut, 1882-1887.

formation of a *société en commandite* in 1880.[44] Under the statutes of this arrangement, future management was to be confided to three *gérants*, or directors, appointed from among the new shareholders' midst. Thus when Madame Boucicaut died seven years later, the Bon Marché escaped the fate that A. T. Stewart's had met, and, passing into secure and knowing hands, was to be governed under this system for the next three decades.

From this point, an overview of the Bon Marché's evolution until the First World War is primarily one of still further growth whose details need only be sketched. As the population of the Paris region continued to grow until it had passed the 2,500,000 mark by the turn of the century;[45] as the wealth and purchasing power of the country continued to increase;[46] as provincials and foreigners continued to flock to the capital, especially during the world's fairs of 1878, 1889, and 1900, each of which produced a substantial jump in the turnover of the store;[47] as public transport became ever more convenient with the addition of tramways in the 1870s and then with the first métro lines after 1900;[48] as new inventions like the tele-

[44] A *société en commandite* was a commercial company with sleeping partners. Some were relatively indistinct from family firms or traditional limited partnerships. Others were medium to large partnerships with share distribution that often was adopted as a means to increase the firm's capitalization. In contrast to the limited liability corporation (*société anonyme*), however, the directors of a *société en commandite* were financially responsible for the firm's obligations. That many French companies preferred the *commandite* form even after 1867, when restrictions on *anonyme* registration were lightened, undoubtedly derived from the tighter control of the directors in the former, the greater sense of corporate privacy, and restrictions and limitations that could be placed on shareholding. For many family firms, the *société en commandite* could also be the best means for increasing one's capitalization without diluting all of one's control. For a more detailed discussion of the *société* Madame Boucicaut created, see Chapter III and Chapter IV.

[45] Chevalier, *Formation*, p. 284.

[46] See figures on the number and holdings of savings accounts in de Lavergne and Henry, *Richesse*, pp. 182, 187.

[47] These fairs drew 16,000,000, 32,000,000, and 50,000,000 visitors respectively to Paris. E. Levasseur, *Histoire du commerce de la France*, vol. 2 (Paris: Librairie Nouvelle de Droit et de Jurisprudence, 1904), p. 99.

[48] In 1902 more than 450,000,000 passengers were carried by some form of

phone, the electric light, the cash register, and the escalator increased the efficiency, safety, and ease of shopping in a department store; and as a host of new products, from the bicycle to the cinematograph, broadened consumer incentives; so too did the Bon Marché experience a period of ever-increasing expansion. Sales volume, which had reached 123,000,000 francs at the time of Madame Boucicaut's death, passed the 200,000,000 mark in 1906. Employees, who had numbered 1,788 in 1877 and then 3,173 in 1887, numbered 4,500 in 1906; while the full count of persons employed in some capacity at the Bon Marché in this year was near 7,000.[49] In turn this growth, reflected particularly in the addition of new departments and in the enlarging of offices (by 1906 there were several thousand persons working at the store who were not directly involved in the selling process), led to continual plans for store rearrangement, purchases of surrounding structures, demolitions, and the erection of new buildings. At first such activity was intended primarily to regroup expanding offices and services and to shift these and workshops to secondary buildings so that the main house could be reserved for maximum selling space. But in 1899 it came to include the building of an annex across the rue Babylone intended for office and warehousing space and merchandise display—especially that of bulk goods like furniture. Then in 1912 a major extension was opened directly across the Sèvres-Bac intersection and joined to the original building by an underground passage.

Parisian public transport. Lagarrigue, *Cent ans*, p. 99. In 1909 the métro alone was carrying 254,000,000 passengers, and by 1914 120 kilometers of *métro* line were in operation. Most of this construction, however, was on the Right Bank. Anthony Sutcliffe, *The Autumn of Central Paris* (London: Edward Arnold, 1970).

[49] Lescure, "Naissance," p. 28; B.M., Sales Totals and Net Profits 1887-1906. For the period after 1887 there are no progressive statistics on employees at the Bon Marché, but a report of the *Assemblée Générale Ordinaire* (hereafter referred to as AGO), 28 August 1906 refers to a current total of 4,500. Like earlier totals given in this study this figure includes only sales and office clerks, and part of the service personnel who were referred to as *employés* by the store. The 7,000 figure is taken from B.M., *Livre d'Or*, 1907.

Overall, these were the golden years of the Bon Marché, a time when the left-bank store was unchallenged in its primacy among all the great Parisian emporia. When in 1910 the Bon Marché sold merchandise worth 227,000,000 francs, it far outdistanced its nearest competitor, the Louvre, whose sales volume that year reached only about 152,000,000 francs. Future giants such as the Printemps, the Samaritaine (founded in 1870), and the Galeries Lafayette (founded in 1895) were still selling at levels the Bon Marché had surpassed nearly three decades earlier.[50]

[50] In 1910 the Printemps had a sales volume of 100,000,000 and the Samaritaine 110,000,000. Levasseur, *Histoire*, vol. 2, p. 451. In America Macy's sales volume in 1914 was 17,000,000 dollars and Marshall Field's retail volume in 1906 was 25,000,000. Only Wanamaker's combined operation in Philadelphia and New York was perhaps as large, or larger, than the Bon Marché. No published sales figures for this period are available, however.

II · THE "GRAND MAGASIN"

IF WE WISH TO REGARD the Bon Marché as standing at a cross-roads of bourgeois culture, we must first see in what directions the conceptual signposts were pointing. The concepts—mass society, bureaucratization, rationalization—need to be made tangible, to be translated into the workings of the *grand magasin* that the Bon Marché had now become. In what way was the Bon Marché a mass marketplace? How did the machine work? How was the strategy of mass retailing converted into the structure of a rationalized operation? The answers to these questions may be found by looking first at the merchandise the Bon Marché sold, then at the store's methods of finance and purchasing, and finally at the firm's administration and organization.

MERCHANDISE AND THE MASS MARKET

The department store grew in two ways. First, by stressing stock-turn and low prices, it increased sales volume enormously. Secondly, it diversified into new lines. In France, diversification nearly always occurred through the introduction of new lines in an already existing department. When sales of these lines expanded to the point that they merited a department of their own, a split from the original department occurred. Rarely were totally new departments created from scratch. It was partly for this reason that the French stores appeared to lag behind their American counterparts. The Macy's of 1870 was considerably more diversified than the larger French stores, containing departments that would not appear across the Atlantic for another decade.[1] Yet the variety of merchandise to be found at the Bon Marché could also be considerably greater than its departmental listings suggested, especially if one explored the odds-and-ends categories of articles of Paris or the *mercerie*.

We are told that Boucicaut resisted expansion beyond the standard dry-goods and fashion lines,[2] but this was not completely the case. If he did announce that his new store was intended for a great trade in *nouveautés* (dry goods), this term would always form part of the Bon Marché's identity. Even after the turn of the century, when merchandise diversification was relatively akin to the contemporary department store's, the firm would continue to refer to itself as a *grand magasin de nouveautés*. Nor did Boucicaut shrink from proclaiming that "everything useful, convenient, and comfortable that experience has been able to produce" could be found at this new emporium. For the times, the claim was outrageous, mere puffery. Behind the publicity was a far more cautious Boucicaut and a far less diverse Bon Marché. But the statement was suggestive of future pretensions, and if Boucicaut ventured into new lines only gradually, indeed somewhat timidly, his progress in that direction was nevertheless constant. When Boucicaut entered the Bon Marché, the store carried shawls, cloaks, and tippets; garment linings and millinery items; a *literie* (perhaps beds, perhaps bedding); a *mercerie* section; and assorted fabrics and cotton goods.[3] Thirty years later, at the time of Zola's visit, the Bon Marché maintained thirty-six separate departments. How this evolution occurred bears some repeating.[4]

---

[1] The one potential exception was the *Magasins Réunis*, a project providing a common source of housing, heat, light, and publicity for 150 separate shops gathered together and catering to nearly every imaginable consumer need of the time. The venture failed miserably, collapsing soon after its inauguration. *La Presse*, 10 January 1867; Jeanne Gaillard, *Paris la ville, 1852-1870* (Paris: Editions Honoré Champion, 1977), pp. 544-47.

[2] D'Avenel, "Le mécanisme," pp. 356-57.

[3] *Annuaire-Almanach du commerce*, 1852.

[4] The following account comes primarily from a review of Bon Marché cata-

One route of diversification was through expansion of existing dry-goods and clothing lines. In the 1860s a ready-to-wear department was added, initially confined to garments such as cloaks and overcoats. By the end of the decade, however, the department was offering bathing suits and various fashion dresses, although the latter apparently were models cut to individual measurements. Advertisements in the 1880s for "dresses completely made" suggest that ready-to-wear was beginning to encroach even on the fashion trade.[5] Meanwhile men's wear, first introduced as shirts and ties in the 1860s, was substantially expanded during the following decade, while the 1870s further witnessed the addition of a separate children's section and the introduction of A. Boucicaut gloves, the first in a long line of Bon Marché trademarks. Another route of diversification led from the introduction of rugs in the 1860s, and perhaps beds as early as the 1850s, to tables, chairs, upholstery, and great lots of Oriental rugs in the 1870s, to integrated room sets, deluxe cabinet work, country furniture, and even camping ware in the 1880s. Finally, a third route brought an increasingly disparate set of goods together under one roof. In the 1860s Boucicaut was selling umbrellas, change purses, hairbrushes and toothbrushes, fans, scissors, stationery goods, combs, bracelets, ribbons, and Chinese and Japanese specialties, nearly all of these items carried within the *mercerie*.With the opening of the new store, the tempo towards this sort of diversification increased. In 1872 a travel-goods counter appeared. In 1875 Boucicaut installed a perfume department.

---

logues in the Bon Marché archives and catalogue holdings in the Bibliothèque Nationale. Bibliothèque Nationale, 4 WZ 3264; Fol. WZ 211; Fol. WZ 212.

[5] Catalogues in the 1870s are vague concerning the extent that ready-to-wear had penetrated dress-making and other fashion items. On the one hand evening gowns, wedding gowns, and other dresses continued to be available on individual demand and cut to fit the client. There is, however, a letter from Boucicaut to his secretary (one of the very few still extant) calling for greater publicity concerning the store's ready-to-wear dresses. B.M., Letter of Aristide Boucicaut to M. Karcher, 16 September (?) 1876.

Meanwhile, future departments were anticipated with the introduction of lines in fancy leather goods and very possibly silverware. Then in the 1880s two of the principal mainstays of the modern department store—stationery and toy counters—were added, while shoes, not traditionally a part of *nouveautés*, received a department of their own. Still further innovations included counters for jewelry, brushes, and articles for horses. As a result, by the 1880s department stores like the Bon Marché and the Louvre were coming to be referred to as great *bazars* as well as *grands magasins*, the former a term originally reserved for a format that specialized in household wares and furnishings, cutlery, toys, and assorted knick-knacks.[6] So, for all their reputed aversion to diversification, the Boucicauts had drawn, by the time of their deaths, the outlines of the modern merchandise mart.

Their successors were to fill in these lines, turning the Bon Marché into a market approximating that of department stores today. This is not to say that there was either a decreased interest or lack of innovation in clothing or dry goods. These lines were to continue to predominate among store merchandise to the point that forty-one of the fifty-two major divisions at the Bon Marché in 1906 basically involved such goods. But the most notable feature of the Bon Marché after 1888 was the enormous proliferation in the variety of merchandise offered for sale; indeed, the annex of 1899 and the building of 1912 were in large measure constructed to house the ever-expanding new lines. A list of "principle articles sold at the Bon Marché," printed in a house publication of the mid-1890s, revealed how varied store merchandise had become. Altogether, more than 200 items, from household wares to sport and garden goods to kitchen utensils to baby carriages, were offered for sale. With the turn of the century there was still further expansion into house, kitchen, and

---

[6] Like *magasins de nouveautés*, firms specializing in these sorts of wares underwent significant expansion in the middle years of the century. One house, *A La Ménagerie*, occupied a three story building by 1868 that was divided into twenty-one departments of household wares and furnishings. Catalogue, *A La Ménagerie*, 1868, Bibliothèque Nationale, 8 WZ 1716.

cosmetic wares, telephones, tea (at the China counter), photography goods, toilet paper (Bon Marché trademark), musical instruments, paint, and cinematographs. By 1914, then, there was little in the way of consumer goods that one could not buy at the Bon Marché.

A list of this sort does not in itself recreate the marketing strategy of the Boucicauts and the men who succeeded them. Alone it does not permit us to reenter their world of decision-making, to piece together the temptations and prejudices that weighed on the Boucicauts' minds or to reproduce the suggestions, reports, and deliberations that determined if new lines would be added or old lines discontinued. From it we cannot reenact the tension, exhilaration, and at times disappointment that accompanied the introduction of new counters and departments. Nor can we extract from it the intangibles—the comprehension of market trends, the flukes—that informed their calculations. In short, it does not permit us to reassemble the complexity of the history of merchandise diversification as it occurred at the Bon Marché. In the absence of further documentation, that is a story that simply cannot be retold.

But the list does reflect, in a significant way, what we mean when we refer to the department store as a mass retailer, or mass marketplace. It reflects, first of all, as we have earlier suggested, on the pattern of growth that brought this development about. It adds some flesh to the bones of sales volume figures, reminding us that the Bon Marché grew through a series of investments and experiments in how best to employ the profits that its new sales practices were generating, how best to sustain and further previously achieved levels of success and dynamism. In other industries in the nineteenth century, such decisions tended to lead to the building of new plants, or to backward and forward integration, or to mergers. At the department store the path of growth lay, as it would for most enterprises in the following century, in diversification, in the selling of new lines of merchandise. Secondly, the list reflects the sheer numbers of customers—the mass clientele—who in turn gave meaning to the term mass market. Mirrored in the tens of departments and hundreds of lines of merchandise are the 10,000 clients that probably entered the store on good days in the 1880s, or the 15,000-18,000 persons that Georges d'Avenel, a decade later, suggested passed daily through the doors of the Bon Marché and of the Louvre, or the 70,000 clients who perhaps came on the days of special sales.[7] In future sections we shall return to this clientele, seeing who they were and how their lives and life style became intertwined with the life of the store. Finally, as we run down the list of merchandise that came to find its way to the shelves and counters of the Bon Marché, we can begin to grasp in what way the department store had come to function as a mass marketplace for an emerging mass society. We can see that what constituted the mass market were not only the vast numbers of sales and consumers, but the vast range of consumer goods that were now on display. We can see that the prodigious sales figures represented an increasing turn towards the purchase of comfort, amusement, and luxury. And thus we can see the essential reality of the mass market—a new commercial concept designed to accommodate (and induce) a society that more and more would seek its identity in the variety of goods it consumed.

FINANCE AND PURCHASING

In their heyday, department stores often provoked charges of financial feudalism, as if their success resided alone in their ability to mobilize large sources of capital. For many this was simply a label of convenience or desperation, a willingness to accept the most malevolent implications of the equation that money equals power. But in a way the charge was not far off the mark. Mass retailing and the financing of mass retailing were interrelated at the most fundamental level of the revolution in merchandising. And the ability of the department store to finance and to supply itself (the latter closely allied to the former) on a massive, regular, diverse, and inexpensive

[7] Zola, NAF 10278, p. 75; D'Avenel, "Le mécanisme," p. 354. Zola's figures (including the figure of 70,000 for special sales days) appear in his notes on the Louvre, but can most likely be applied to the Bon Marché as well.

scale *was* integral to the success of the enterprise. What is more, the means by which these operations were carried out pointed to the growing integration of independent market processes within the confines of the *grand magasin* itself and to the subsequent control that the department store came to exercise over other market sectors.

The relationship between mass retailing and its financing was a simple one. Rapid turnover, the most basic of new merchandising practices, was combined with a policy of cash sales only. As a result, the flow of cash into store coffers was both constant and plentiful. Accounts receivable and similar *bêtes-noires* that haunted smaller operations were simply not a problem. Once the mechanism of low margins, low prices, high stockturns, and high volume was set in motion, operating capital became readily available.

How other financing was arranged during the early years of the Bon Marché's rapid growth is uncertain. But it is likely that such projects as the 1869 building were paid for, at least in part, from savings that employees placed with the firm for a return of six percent interest. By the 1880s this savings program had evolved into merely a service for encouraging thrift among the work force. But then later expansion—especially the acquisition and construction of new buildings—was financed through statutory deductions from the net profits and from the creation of a reserve fund that eventually grew to 40,000,000 francs.[8]

Thus in a variety of ways capital at the Bon Marché was internally generated. In keeping with the French practice of *autofinancement*, the store's owners and managers tended to reject dependency on outside financial sources. But they were not averse to tapping such sources if the dependency relationship could be reversed. This was the case in their dealings

---

[8] Gaillard suggests that Boucicaut borrowed from the Crédit Foncier in 1869. This is possible, although Bon Marché archives make no mention of a loan and Gaillard offers no documentation (it is not clear from Gaillard's remarks whether Boucicaut actually did take a loan or simply was in a position to receive one at a favorable rate). In any event, house records reveal no pattern of borrowing after this date. Gaillard, *Paris*, p. 533.

with suppliers. Because the department stores bought in quantity, because they bought regularly, their special sales alleviating the layoffs and shutdowns that came with slack seasons, and because they bought from labor-intensive industries consisting of small and medium-sized firms, they were in a position to dictate the terms of supply. Not surprisingly, their first use of leverage was to demand lower rates, which furthered the department store's competitive edge. In itself this was not a severe demand. Suppliers were merely being asked to adopt the same principle of low margins and high stock-turn that the *grands magasins* had already applied to the retail market. But with lower rates came more subtle mechanisms of control. Department stores bought on credit, interest-free, thereby shifting to the manufacturer the initial financing of supplies. By the time the credit came due, the goods had frequently been sold, again illustrating the linkage between turnover and capital. The stores also required that deliveries be staggered; so that in still another way operating costs—this time the costs of warehousing—were largely shouldered by the supplier. And it was not uncommon for *grands magasins* to extend their own credit to financially troubled manufacturers, generally at the rate of one percent per month. This could lead to permanent control over the manufacturer and to still more favorable concessions in addition to the high interest return. To the Bon Marché's credit, it was always known for its scrupulous dealings with manufacturers. Contracted conditions were always honored and kickbacks to its buyers were never tolerated. Nor do house records indicate that the Bon Marché directly extended loans to its suppliers. Still, credit buying and warehousing demands were considered within the range of proper business conduct and played a significant part in the store's financing and purchasing. Ultimately they too permitted the Bon Marché to sell in mass quantities and at low prices to its clientele.[9]

[9] D'Avenel, "Le mécanisme," p. 344; Paul Passama, *Formes nouvelles de concentration industrielle* (Paris: Bibliothèque d'Economie Politique et de Sociologie, 1910), pp. 136-37; B.M., *Conseils Généraux*, 1891-1911, passim.

The power that department stores came to wield over suppliers, and the subsequent benefits that accrued to store and consumer alike, followed from the internalizing within the store's own operations of what had previously been separate and multiple market transactions. In the past, manufactured goods had reached the retailer only after passing through a variety of middlemen. Between factory and shop lay commercial travellers, wholesale representatives, and most likely still more commercial travellers. Whether wholesaling of dry goods and housewares began to follow the same pattern as occurred in the United States toward the middle of the century, where the telegraph and railroad gave rise to large-scale jobbing firms with extensive purchasing and sales networks, is uncertain. But in the textile trade there did emerge a number of powerful wholesaling houses who provided advances to manufacturers (and presumably credit to retailers), established a communications system between market and factory, and offered the indispensable service to retailer and producer alike of gathering together the variety of products that a variety of factories was capable of manufacturing. Developed as these wholesaling networks had become, however, the department stores preferred to build buying organizations of their own. Rapid turnover and high sales volume required tight control over the flow of their supplies, and the stores did not need the credit that wholesalers could provide. Consequently, they began to maintain their own representatives in the field, the Bon Marché, for example, establishing purchasing houses at Lyon, Roubaix, St. Etienne, and London (until 1894). More important, they established direct contacts with manufacturers by dispatching their buyers (department heads) on a regular basis to the factories themselves. The buyers thus came to carry out the functions that middlemen had performed, while their knowledge of consumer trends enabled them to assume an active,

---

Not all purchases were made on credit. The department stores could also use their substantial cash reserves to win still further concessions from suppliers. Zola, NAF 10278, pp. 197-98.

even dominant, role in determining what was to be produced in the future.[10]

As they moved upstream, the *grands magasins* also entered into production of their own. This did not mean the acquisition of factories themselves, a route the department stores were reluctant to follow. But integration backwards did come to take two other forms. First, many stores became entrepreneurs much in the fashion of the old putting-out system. Gathering about them a network of small workshops or individual workers, they passed on a variety of goods that would have to be sewn or finished by hand. Arrangements of this sort included work on lingerie, shirts, some ready-to-wear, and cabinets. Dresses made to measure or requiring final individual touches were also often completed in this way. Some stores had the work done by workshops for young girls at convents, and in Belgium it was not unknown for work to be farmed out to the prisons.[11] However the Bon Marché, despite its religious connections,[12] preferred to rely upon small workshops of several people, upon intermediaries who passed the work on to individuals at their homes, or directly upon workers themselves, many of whom passed daily at the Bon Marché to receive orders or to be handed merchandise in need of completion.

The advantages of the system were numerous. It permitted the Bon Marché to meet the qualitative and diverse needs of its clients in regard to certain major items it sold. Expenses were the responsibility of the workshop or workers, and the work came cheaply, paid according to piecework at sweating system rates. The store retained maximum control over its orders, a necessity for a house that vaunted its hand-sewn

[10] André Saint-Martin, *Les grands magasins* (Paris: Librairie Nouvelle de Droit et de Jurisprudence, 1900), pp. 101-02; Claude Fohlen, *L'Industrie textile au temps du second empire* (Paris: Plon, 1956), pp. 146-48. For a detailed discussion of wholesaling in America, see: Chandler, *Visible Hand*, pp. 19-28, 215-24; Glenn Porter and Harold C. Livesay, *Merchants and Manufacturers: Studies in the Changing Structure of Nineteenth-Century Marketing* (Baltimore: The Johns Hopkins Press, 1971).

[11] Saint-Martin, *Grands magasins*, pp. 120-21.

[12] See Chapter V.

goods. Finally, the house could bypass state regulations, since it was not the habit to hold inspections in the homes of individual workers.

Meanwhile, the Bon Marché set up its own *ateliers* or workshops within the store itself. There were workshops for shirts and men's clothing; for trousseaus, baby clothes, and white goods; for women's hats and ready-to-wear items such as coats or cloaks; for made-to-measure clothes like skirts, blouses, evening and wedding gowns; and, finally, for wall hangings, upholstery, mattress and cabinet work. A number of these workshops dated from the 1860s and the early 1870s, and by 1890 there were more than 600 workers, both men and women, employed on the house premises in Bon Marché *ateliers*. Such workshops, however, were often only the core of the wider workshop network, since much of their work was completed on the outside, or vice versa.

ORGANIZATION

"All department store history," wrote one commentator at the turn of the century, "is dominated by this idea. . . . Circulate the capital as often as possible."[13] This was, in truth, the essence of the undertaking. The Bon Marché worked because it accelerated the flow of goods from the producer to the consumer, high velocity turnover generating high volume sales and rapid cash intake. But the Bon Marché also worked because it designed an organization to manage these flows. As the velocity and volume of operations increased, and as transactions were internalized to speed still further the stream of merchandise from factory to market, the Bon Marché developed the mechanisms necessary to coordinate and administer what had evolved into a complex set of processes. Only after it had accommodated its structure to the strategy it pursued did the mass marketer function effectively, and efficiently.[14]

[13] Saint-Martin, *Grands magasins*, p. 30.

[14] For the basic statement on the relationship between strategy and structure, see Alfred D. Chandler, Jr., *Strategy and Structure: Chapters in the History of the American Industrial Enterprise* (Cambridge: M.I.T. Press, 1962).

Management of flows began with coordination, the allocation of tasks among a variety of sectors and then the linkage of these sectors in a systematic way. Through this network of interlocking activities, the Bon Marché scheduled the rapid and steady passage of goods and paper, and performed the multiplicity of services that its clientele had come to expect of the store. Just how far the system extended beyond the direct selling process, and how methodical it had become in the coordinating of operations, can be seen if we follow the course of the flows from beginning to end.

There were two principal routes that these flows took, one of merchandise, the other of paper.[15] The first began at the receiving service, where the goods the store bought were delivered in bulk (by Madame Boucicaut's death a single year accounted for 87,000 parcels with a combined weight of 6,000 tons). Here crates and packages were weighed and opened before members of the departments for which they were destined, the contents examined, and the merchandise forwarded either to the reserves or directly to the selling floor. Once on the floor, the goods were displayed and then, of course, sold, this latter process entailing several transactions beyond the actual selling itself. First, the seller led the client to a cashier (73 in the time of Zola), where he cried out the sale and price to be paid. The cashier then wrote this down in a book at his counter and called back the terms to ascertain he had heard them correctly. On particularly heavy days a third person—*débiteurs*—acted as an intermediary to free the seller for his principal duties, these *débiteurs* being drawn from less burdened store sectors.[16] Finally, when the notation had been made and money exchanged, the sale was completed.

If the client carried her purchase home, then this was the end of the merchandise route. But if she preferred delivery, there were still several operations to be performed. First, the package was wrapped by garçons and then transmitted below to the central depot, a service that occupied 130 men in

---

[15] Most of the subsequent details are drawn from Zola's notes of 1882.

[16] By the 1890s the position of *débiteur* may have been permanent.

1906. Here the package was sorted and classified according to destination, and then loaded onto wagons for final delivery by coachmen and delivery boys. This in itself was a substantial operation. Eighty to 100 horses, with 30 to 40 wagons, were in use by 1876, the number growing to 150 horses and double the wagons twenty years later.[17] Intended to be as comprehensive and as efficient as possible, this service entailed 5 separate departures from the depot daily. In 1876, 93 suburbs, towns, and outlying villages received direct deliveries; in 1912 they numbered 600.

The route of paper began as well with the arrival of goods that were shipped by suppliers. The invoice was accepted by the receiving department, forwarded to the department head for approval and signature, and then sent again upstairs for a check by the verification bureau, and then for payment by the cash house. This latter office, known as the *caisse centrale*, functioned as well as a central accounting bureau where final records were kept. Fifteen men worked on these records in 1882, nearly 50 in 1906. A second route of paper followed the sale of the goods. Here three operations occurred between the offices and the selling floors below. First, notebooks in which sellers kept track of their sales were forwarded to a control office for the computation of commissions. At the same time this office (composed of 30 men in 1882, 109 in 1906) received the cashiers' notations and verified their totals daily. Thirdly, the cashiers, after totalling their receipts, transferred their take to the head cashier. He then added up the total for the entire house, and with the aid of assistants carried the cash to the *caisse centrale* above. We may also assume that a fourth operation, a check between the control office and the cash house, also took place.

There was one further route of merchandise and paper that was largely independent of each of these others. This was the operation of a mail-order department, whose workings can be appreciated only when we realize the extent of its trade.

---

[17] The firm was skeptical about the advantages of motor cars, but a few were introduced after the turn of the century.

The Bon Marché was like a great consumption empire, drawing to its center a cosmopolitan throng, conquering its provinces with its promotional legions, and then reaping the tribute from its outlying territories. The firm thought of provincials and foreigners as subjects to be won, and solicited them as eagerly as it did the Parisians. For mastering the former it relied upon the press, and the national rail system to herd them to Paris. Indeed while all the *grands magasins* scrambled after this market, the Bon Marché especially became known for the trade.[18] To win the latter, it again turned to the press, this time the foreign newspapers that were printed in Paris (the cream was culled by searching arrivals columns and then issuing invitations to their hotels—what pathetic soul in the depths of the bureaucracy was responsible for this scheme is fortunately not documented).[19] More important still were the great world's fairs and the mass audiences they drew to the heart of the capital (all empires must have their spectacles—a subject about which we will have more to say later). That the new annex was scheduled for the turn of the century tells us how eagerly these extravaganzas were awaited by the store.

But the greatest source of the empire's prosperity lay not in bringing its subjects to the center, but rather in bringing the center to them. In part this was accomplished by going abroad, by exhibiting displays at foreign world's fairs or by opening agencies in distant city markets.[20] Most of all it was accomplished through the practice of mail-order, the Bon Marché maintaining a service by 1871, and perhaps as early as the decade before. The mailings were massive. In 1894, for the winter season alone, 1,500,000 catalogues were sent out

---

[18] Zola, NAF 10278, p. 209.

[19] These newspapers included the *New York Herald*, the *American Register*, and Galignani's *Messenger*.

[20] The firm went so far as to mount exhibitions at the world's fairs of Chicago and St. Louis, despite what was considered an excessive cost. See *Conseils Généraux*, 7 November 1892, 17 November 1902. Agencies were established just before the war at Algiers and Buenos Aires. These were not branch stores, but rather intended to publicize the firm and to handle complaints concerning merchandise or service.

by the store, 740,000 destined for the provinces, 260,000 mailed abroad.[21] In 1910, for the white sale alone, the provincial figure reached just shy of 1,000,000.

The store did its utmost to make the trade work. Instructions for ordering were printed in catalogues, and exchanges or returns were readily accepted. For France, "Alsace-Lorraine," Germany, Italy, Switzerland, and Holland, all purchases of twenty-five francs or more were sent free of charge, except for items that were bulky, such as furniture. Elsewhere there were similar arrangements, depending on the distance or value of the goods. Catalogues also contained pictures and descriptions for taking one's measurements, and clients were encouraged to stop by the store when they were in Paris to have their measurements placed on file. Moreover the store was willing to mail-out selections of shawls, lingerie, and hosiery for inspection on request, although the return of these goods was at the charge of the client. In addition cloth and carpet samples, often simply attached to the mailing of catalogues, were sent out in the tens of millions each year. Just how successful these efforts became can be seen by examining the following tables:

TABLE ONE[22]

Dates	Sales Volume	Mail-order	Paris
1871-72	33,949,621	5,079,839	—
1876-77	72,693,993	13,196,974	—
1886-87	123,234,523	17,320,302	13,338,532
1895-96	159,420,596	26,463,062	19,662,714
1902-03	188,455,416	33,293,982	25,160,119

Mail-order, then, was a serious business for the Bon Marché, and its procedures had to be systematically organized to keep the flows moving as rapidly as possible. By the time of Zola there were several hundred men working in this service, some of whom simply opened the thousands of let-

[21] It was not uncommon to print the catalogues in the language of the country to which they were sent.

[22] The figures for "Paris" represent purchases made at Paris by provincials and foreigners but mailed to the clients at their homes, most likely C.O.D. B.M., Mail-order Statistics, 1895-1903.

TABLE TWO
VALUE OF PACKAGES MAILED
IN FISCAL YEAR 1902-1903[23]

Provinces	50,229,105	Holland	304,074
Algeria	1,208,371	Italy	294,333
Corsica	178,786	Spain	197,807
Tunisia	163,350	Central America	167,702
Other Colonies	790,803	Foreign Colonies	158,787
England	1,084,899	Scandinavia	152,045
Switzerland	776,955	Turkey	147,698
South America	771,180	North America	136,998
Germany and		Austria-Hungary	132,956
Luxembourg	547,580	Russia	87,361
Belgium	461,262	Portugal	78,441
Bulgaria, Rumania,		Greece	62,640
and Serbia	345,578	Others	569,664

ters that arrived each day. Others then read the letters and began the process of expediting the goods. First, they classified the order by nature of the command, and then sent it to the department that carried the item. Later, once the department had forwarded the order back to the service, they checked to see that it had been properly filled. Finally, the order was sent off to be packed and then forwarded to the depot, where it was prepared for delivery to the correct railroad station. Meanwhile the service's own accounting divisions processed the paperwork that was so largely independent of the other selling network, although we may assume that final receipts and notations were ultimately transferred to the *caisse centrale*.

Working with mail-order were several other services designed to further the effectiveness of its operations. One

---

[23] *Ibid*. These figures include packages mailed after purchases in Paris. In some instances they are likely to be well below the total number of sales made to a particular national clientele. For instance, council records frequently refer to a numerous American clientele which must have accounted for well beyond the 130,000 francs listed above. In the era of ship travel and steamer trunks, there was little reason for Americans to have goods forwarded home later. We may also assume that a fair portion of foreign clients were in fact residents of Paris.

of these, a correspondence bureau composed entirely of women, was responsible for answering the written queries that the clientele sent in. These women were expected to have a certain level of education (including in some cases knowledge of a foreign language), a respectable hand, and, we might suppose, a talent for suppressing their natural sense of humor. There was also a service to cut and paste the samples that accompanied store catalogues. This sector too was largely composed of young women, numbering approximately 150 by the late 1880s.

The production of catalogues, however, was the responsibility of publicity, a service that worked not only for mail-order, but also for the selling departments and the house as a whole. How it functioned, especially in the matters of initiative and execution, is a subject about which we know far too little—although it is clear that much of the work was done with the collaboration of the individual department heads. As a service, publicity was part of a wider network of individual store units, each of which, in its own way, helped to keep the machine working. These included a complaints service (humor here was more likely at a premium), interpreters, and inspectors who doubled as floorwalkers and a security force, this latter duty including the policing of the work force. There were also firemen who doubled as nightwatchmen, packagers, stablehands, cooks, electricians and mechanics, and a service charged with delivering unfinished goods to the outside workshops. We might also add that the house relied on the concierges of Paris to supply information and to help distribute catalogues. This service was provided for the customary bribe that polite people refer to as Christmas gratuities.

There was one other service whose multifarious duties were indispensable to the movement of flows through all sectors of the store. This was the garçons, a misnomer for a group of fully grown men who numbered 350 by 1882. Primarily, the garçons performed the heavy labor at the Bon Marché. They cleaned the building, assisted in the kitchens and eating rooms, carried packages down to the basement from the cashiers and mail-order, worked in the receiving service and the central depot, and assisted clients who needed help with their bundles. Garçons were also stationed behind the cashiers to wrap packages for customers or to do the initial packaging before delivery to the depot. They acted as messenger boys between departments and services, and finally they accompanied the coachmen on delivery runs or were sent out with their own hand pulled carts. In a sense it was the garçons who made the system work, providing as they did the communications network between one division and another.

A second dimension to the management of flows was the creation of layers of managerial authority. Organizational design called not only for units to process operations, but for units to supervise, plan, and control. Indeed, systematic coordination was made possible only once an administrative structure had been firmly established.

Not surprisingly, given the strategy of diversification by lines, the store's basic administrative unit became the department. Run by a department head and by several assistants who were known as seconds and who were ranked hierarchically (a chain of command repeated in offices and services), the department was practically an affair all its own. Each department head received his own budget, bought his own merchandise, and hired and fired the personnel in his charge. He further, of course, supervised sales except during trips to the factories, when the ranking second took over command. This meant that it was also the department head who set the rates of mark-up and mark-down and who prepared the displays and departmental advertising. Finally, as administrator of the basic sales process, it was equally the role of the head of the department to function as coordinator with the central store services.[24]

For more complex matters of store administration, there were several higher levels of authority, beginning with a body of administrators collectively known as the council. The origins of this council are obscure, although we may suppose

[24] There were no leased departments as occurred in the United States.

that in the early years of the firm Boucicaut, in a rather loose manner, organized, planned, and oversaw affairs and that he was assisted by several men whose opinions he valued and whose talents he respected. Then, perhaps in the 1860s, certainly by the early 1870s, this relationship was formalized with the creation of a general council of administration. Again we may suppose that Boucicaut remained the ultimate authority, most likely chairing all meetings of the council. Otherwise each administrator was allocated precise managerial duties for specific departments and offices or services. The administrators became the line authority between their basic units and the center, and were responsible for the performance of the sectors assigned to them. Their more specific duties included supervising the distribution of overhead and keeping a careful eye on their departments' rates of markdown. In a more general way they provided the channels of coordination for operations that extended beyond the departmental level. As a group, the council met on a regular basis, discussing such matters as general expenses, plans for new operations or departments, affairs concerning employees (including promotions), and the allocation of resources (space and personnel) according to seasonal demands. Later records suggest that from time to time commissions were selected among council members to draw up plans affecting combined spheres of operations. Individual administrators, it would also appear, could be charged with this function or could initiate proposals of their own. The size of the council varied over the years, numbering 11 members in the 1880s, about 15 at the turn of the century.

Following Boucicaut's death, the council perhaps reached the height of its authority, since neither Boucicaut's son nor his widow showed much interest in day-to-day management. Then, following the death of Madame Boucicaut, two new formal command groups were established. First there were assemblies of shareholders, although these were concerned primarily with institutional matters rather than with daily business. Secondly, a triumvirate of *gérants*, or directors, was created. We shall have occasion to discuss both the assemblies' and the directors' respective positions and power in a subsequent chapter. Here it is sufficient to note that the directors formed a new central executive, the principal director chairing the council and each of the three assuming ultimate responsibility for the administration of the different store sectors. As usual, a principle of division of labor prevailed, one *gérant* concentrating on financial affairs, another on selling departments, and a third partly on the one division, partly on the other.

This, then, was the organizational structure devised by the Bon Marché to process, coordinate, and administer its operations. By formal standards it was a hybrid design, combining a multi-divisional model's decentralizing tendencies with equivalent functionally centralized features. It was also, in some respects, a casual one, for, as systematic as components of the design could become, organizational planning in a comprehensive way was simply not part of the Bon Marché's thinking. There was little interest at the firm in organization per se, little reflection on management as a subject all its own. Indeed no organizational charts are to be found in the store records, and I doubt that any might once have existed. Consequently, lines of authority could be defined only unclearly, especially in matters of cross-store operations. If a dispute arose between two separate sectors or between two departments—perhaps over selling space or the allocation of new mechandise—the issue was likely to go all the way to the council before a final decision could be made. Nor was anything created in the way of a staff that could ease the lines of cross-store coordination, or ease the preparation of new plans and procedures. And the directors could occasionally be terribly overburdened, fully immersed as they were in day-to-day affairs. Where was the time for independent thinking, for overall appraisal or for the planning of strategy? This was one organizational question that did, for a time, occasion some study,[25] although no change came about until after the war.

[25] B.M., *Assemblée Générale Extraordinaire* (hereafter referred to as AGE), 14 December 1909; AGE, 11 March 1910.

Despite these shortcomings, the design was a sound one, and reflected a grasp of the particular conditions that followed from a department store's mass-marketing strategy. Through decentralization at the departmental level the Bon Marché could fix responsibility for its most essential operations, and coordinate buying and selling for a wide range of merchandise. There was no need to develop a more complete divisional form, as would later be the case when diversification came to the mass production industries. The problem of marketing a variety of product lines simply did not produce the same strains at the department store to warrant autonomous services and offices for each set of departments. By the same token, because so much coordination occurred within the selling departments themselves, there was less pressure to establish line and staff procedures. And if the load on directors could at times be a heavy one, there was nevertheless little need to remove them completely from operational affairs. Running a department store was just not that strategically demanding once the overall system had been set into motion. Most strategic thinking—like the introduction of new lines—was likely to originate at the departmental level, again a condition for which the Bon Marché was more than adequately prepared.

There was one other dimension to the management of flows beyond the design of an organizational structure. This was the incessant push towards greater efficiency, the penetration of a broad rationalizing process into all spheres of store operations. Not that the Bon Marché self-consciously pursued a policy of rationalization anymore than it thought about administrative affairs. Only at the end of the 1920s would rationalization become a part of the house vocabulary or an efficiency engineer be employed by the firm. Still, there was little difference between such an outlook and the mood of the pre-war Bon Marché, where a director could remark, almost offhandedly, that council members should "seek out improvements in our way of doing things, seeing notably if it would not be advisable to simplify certain work methods or to divide the work in a better way so that it will be more quickly executed, the duty being to seek constantly to do better."[26]

One means of dividing the work in a better way was to break down store sectors to keep them from becoming too unwieldy for individual management. This principle was most apparent in the creation of new departments out of old ones once sales volume for one set of goods reached a certain level. Mail-order was also divided into two sections, one for foreign clientele and one for provincials, the latter section further divided into a first and second division. By the turn of the century, additional central accounting branches were created to handle the increased flow of paper. And at the same time, as bureaus and services were divided into more manageable units, efforts were made to group together office space so that transactions between them could be processed more readily.

There was a certain protean quality to rationalization at the Bon Marché. In the delivery service it led to the partition of Paris into ten divisions to simplify classifications in the depot and to avoid duplication of routes as much as possible. In mail-order it was manifested through files on past purchases to increase the efficiency of mass catalogue mailings. Elsewhere it took the form of special symbols and colored paper, each symbol or color corresponding to a particular operational variation to make the flow of paper more rapid and more easily classifiable. By the end of the century it began to appear more and more frequently in the guise of technology adapted to the organizational needs of the firm. Telephone lines were increasingly installed for interservice communication or for communication between sectors such as departments and their workshops. Sliding chutes, turning tables, and what must have been a form of conveyor belt were used to funnel packages to the central depot. Technology, in fact, became so important that in 1910 Edouard Hocquart, the

[26] B.M., *Conseils Généraux*, 26 December 1906.

store engineer who had devised the belted system and installed the first escalators in the house, was named to the council.

Rationalization also took the shape of methods of control designed to monitor performance of both individual units and the store as a whole. One commentator in the 1890s remarked that statistics were not especially stressed at the firm, but this simply was not the case. As we have already seen, precise procedures were established no later than the 1880s to assure a constant flow of daily store data into the central accounting office of the store. A set of mail-order records from 1895 to 1903 further reveals an extensive breakdown on sales, expenses, and operations by sectors and months and includes, as well, comparisons with the figures of the previous years for each of these areas. And if still further accounting records are no longer available, we nevertheless do know that certain essential (and relatively refined) statistical operations were, in fact, being performed. We know, for instance, that comparative sales data—by department—were regularly computed, perhaps even monthly, and, more important, that general expenses (including overhead) were apportioned on a departmental basis by at least the turn of the century. We also know that considerable attention was given to the computation of inventories, and that both the cost of goods and current market prices were taken into account. Above all, we know that by computing rates of stock-turn for individual departments, Parisian department stores had, by the 1880s, acquired the capacity to evaluate both the overall success with which store flows were being managed and the performance of individual units in this process.[27]

Perhaps most symbolic of rationalization at the Bon Marché was the *blanc*, the great white sale that occurred in late

---

[27] D'Avenel, "Le mécanisme," pp. 346, 352; B.M., *Conseils Généraux*, 12 July 1898, 7 August 1901, 23 August 1901, 28 August 1908; Zola NAF 10278. Zola's reference to turnover by department comes in his notes on the Louvre, but there is no reason to doubt that the same computations were being made at the Bon Marché—especially since an earlier reference to the initial importance of turnover comes in his notes on the latter store.

January or early February as a diversion from the winter off-season. During the first day of this sale the store could expect to gross three times as much as on an average good day, while the excess for the week as a whole might well come to 1,000,000 francs or more.[28] Thus the *blanc* was the single most important sales week of the year for the firm, and as such came to merit special attention and preparation. Long detailed reports, increasingly refined over the years, were drawn up after each sale to be used as a guideline for the following year.[29] These reports were meticulously put together, discussing difficulties that had arisen during the past sale and making suggestions for avoiding them in the future. It was also the purpose of these reports to define the duties of each service (with particular attention to special arrangements for the overloaded depot) and to determine the allocation of space and employees from one service or department to another. Then, well in advance of the actual sale, the reports were passed out and a *blanc* commission formed to finalize details. Begun thus as a mere merchandising gimmick, the *blanc* soon came to be the most organized week at the store, a model of the sophisticated sort of planning that Bon Marché directors and administrators were capable of producing.

So ultimately organizational design at the *grand magasin* came to mean the bureaucratization and rationalization of retail trade in France. Extreme division of labor, a corps of middle and top managers, and an inexorable impulse towards seeking the most efficient means of carrying out operations were the components that made the department store work. Together with the mass display of a wide range of merchandise under one roof, the successful coordination of wide-ranging and complex sets of procedures underscored the transformations that the new emporia brought to the marketplace. But bureaucracy and mass retailing were also developments that carried far beyond the world of business op-

[28] B.M., Karcher Letters.
[29] When these reports began is not known, since Council records, where they appear, are only available from 1891 on. Reports on a far smaller scale were also drawn up for several of the other special sales.

erations, developments that affected individuals as well as markets. Indeed they very deeply affected a fair proportion of the bourgeois community, from businessmen to employees to consumers to the public at large. And in the end the success of the *grand magasin* depended on the willingness of each of these groups to come to terms with these fundamental changes that the department store was bringing to their world. This process of change, then, the human as well as the structural, is a subject to which we must now turn.

PART TWO

Internal
Relations

III THE BOUCICAUTS

FEW STEREOTYPES are as evocative of nineteenth-century French bourgeois culture as the French bourgeois family, bastion of respectability, bearer of status, instrument of social exchange and ambitions. It was through family values, allegiances, and relationships that the bourgeois engaged in and found meaning in his daily milieu. The family was a veritable institution, the ultimate arbiter of success or failure. It stood at the very center of the nineteenth-century frame of mind, and as such it penetrated another institution equally a foundation of nineteenth-century bourgeois society—the French business house.

Traditionally the two were inextricably intertwined in that rudimentary form of the French family firm, the small family shop. Here the enterprise was literally an extension of the household to which it belonged. The family lived and worked within a single building, the *patron* and wife forming a surrogate family for those assistants whom they took in their charge. Some went still further, engaging their daughters to their senior employee and thus making him their sucessor when they retired.

But the French family firm knew no set limitations, and, as the century progressed and business expanded, the penetration of family relationships grew with it. This was particularly true of the French textile industry, where nearly all firms were family controlled and where the world of family lent substance and coherence to the world of business, fixing the conventions and defining the roles that pegged the businessman's endeavors to his broader cultural setting. Yet it was also true of nearly all other sectors, where, if not every enterprise was a family concern, many shared in the ethos of family relationships. Even in heavy industry, where capital demands were enormous, the family firm was common, indeed often to be found among the leading concerns. When businessmen did turn to capital associations like *sociétés en commandites*, they often did so in a way that retained a strong element of family control or, at the very least, control by the founders. *Sociétés anonymes*, or limited liability corporations, existed from the beginning, but their development was slow until late in the century, and the typical form remained the family firm, or some variation of it. Within the enterprise the family ambiance was intense. Often managerial and technical assistants were drawn among relatives, including the sending of children to the best engineering schools. In the realm of worker relations, the family spirit remained pervasive, again bringing cohesion to the businessman's world and to the conditions of authority that he attached to it. Highly personal and often highly paternalistic—increasingly with an eye to fixing and disciplining an industrial work force—the family affair remained wedded to those household traditions that informed the very idea of the firm.[1]

[1] Daumard, *La bourgeoisie*, pp. 325-55, 394-401, 458-77; André-Jean Tudesq, *Les grands notables en France, 1840-1849* (Paris: Presses Universitaires de France, 1964), pp. 261-64, 422; Jesse Pitts, "Continuity and Change in Bourgeois France," in Stanley Hoffmann et al., *In Search of France* (New York: Harper and Row, Harper Torchbooks, 1965), pp. 249-54; David Landes, "Religion and Enterprise: The Case of the French Textile Industry," in Carter, *Enterprise*, pp. 41-86; Fohlen, *L'Industrie textile*, pp. 84-85; Jean Vial, *L'industrialisation de la sidérurgie française 1814-1864* (Paris: Mouton, 1967), pp. 178-79, 388, 391-96. According to Vial, only five percent of siderurgical firms were *sociétés anonymes* by mid-century—p. 186. The de Wendel concern was strictly family-owned. Le Creusot under the Schneiders was structured as a *société en commandite*, but by 1855 Eugène Schneider was majority shareholder. Alfred Desseilligny, who was an engineer and director of the firm from 1853 to 1866, was Schneider's nephew. He married Schneider's daughter in 1858. After Eugène's death the firm passed into the hands of Eugène's son, Henri. See Joseph-Antoine Roy, *Histoire de la famille Schneider et du Creusot* (Paris: Marcel Rivière, 1962). Stearns suggests a somewhat different approach to business organization by mid-nineteenth century, but I think he seriously overstates the degree of bureaucratization existing at this time (certainly relative to what was to come later)—he gives no figures or documentation on this—and underestimates the extent to which family relations pene-

The bureaucratic capitalism of a venture like the department store was an intrusion into this world. It was an intrusion into the close proximity between management and ownership. It was an intrusion into the family tenor of employee ties that had rarely been subjected to such a rationalized environment. And in the particular case of the *grand magasin* it was an intrusion into the expectations of white-collar workers for whom bourgeois status implied a house of their own. So, for the Boucicauts, building the Bon Marché required more than pioneering marketing strategies and administrative structures. There was also a need for more complex business roles to adapt to the management of an organizational endeavor and a need for more complex employee relations to form, shape, and integrate a mass bureaucratic work force. How to respond to these challenges, how to redirect the internal cohesion of the French family firm, and how to do so in a cultural milieu where household values remained highly prevalent and prized, were the essential questions that the Boucicauts were forced to ponder as they set about building an associational frame to match the one of glass and iron.

Building Organization Men: The Base

Internal relationships at the Bon Marché centered on the creation of organization men. This was the foundation upon which all other blocks of an associational structure would now have to be raised. To build such a work force the Boucicauts turned to a mix of rationalized work policies and institutionalized paternalism. The former of these, their system of work, must be considered first.

---

trated new business forms in France. On the other hand he does bring out the personal and paternalistic climate of the early industrial period. Stearns, *Paths*, Chapters 1 and 4, and pages 129-32. For more discussion on early paternalism see below, p. 88. On small shopkeepers see Balzac, *La maison*; Zola, *Au bonheur*; Daumard, *La bourgeoisie*, especially pp. 446-52 (there is however some variance between Daumard's figures on marriage between employees and the daughters of *boutiquiers* and the picture presented by novelists like Zola—p. 382).

Most clerks were drawn from the lower middle class, very often the sons and daughters of small shopkeepers, although garçons and other employees who performed manual labor tended to come from peasant stock. Both groups were predominantly provincial in origin, the garçons almost exclusively so, while approximately four-fifths of the clerks were born outside Paris. The one exception was women employees, who far more frequently came from the capital. But women clerks at this time were a distinct minority. When Zola visited the Bon Marché in the early 1880s, only 152 women were selling in the store, and these were confined to a few departments such as ladies' lingerie or trousseaux.[2]

Few clerks, if any, entered the Bon Marché as novices to their profession. Like the young man who was born in Calvados, worked for a year at the Belle Jardinière in Rouen, then moved to Paris, where he spent eleven months at the Pauvre Diable, ten at the Coin de Rue, and eight at the Louvre before entering the Bon Marché, or the *blanc* salesman who was born in the Basses Pyrénées, began his career at the Maison Blanc in Pau, worked for a year at another store in Bordeaux, and then spent four years in *service militaire* before working for the Boucicauts, all Bon Marché clerks had some previous selling experience.[3] This was a store requirement. It was a requirement that the Boucicauts could make because high salaries and other favorable conditions attracted a surplus of applicants to Bon Marché positions, and it was a requirement that enabled the Boucicauts to rely on other stores for their salesclerks' initial training. It was also a requirement through which the Boucicauts could underscore from the very beginning that the Bon Marché work system placed a substantial premium on the employee's performance. Further stressing performance in a trade that often

[2] Pierre Giffard, *Paris sous la troisième république: les grands bazars* (Paris: Victor Havard, 1882), p. 73. B.M., Employee Dossiers; Zola, NAF10278, p. 50. Of ninety-nine clerks who entered before 1887 and whose dossiers were checked, twenty were born in Paris and three in foreign countries. Of twenty-nine garçons, coachmen, etc., only one was born in Paris.

[3] B.M., Employee Dossiers.

chewed up its work force by middle age, the Boucicauts did not tend to hire persons over thirty years old, although this did not become iron-clad policy until at least the mid-1880s.[4]

The recruitment process itself initiated employees into a network of procedures, specialized functions, and delegated decision-making. An applicant presented himself not to the owner but to the head of the department for which he was applying. Here his appearance and references were checked and his name, age, place of birth, recent work experience, and Parisian address noted in a special book. A *casier judiciaire* or record of previous arrests was also required. This information was then recorded in a general register and an inspector was charged with any additional investigation that might be deemed necessary (further initiating the employee into the inspector's surveillance net which would enmesh him more completely once he entered the firm). The final decision on hiring, however, belonged to the department head. Recommendations were essential, again underlining the stress on performance. Often these would come from acquaintances in the hierarchy, a member of the family who worked for the store, or from outside sources of influence. But past employers would nearly always be checked to confirm the applicant's aptitude, conduct, and moral character.

Procedures were a way of life at the Bon Marché. Employees were recruited according to store procedures, they were fired or retired according to store procedures, and in between they were expected to work according to store procedures. For some, particularly when nettled by procedural pettiness or by that special ability of procedures to gainsay common sense, the regulatory mania of the store must have appeared as sheer bureaucratic madness. But bureaucracies, like games, thrive on such insanities, and the Bon Marché was no exception. If salesclerks, for example, did not learn

---

[4] The refusal to hire employees over thirty was common to most large stores in Paris. See Léon Bonneff and Maurice Bonneff, *La classe ouvrière* (Paris: Publications de la "Guerre Sociale," 1911), p. 38; P. du Maroussem, "Les grands magasins tels qu'ils sont," *Revue d'Economie Politique* (1893), p. 958.

the cryptic language of the store's symbolic markings, if they did not learn to place these markings on the right forms in the right places (and to do so legibly), and if they did not learn to follow the precise routine of calls and countercalls with the cashiers, no matter how silly they may have felt on certain occasions, then there was little likelihood that either bookkeeping, or delivery, or even their own payment could be carried out effectively. The same sort of standardization was equally essential for the work in the offices, and even for the work of the poor garçons, who received instructions on how to prepare their packages and papers before going on delivery, how to fill out receipts, and what to do when no one was at home. Rigid as this obsession (and its enforcement) might have been, it was the only way that the Boucicauts could hope to make their work force conform to their rationalized organization.[5]

Procedures served still another function; they helped to form a new kind of seller. Prescribing the one right way of selling permitted the Boucicauts to wean their employees away from the old habits of haggling and cheating still rampant in the small shops of the country. It also permitted the Boucicauts to set personal standards for a work force that now represented the firm in its dealings with the public. Such standards were absolutely essential in a business environment that stressed service and the idea of shopping for the pleasure of consuming. They could also be advantageous for a store that now was selling mass-produced goods and whose very name added a common, if practicable, touch to its image.

Thus the Boucicauts dictated a uniform code of behavior that ranged from the employee's appearance to his selling of merchandise. Absolute courtesy was demanded at all times, and the employee was warned against any negligence in his dress or language. He was also obliged to respond to all questions with "the greatest of readiness," never to lie about the

[5] By at least 1876 Boucicaut was issuing a "General Information and Interior Regulations" pamphlet intended apparently for both the general public and the personnel.

merchandise, and to remain by the client's side until he or she had finished shopping in his department. Smoking, needless to say, was expressly forbidden. These rules applied to all employees in contact with the public. Consequently, delivery boys who remained representatives of the firm during their errands outside the store were also instructed to be polite and were advised on such diverse matters as how to station their hand-pulled carts or the proper manner of riding in the coach (safety was also of concern here).

The Boucicauts further shaped their employees' selling behavior by paying them in a way that broke with traditional patterns and that linked salaries to the dynamic climate of the firm. In small shops employees were paid almost solely on the basis of a fixed salary. But at the Bon Marché commissions formed the most substantial part of a salesclerk's pay. Zola claimed that the commission, on the average, was more than double the regular salary, so that a seller earning from 1,200 to 1,500 francs annually on a fixed salary might, on the whole, receive 3,600 francs in a year. Exceptional sellers with the same salary could rise as high as 6,000 or 7,000 francs annually, although this was rare.[6]

Such overall salaries were of course a critical factor in the Boucicauts' ability to attract large numbers of applicants and to set special demands for admission to the firm. Yet this was not the only purpose they served. If traditional small shops used commissions sparingly, this was because they simply were not compatible with time-consuming bargaining or the finessing of high profits from individual sales. But in a selling environment that fed on vast sales and rapid turnover, commissions were compatible. Indeed they were so compatible that, if used generously, as they were by the Boucicauts,

[6] Employee dossiers for the period do not include commission earnings, but figures from the turn of the century tend to bear out Zola's observations and suggest, in fact, even higher commission averages. These dossiers also suggest that perhaps some office clerks and even some garçons were receiving a form of commission, although there is no clarification on this matter and it is only in a few instances that such references appear. Zola, NAF10278, pp. 11, 13, 19; B.M., Employee Dossiers.

they could acclimate the work force to a new selling role that emphasized, not artistry and persuasion, but quantity and speed as the measurement of performance. And commissions fit the new selling environment in still another way: they fostered individualism and competitiveness. They were a frequent cause of quarrels between clerks, and, if they might produce some nasty moments, they also interfered with unionization efforts.[7] Perhaps still more important, by tying salaries to competitive behavior, commissions could infuse the sales force with the dynamic spirit that lay at the heart of the revolution in retailing. For the Bon Marché employee, the sluggishness of the small shop was to be a thing of the past.

The competitive spirit was reinforced by the Boucicauts' decision to fill all positions in the hierarchy through promotion from the ranks. This policy again served to immerse the work force in the dynamism of the organization by tying rewards to competitiveness, performance, and effort—a "struggle for life" as two observers of department stores noted in the 1880s.[8] At the same time the possibility of promotion provided a crucial link in the efforts of the Boucicauts to transform their employees into organization men. In the past, most young men had entered small shops with the expectation of eventually succeeding to a house all their own. Now the Bon Marché was suggesting an alternative to these aspirations by proposing instead that employees perceive of their future within an organization. To become a second, department head, administrator, and later director, to work one's way up the organization and achieve success within it was the new ideal that the store extended to its personnel. And those who made it to the top, passing through positions far more complex and lucrative than any situation an independent shopkeeper might enjoy, would never cease in later years to remind the lowly of their own humble origins. To-

---

[7] The employee movements were aware of this and wished to do away with the practice altogether. See A. Artaud, *La question de l'employé en France* (Paris: Georges Roustan, 1909), p. 235; André Lainé, *Les demoiselles de magasin à Paris* (Paris: Arthur Rousseau, 1911), p. 56.

[8] Giffard, *Grands bazars*, p. 210; Zola, NAF10278, pp. 82-83, 194.

gether with pension programs that would later be established, the policy of promotion suggested that to enter the
Bon Marché was to enter a career, and by 1890, perhaps earlier, the store was receiving applications stating that "my aim
in entering your honorable house is to create for myself a
definitive situation."[9] Career also meant subservience to the
regulations of the house. To rise meant to display obedience
and loyalty as much as talent, and the successful ones would
also vaunt their "devotion" alongside their "intelligence"
and "industry." Like the rivalries it produced, the temptation
of promotion again offered excellent opportunities for maintaining control over the personnel.

No work policy, however, could so effectively control
employees as the spectre of dismissal. Firing was a tool that
the Boucicauts used unhesitatingly and implacably in shaping their work force, and the very frequency with which the
ax fell reflected how rationalized their work system had become. Of the nearly 400 persons who entered the store in
1873, 39 percent were fired in their first five years. If the
number of voluntary departures (43 percent) is also taken into
account, the figures are still more striking.[10] In its broadest
form the intensive use of this power underscored the
Boucicauts' desire to exert their authority at will.[11] More
specifically it was directed at two particular ends: the enforcement of the performance principle for which the
employee had been hired and the assurance that organizational standards and discipline would be respected at all
times.[12]

By weeding out inadequate employees, the Boucicauts
made it clear to incoming personnel that their employment

[9] B.M., Employee Dossiers.
[10] B.M., Employee Register 1872-1878.
[11] By at least the 1890s the Bon Marché had a standardized letter-contract
wherein the applicant acknowledged that in the *commerce de nouveautés* trade
it was customary for either party to terminate employment "without previous warning and without compensation on either part." B.M., Employee
Dossiers.
[12] The following discussion is based on information found in the Bon
Marché employee register of 1872-1878 and employee dossiers.

hinged on their contributions to the success of the firm. Employees who were dismissed during their first year were frequently regarded as "weak," "very ordinary," a "cold seller," or a "mediocre seller." Two men who were fired from the fancies department in 1875 received the respective notations of "not sufficiently accustomed to the fancies trade" and "very ordinary employee unable to accustom himself to the House." Another man who was considered a "good employee" was nevertheless released because he was "insufficient for the bedding [department]. Too accustomed to the practice of the speciality [trade]." Inadequacy was defined therefore both in regard to selling ability and accommodation to the practices of the department store, and failure to produce on either score was reason for dismissal.

Inadequacy could also constitute the commission of errors. A clerk in ready-to-wear was fired in 1873 because he wrote out a sales slip for 35 francs instead of for 125. A coachman who had two accidents was dropped, and office employees had to be careful not to make too many mistakes. Moreover the persistence of off-seasons meant that even skilled employees could be let go if the firm no longer needed their services. Trade slackened twice a year, from June to September and from December (aside from toys and fancy goods) to February. Some department stores were notorious for wholesale dismissals during these periods. At the Bon Marché employees were more fortunate, for figures from 1873 and 1877 do not reveal great increases in the frequency of firings. Still, except for occasional great sales, when the store strained to meet its service requirements, the employee, particularly the newcomer, must have sensed his vulnerability before this beat of the market.

But the most frequent cause for dismissal was a break in the disciplinary or procedural structures of the store. In the bureaucratic environment of the Bon Marché, where the work force was coming to number in the thousands and where authority was dispersed among a host of middle and lower managers, discipline could be maintained only if the personnel learned to respect the orders of all their superiors. They had to respect not only the authority of their *patrons*, whom they now rarely saw, or the authority of the administrator responsible for their store sector, but also the immediate line authority of their second and department head and the supervisory authority of the hated inspectors. In this way alone could the store expect to function properly. Insubordination was simply not tolerated. Refusal to obey an order was immediately punished by dismissal, and employees might often be fired for as little as "talking back" to their second. Not even "good employee[s]" were spared. Similarly, employees who missed work or who failed to respect established procedures were discharged, for the issue of authority was closely tied to the store's complex division of labor, where a breakdown anywhere along the line could impede the functioning of the entire organization. Indeed the least failure to adhere to store regulations was apparently viewed as a threat to the authoritative and operational structures of the store and was rigidly dealt with. For instance, garçons who were lodged by the house and slept out without permission were let go. Even employees who at lunch poured two cups of coffee instead of one could be fired.

Absolute respect for orders and procedures further entailed the enforcement of service and behavior codes, and those employees who failed to abide by one or the other were also released. If, as we shall see, the store ambiance might seduce clients into excesses as shoppers, the clients themselves might tempt the personnel to abandon moderation in less businesslike ways. By Bon Marché standards the first sin (if accompanied by cash) was perfectly acceptable, the second inadmissible; and sales clerks who in the discreet language of the house touched a client in "an indecent way" or who displayed "vulgar thoughts vis-à-vis a client" were immediately dismissed. More often dismissal was simply a matter of having "discontented a client" or "lack of courtesy towards a client" or not having been as presentable (*"maltenu"*) as the store would have liked. Likewise, employees who broke the rule that merchandise should sell itself and who compromised the store's reputation for honesty by giving false information were let go. So firing again was linked to shaping a work force that could fit the new retailing ways of a *grand magasin*.

Yet meddling with employees' personal habits went still deeper, to a concern for that fundamental tenet of bourgeois culture—respectability—and its adaptation to a new bourgeois milieu. Undoubtedly the Boucicauts' own moral standards were strongly at play here. Each was a practicing Catholic and both Zola and a store cashier noted a reign of virtuousness at the Bon Marché.[13] But anxiety over respectability also touched upon more paramount matters, given the store's clientele, the quarter in which the store was situated, and attacks on the "immorality" of department stores as a whole—matters we shall also have reason to consider in future chapters. Hence the Boucicauts did not hesitate to correlate private character with public behavior (and public image), and among notations in the employee register could equally be found: "Good employee. Married, separated from his wife and living in marital fashion with another woman (this situation does not permit us to keep him)"; and "Left voluntarily. Lived with a woman with a bad past. Had to choose between the woman or the House. Good employee"; and, in regard to a saleswoman, "Good employee. Fired because we learned that she was living in marital fashion and not with her parents." Furthermore, like the severity tendered towards the smallest rule infraction, any form of misbehavior was regarded as a threat to the functioning of the store. To be sure, the employee who was fired *"pour avoir pissé au sous-sol"* exceeded tolerable limits. Yet there were also instances of employees who were dismissed for such light offenses as "having hidden the umbrella of one of his comrades" or for playing with eating-ware at lunch and breaking a carafe in the process.

As stringent and omnipresent as store firing policy was, there were nevertheless several qualifications affecting its

[13] Zola, *Au bonheur*, p. 172; Petition, Le Gouriéric to the Ministère de l'Agriculture, du Commerce et de Travaux Publics, 18 June 1868, Archives Nationales, F12 5095.

application. For one thing, many of the less serious offenses may well have represented an excuse for ridding the store of unwanted or unneeded personnel rather than representing established policy. And, despite the emphasis on performance, the store by no means rid itself of all but the choice employees, for many persons who later left on their own received the notation of "ordinary employee." Also, many persons who were fired were later rehired, either shortly afterwards or perhaps a year or two later. There was in fact a rather frequent pattern of entering, leaving, and re-entering the store. Still, the fact that an employee knew that he might be able to return did not necessarily impede the factor of control, for often he re-entered at a lower salary and perhaps lost his rights to accumulated benefits. Finally, the Boucicauts did not tend to fire employees of long standing except for direct acts of insubordination. After five years with the firm and especially after the ten-year mark those employees who left generally did so on their own. Age must have played a role here, for employees over thirty would certainly be careful, given a market that refused to offer them employment in all but the smaller stores or shops. But the rarity of dismissals of older employees was also likely to have resulted from an extensive paternalistic atmosphere that was equally a part of the Bon Marché work environment and wherein integrated relationships between the *patron* and the personnel required responsibilities on the part of the former as well as the latter. And employee behavior itself was likely to have been affected by this paternalistic atmosphere and to reflect an integration into the house and an adaptation to the system, its demands, its regulations, and its authority structure.

Bon Marché paternalism was a complex affair. On one level it was oriented towards the Boucicauts' own adaptation to the new commercial enterprise they were building and on another towards the adaptation of the bourgeois public to the changes that this entailed. Each of these aspects will be examined further on in this study. On a third level it can be traced to intentions of benevolence and duty, a genuine sentiment of responsibility for the social and moral welfare of those persons in their charge. The Boucicauts' programs and deeds garnered medals from the juries of universal expositions and the French Academy of Moral and Political Sciences. Le Play's disciples stated that the store "offered probably the most complete example of what the paternal regime can produce when applied with generosity."[14] Even the leaders of the Chambre Syndicale des Employés—the commercial employees' union—were forced to admit that Bon Marché employees were the most favored of their profession, and the league of small shopkeepers that virulently opposed the department stores was always judicious in its personal treatment of the Boucicauts.[15]

Yet paternalism in France was also coming to be tied to the functional needs of employers engaged in building new kinds of work forces. In the 1840s and 1850s the textile mills of Alsace and Franche-Comté had begun to experiment with cheap company housing, company provident funds (to provide aid in the event of illness or other personal catastrophes), and company pension programs as a means of assembling, fixing, and controlling an industrial work force and preserving solidarity between the men and their *patron*. Railroads, pioneers in so many other facets of big business, also turned relatively early to paternalism, especially to pension funds, to recruit, stabilize, and discipline their personnel—problems that were particularly acute for companies of their size and geographical dispersion. Some manufacturing concerns set up technical facilities to produce the skilled laborers their plants required. At Le Creusot, where social programs were exten-

[14] Quoted in Giffard, *Grands bazars*, p. 226. The philanthropy of the Boucicauts was discussed in almost every account of them or the Bon Marché. For a summary of this view see articles on the Boucicauts in *Grand dictionnaire universel du XIX siècle*, Deuxième Supplément, p. 626; D'Yderwalle, *Au Bon Marché*. Prizes were won at almost every international exposition, including a *Diplôme d'Honneur* in 1878 and a *Médaille d'Or* in 1889. In 1900 the firm was *Hors Concours–Membre du Jury*. From the Academy of Political and Moral Sciences the store received the *Prix Audéoud* in 1888.

[15] Préfecture de Police, Ba 153, report of 30 July 1886; for the view of small shopkeepers see "A Monsieur Vte. d'Avenel," *La Revendication*, 15 March, 15 June, 1895.

sive, nearly a quarter of the paternalistic budget for 1869 went to education.[16]

At the Bon Marché, paternalism was to follow this path as well, in some ways responding to problems very much similar to those which manufacturers faced in the early stages of industrialization, in some ways responding to the more complex problems that a bureaucratic setting now imposed. Thus, for example, paternalism was interjected into the Bon Marché's rationalized work environment because it could complement the recruiting and shaping of a department store work force. This was clear from the beginning, when Boucicaut declared at the cornerstone laying that he wished "to give to this unique building a philanthropic organization," thereby identifying his paternalistic intentions with the conceptual design needed to create a *grand magasin*.[17]

Paternalism was also interjected into the rationalized work environment of the Bon Marché because it could further the disciplinary structure of the store. Again the 1869 origins of a broad paternalistic scheme were significant, two citywide strikes of commercial employees occurring in that year and the dedication itself coming only one week before a near total walkout of the work force. These events began with the formation of an employees' Chambre Syndicale in 1868. The following year, claiming over 5,000 adherents, the movement threatened to strike in May if the new stores did not agree to a Sunday closing. The employees got their way, many major stores acquiescing to their demands, those that did not being forced to close for lack of personnel.[18] Encouraged by these

[16] Henri Hatzfeld, *Du pauperisme à la sécurité sociale, 1850-1940* (Paris: Armand Colin, 1971), pp. 109-31; Fohlen, *L'industrie textile*, pp. 86-88; Caron, *Histoire*, pp. 322-23; Lévy-Leboyer, "Innovation and Business," pp. 94-95; Charles Gide, *Cours d'économie politique* (Paris: Librairie de la Société du Recueil J.-B. Sirey, 1909), pp. 671-72.

[17] In the 1860s a less formalized paternalism existed at the Bon Marché. According to Le Gouriéric's petition, employees received payment during long illnesses and their widows were allocated pensions if no positions in the store were available.

[18] The Bon Marché apparently had been closed on Sundays for a number of years and does not seem to have been affected by this phase of the strikes.

results, the Chambre Syndicale then engaged on a new venture that would be a long, bitter, and eventually disastrous struggle. In October a demand was made to limit the work day to a strict twelve hours. This time the *patronat* rejected the proposal, Sunday work again became an issue, and two-thirds of the 12,000 clerks in Paris went out on strike. The strikers held fast, but the stores countered by hiring women employees for the first time in significant numbers, the Louvre receiving a shipment of a hundred girls, compliments of the Assistance Publique. Employee plans to open cooperatives never materialized, and eventually the duration of the strike sapped morale. By December it sputtered to an end with no substantial results.[19] Still the strike provided an ominous background against which the new building was launched, and the lesson was not lost on the Bon Marché's owners. In preparing their "philanthropic organization" the Boucicauts were also to make certain that numerous options remained open for exerting leverage over their personnel.[20]

But, above all, paternalism was interjected into the Bon Marché's work environment because of the tensions and difficulties which that environment produced. This is a subject that requires a deeper look at the Boucicauts' work policies and the conditions they created for the Bon Marché employee.

The strains the new work system generated as the Bon Marché expanded into a full-scale department store could be seen in the large numbers of persons who left on their own. For example, 43 percent of the group who entered in 1873—the year after the first section of the new building was opened—left before five years, and of these a considerable portion did so in the first year. To be sure, the reasons behind this flight could be as varied as the causes for dismissal (and

[19] Sunday closings also appear to have been a casualty of the strike. At least the issue again became a heated one towards the end of the century and was not resolved until 1906.

[20] For accounts of the strikes see Office du Travail, *Les associations professionelles ouvrières*, vol. 4 (Paris, 1904), pp. 614-20; Artaud, *La question*, pp. 124-27, 253-57; "La grève des commis," *L'Illustration*, 30 October 1869.

many reentered the store). Women often left to get married and army draftees might frequently not return, although quite a few did as their jobs remained available. There were also clerks who had been sent by their fathers to learn the new merchandising practices, and who then returned to the provinces to assume control of the family business. Others simply felt that they had learned enough to begin their own store, and left "to establish" themselves. But for the most part departures were simply listed as "left voluntarily" and probably reflected, as did the large numbers of persons who were fired for insubordination or failure to respect the rules, a feeling of discontent with the work system itself.

The tensions of working in a department store were illustrated by the salesclerks' pay. Many clerks entered the Bon Marché because overall salaries were far higher than what one could earn in the smaller stores or small shops. Nor did the status temptations of a middle-class career entail financial sacrifices. This was a white-collar curse that would come only with the following century. Compared to other working men, most of whom were fortunate to earn five or six francs a day, department store clerks were considerably well off. An income of 3,500 to 4,000 francs a year in nineteenth-century France was sufficient to enable one to live a modest bourgeois existence, especially if one was fed on the job.[21] Annual salaries rather than daily wages were still another attractive feature. But the Bon Marché salary, for all its promise and security, nevertheless entailed a great deal of uncertainty and stress for the salesclerk.

The principal problem was the commission. This, admittedly, did not affect office clerks who worked on straight salary. They often entered at several hundred francs a year, re-

[21] Ministère du Commerce, *Annuaire statistique de la France* (Paris, 1882), pp. 332-33; *Ibid.*, 1890, pp. 258-59; Theodore Zeldin, *France 1848-1945*, vol. 1 (Oxford: Clarendon Press, 1973), pp. 210-11; Marguerite Perrot, *Le mode de vie des familles bourgeoises 1873-1953* (Paris: Armand Colin, 1961), pp. 167-75. Perrot notes that food costs of low income bourgeois families were substantial, running as high as 40 percent of their budget. On the Bon Marché food service see below, p. 106.

ceived rather large annual increases so that they might earn over 2,000 francs after five years, and, if they stayed long enough, eventually rose to perhaps somewhere between 3,000 and 4,000 francs. But the fixed salary of sellers was often quite low. While there were a number of sellers who entered at or attained the relatively high pay of from 2,000 to 3,000 francs a year, they were the exception and may not have been on commission at all. Most sellers began at a salary that fluctuated from 300 to 800 francs and some entered *au pair* and received no pay for the first several months. Annual increases were customary, but a maximum of from 1,200 to 1,500 francs appears to have been the norm.[22] Thus salesclerks were dependent upon their commissions to escape a working-class standard of living, and this in turn meant that they were at the mercy of the clientele's whims. The fate was not enviable. How many nightmare stories must have circulated daily through the halls of the great store, recounting the exploits of those shoppers who had to try on every dress or shoe or glove in the house, only to purchase in the end a mere trifle at best, or nothing at all, or perhaps several thousand francs worth of goods, all of which were returned the following morning? How many customers were garroted, guillotined, hung by their thumbs daily—in the wishful minds of frustrated sellers? The fantasies of newcomers who had lowest priority in "the line"—a system of rotation for waiting on clients—must have been especially gruesome.

Commissions also posed a series of conflicts for salesclerks. There were conflicts between each other and between competing departments over the quest for commissions, conflicts with office clerks who received bonuses for detecting faulty commission claims, and conflicts between the desire to sell as much and as often as possible and the need to maintain a posture of honesty at all times.

Even if the insecurity, conflicts, and forced tempo produced by commissions could be offset by the greater salaries

[22] B.M., Employee Dossiers; B.M., Employee Register.

one could earn, not all clerks who averaged perhaps 3,600 francs a year lived far beyond the precarious edge. For many it was an unstable life. Bachelors often congregated in special hotels for clerks. Others who had their own lodgings changed their addresses with great frequency (to avoid paying rents?).[23] Occasional requests to the House for aid suggest that salaries offered little leeway for coping with unexpected needs.[24] In some respects these conditions were a consequence of the clerks' adopted life style. Employees were notorious habitués of the music halls and cabarets, and their average annual expense on clothing and cleaning might reach 400-500 francs.[25] Yet clerks were also expected to be well dressed for work, and all had middle-class pretensions, so that even the frugal employee was obliged to spend a fair percentage of his salary on his attire.

Employees who might work fifteen to sixteen hours per day in small shops also entered the Bon Marché for its shorter workload. But the hours were long, nevertheless. In the summer the work day extended from 7:30 in the morning until perhaps 9:00 at night, and in the winter from 8:00 in the morning until 8:00 at night (by 1889 the latter hours were maintained year around). And if the work day was shorter, the pace was harder. During busy seasons there were few slack moments for clerks or garçons, and on days of great sales the intensity of the tempo could be absolutely maddening. At no time were salesclerks permitted to sit down. Overtime work—without reimbursement—was not unusual. Nor did Sunday closings always mean Sunday holidays. At least in the early years, some or all of the work force were required to spend the day preparing new displays or working on other similar chores. By 1882 this practice apparently had changed, for there are references in Zola to Sunday outings by clerks. Still, certain services like delivery continued to work on Sun-

---

[23] Zola, NAF10278, p. 205; B.M., Employee Dossiers.
[24] B.M., *Conseils Généraux*; B.M., Employee Dossiers.
[25] Chambre Syndicale des Employés de Commerce, d'Industrie et d'Administration, *Améliorations Professionelles/N. 1 Nouveautés* (Paris: 1880), p. 16, in Préfecture de Police, Ba 152.

day, while on the Sundays before big expositions or on inventory Sundays it is likely that most, if not all, employees were expected to work at the House.[26]

Health conditions were another matter of concern. Department stores as a group were criticized for their unsanitary conditions, particularly in regard to poor ventilation and the great quantities of dust that accumulated in back rooms and offices. Tuberculosis rates of commercial employees were reputedly among the highest in Paris.[27] This may have fit the romantic self-image some department store clerks held of themselves, but the consequences were nevertheless dire. Dossiers of Bon Marché personnel entering before 1907 show that perhaps as many as one-fifth left for reasons of fatigue, health, or because of death.[28] It is not surprising, therefore, that the Bon Marché and other stores gradually adopted a policy of not hiring persons over thirty, or that Madame Boucicaut set fifty years as the retirement age when she founded a pension fund. Many employees were well used up by that time.

The tensions of working at the Bon Marché could also be seen in the lure, and disappointments, of the Boucicauts' promotion policy. Undoubtedly most clerks came to the Bon Marché with dreams of one day entering the power structure of the store. Yet only a few persons could ever expect to rise to the level of administrator, and later director, and all the ranking positions together never comprised more than perhaps 10 to 12 percent of the work force. Many employees who entered in the 1860s did rise with expansion. But those who came after 1869 found that opportunities were far less available. By the time Zola visited the Bon Marché, there

[26] La Réforme, 8 October 1869; Zola, NAF10278, pp. 190, 342-45.

[27] Lainé, Les demoiselles, pp. 51-52.

[28] These figures are based on a sample of 224 dossiers over the period. Since these dossiers include a disproportionate number of employees who remained with the store for several years, at least in regard to 68 dossiers of entries before 1877, the one-fifth figure might be adjusted downward somewhat. A downward adjustment might further be in order since a number of persons included in the sick, etc. group were retirees.

were over 2,500 employees and only 200 or so managerial positions.

But perhaps the greatest difficulty that employees encountered at the Bon Marché was the severe regimentation of the House and the impersonality of its bureaucratic organization. Most employees found their identity with the firm as a whole limited to the prescribed procedures that they followed as they carried out their specialized tasks. Thus it was far more difficult for the individual employee to develop a sense of a personal relationship with the House than it was in smaller firms or especially in the traditionalist small shops. When the employee did break out of the rigid specialization, he did so as a pawn, shifted about for specific needs, as on the occasion of great sales when clerks were at a premium and administrators arranged the wholesale transfer of personnel. At the same time, however, the employee was extremely vulnerable to the workings of all the organization and hence to the performance of persons whom he did not know and who worked in sections of the store that he might never enter. This was especially so for salesclerks, whose pay was dependent on the smooth functioning of the depot and delivery, and also the office where commissions were computed. But all employees were subject in some way to the interdependency of a system where a change in hours for a particular service, or even a delay on a given day, could affect another's work schedule and perhaps lead to overtime.

Authority could be equally impersonal. Unlike the small shops where authority was no less pervasive but where it emanated directly from the *patron*, the Bon Marché rarely brought the clerk into contact with Boucicaut himself. Orders were passed through a series of hierarchical levels, each of which demanded absolute obedience. It was also, as has been seen, an authority that regarded the employee merely as an instrument and used him accordingly, discarding him with little hesitation when he was ineffective or insufficiently tractable. It did so as well with little grace. Most clerks were fired with a brief "pass to the cashier, monsieur." In its most extreme form, authority at the Bon Marché was impersonal through its reliance on procedures that bound the employee from arrival when he presented a token of presence and submitted to roll call until departure, when a bell rang and he left through a specified door. Hence there was little room for individual initiative, and this regimentation was enforced by a corps of internal police—the inspectors—who were certainly the most detested persons in the store. These men maintained a constant surveillance over the personnel, exercised absolute authority to preserve absolute order, and were notorious for their ruthlessness.[29]

The extent to which the system could be depersonalizing was most apparent in the conditions of that sub-group of employees, the garçons. These grown men who did the bulk of the physical labor and were paid less than the others—they generally began at 600 francs and received annual 100-franc increases up to perhaps 2,000 francs, with a few exceptions in a higher range—were obliged in almost every respect to surrender their individuality. They were attributed a demeaning title and were dressed in livery to appeal to the clientele. They also were given numbers which they wore on their uniforms and by which they could be identified. There was, in effect, an almost military character to their organization, even to the point where foremen chosen among them were known as corporals. Some were lodged in the store and slept on tops of counters or spread their folding beds wherever they could find sufficient space. To be sure, these "accommodations" were likely to be no worse than the miserable hovels most garçons had probably once called home, or the farm. But then garçons had, after all, come to Paris seeking a better life, and one would be hard put to see sleeping in a department store as the mark of a man on the rise. Not a few garçons, along with coachmen who shared many of their conditions, were fired for drinking.

The Boucicauts created, therefore, a very ambivalent world for their employees. On the one hand, they offered their

---

[29] Zola gives a good illustration of the fear and hatred of inspectors in *Au bonheur des dames*.

work force the prospect of rising to dizzying heights within their organization and of working conditions that were perhaps better than those any other store in Paris could provide.[30] Zola noted that the ambition of all clerks was to be accepted either at the Bon Marché or at the Louvre, and that a return to the smaller stores was looked on as a "downfall."[31] But work conditions at the Bon Marché were also laden with tensions, and if commissions, promotions, procedures, and dismissals could go far towards adapting employees to the bureaucratic and competitive world of a *grand magasin*, they alone could never build complete organization men who would also feel a sense of personal attachment to such a world, or to the firm and *patron* that represented it to them.

And yet integration of this sort was the essential issue that the Boucicauts faced in their relationships with their personnel. It was the essential issue because absolute respect for authority, energetic pursuit of orders, courteous and professional service of clients, and the efficient processing of flows ultimately hinged on some feeling of identity between the lives of the employees and the goals of the organization. And it was also the essential issue because it touched on a matter that ran still deeper than the specific needs of the Bon Marché, although the fortunes of the firm were tied to this as well.

Department stores were creating not only a new kind of work force but a new kind of middle-class man. The middle-class dream had always envisioned a bourgeoisie open to all those whose birth or hard work or education entitled them to a place in it. But in the past the vision of an expanding bourgeoisie had also assumed a corresponding expansion of independent situations. Many bourgeois who came from the lower echelons of the class or worked their way up from the working-class fringe might begin their middle-class careers in salaried positions. Yet, with the exception of those who entered government service, the position of employee was

[30] Employees at the Bon Marché were also not subject to the hated fines that elsewhere haunted their every mistake.
[31] Zola, NAF10278, p. 213.

rarely seen as more than a stepping stone in the stream towards independent proprietorship. Department stores,
insurance companies, big banks, and other big operations
like railroads, however, forced, a change in this current.
Middle-class careers continued to expand, but now more and
more they were being channeled into permanently salaried
positions with an organization and within an impersonal and
hierarchical work environment. The men who entered these
careers continued to identify with bourgeois culture and to
pursue the conventions of a bourgeois life style. But neither
bourgeois respectability nor bourgeois status could cloak the
reality of an occupational milieu remarkably similar to that of
the working class (Zola was in the habit of referring to department stores as "the great steam engine").[32] Unmistakably, the emergence of white-collar work in mass proportions
and under bureaucratic circumstances signaled a qualitative
shift in middle-class life. For many it was a disturbing shift as
well. Indeed if the white-collar worker was to become such a
volatile factor in European society by the turn of the century,
it was largely because of the strains that his working life
placed on his pretensions. Thus, integration of the work force
was the critical issue at the Bon Marché not only because the
success of the firm depended in the end on the employee's
adaptation to his new work environment, but also because it
touched on the question of whether white-collar workers
could be effectively reconciled to the middle-class world that
they would now have to inhabit. On this too ultimately hung
the fate of the house, for not until the underpinnings to a new
bourgeois culture were set firmly in place would its institutional representations themselves be secured.

To establish these underpinnings, to create integrated relationships between the employees and their work was, then,
the most vital purpose that paternalism was to serve in the
Boucicauts' efforts to build organization men. Like a number
of their industrial contemporaries, the Boucicauts recognized
that a new, institutionalized paternalism, reproducing in its

[32] *Ibid.*, pp. 82, 87.

own way the family relations of the traditional business household, could be adapted to far larger, far different, kinds of enterprises as a means of retaining a community spirit within an impersonal and rationalized work environment. The idea may have been a simple one, but its implementation was complex, for the Boucicauts never sought merely to counterpoise bureaucracy with a paternalistic veneer. Rather, they endeavored to blend the one with the other, restructuring and reorienting old household values to correspond to the style and the goals of their rationalized work system. In this way they could correlate their paternalism with their firm's structure and purpose, thus projecting an image of an internal work community to tie the personnel to the House, its leadership, and its dynamic aspirations. Basically wedded to the French household tradition, the Boucicauts were to cope with fundamental changes in their culture, not by abandoning its practices and its tenets, but by redefining these to fit their new needs and new ends.

Perhaps most representative of the ways the various strands—benevolence, formation, control, and integration—were woven together in the Boucicauts' paternalism were two funds that they established for their personnel, neither of which required contributions on the part of the work force (this in itself was a significant example of the Boucicauts' beneficence—similar programs elsewhere nearly always demanded employee participation in their financing). The first, a provident fund, was founded in 1876 and was financed by setting aside a certain sum each year, to be determined by the Boucicauts, from the annual net profits. All employees below the rank of department head or inspector, and who had been with the firm for at least five years, were eligible to participate. An account was opened in the employee's name, and each year a share of the general allocation was deposited in it. Since the fund was intended to provide the employee with a lump sum upon his retirement, the employee could not cash in his account until he reached the age of sixty (fifty in the case of women) or until he had completed twenty years (fifteen for women) of uninterrupted employment at the Bon Marché. In 1886 the age conditions were reduced to fifty years for men, forty-five for women. Thus the money was left to accrue over the years with an annual four percent interest added to it. If the employee quit or was fired, his amount was redistributed into the general fund, unless the Boucicauts chose to provide him with part of his balance.[33] However, women who left the store to marry received their balance in full on the day of their wedding (the Boucicauts, in their bourgeois fashion, were never ones to feel fully comfortable with the prospect of cultivating careers for single middle-class women). An employee who became incapacitated could also draw on his account if he received the Boucicauts' permission. Finally, in the event of death, an employee's account was distributed to his widow and children, although the Boucicauts reserved the right to determine how the money might be used, as they did in the case of all employees who fulfilled their conditions (an option, however, that was rarely exercised).

The creation of the provident fund was followed ten years later by the establishment of a pension fund. This program, initiated with 5,000,000 francs in donations by Madame Boucicaut, guaranteed pensions to employees after twenty years of service with the firm. Male employees, however, were expected to reach the age of fifty, female employees the age of forty-five, before they could begin to draw on the fund. But, like the provident fund, the pension program also contained provisions for temporary financial aid or for full pensions to incapacitated employees or to their widows or to orphans.

These funds formed the capstone of the Boucicauts' paternalistic plans and of all the programs they established were the most extensively praised. Their benefits were substantial. The employee who remained with the firm for twenty years or more could expect to depart with at least several thousand francs from his provident fund account and a pension rang-

[33] In 1877 this provision was amended as follows: employees who left after ten years of uninterrupted service automatically received one-third of their account; men with fifteen years service received two-thirds.

ing from 600 to 1,500 francs a year. Yet the funds were also primed with effective mechanisms for shaping and controlling the work force and for integrating them into the House.

In their most obvious way the two plans were designed to foster stability among the personnel. Offering security in return for a career commitment to the firm, pensions and provident fund benefits were one means of attracting skilled employees and retaining them permanently in salaried positions. Looked at from another perspective, these benefits were also a means of assuring that a substantial proportion of the work force would be composed of individuals who had mastered their positions, proved themselves trustworthy, and familiarized themselves with the complex procedures of the organization. How well the plans succeeded can be seen in the steady progression of membership in the provident fund. When this fund began, only 128 individuals or 8 percent of the employees (1575) had been with the firm for five years or more. Five years later, however, there were 515 adherents (or 22 percent) and by Madame Boucicaut's death 39 percent of the 3,173 employees qualified as five-year men or women. In 1905 when there were perhaps 4,500 or so full-time employees there were 3,181 participants.[34] Moreover, of the 4,417 persons who passed the five-year mark before 1900, approximately 50 percent were to remain with the firm for twenty years or longer.[35]

[34] B.M., *Caisse de Prévoyance* Reports, 1876-1914. If these figures are adjusted back five years so that they are based on the pool of available men and women who could become five-year employees, the progression of percentages from 1871 to 1876 to 1882 is 19 percent, 32 percent, and 50 percent.

[35] Before 1900, 4,417 persons had passed through the fund. These represent all those five-year men and women who potentially could have remained with the firm for twenty years or more during the pre-1914 period. The 50 percent figure was arrived at by adding: (1) the number of pensioners alive in 1914 (933), (2) the number of persons with twenty years' service at that date who had not yet been pensioned (1,013), and (3) 29 percent of number one to allow for deaths of pensioners (271)—1921 pension figures show that while 1,787 pensions had been accorded, there were only 1,275 living pensioners. See B.M., *Règlement général des employés* (1921); B.M., *Caisse de Retraite* Report in AGO, 4 September 1914; B.M. *Caisse de Prévoyance* Reports.

Pensions and provident accounts also meant control. Once the employee accepted the prospect of making his career with the firm in exchange for retirement benefits in the end, he inherently was led to accept as well the work and authority relationships at the Bon Marché. In similar fashion, both funds contained built-in leverage points to reinforce the employee's submission throughout his tenure with the store. The provident fund, for example, offered the employee several occasions to draw upon his balance prior to maturity, yet each of these, aside from marriage, was subject to the Boucicauts' personal approval. The retirement fund, meanwhile, provided a considerable leeway between the minimum and the maximum pension, again to be determined solely by the Boucicauts' good will, so that aging employees who were unlikely to be fired were also unlikely to slacken their pace or their obedience to their superiors. In the event that this *quid pro quo* relationship implicit in the funds somehow escaped the personnel, the Boucicauts did not hesitate to spell it out in more direct terms. Thus at an 1880 report to the personnel on the status of the provident fund, director-designate Gouin could remark:

"Now ladies and gentlemen, allow me on this occasion to recall to you that the constant preoccupation of the founder of our House was always to improve the well-being of his employees. Madame Boucicaut, wishing to continue the work her husband began, has undertaken a heavy task [i.e., the Bon Marché]. In order to deal successfully with this task she needs and counts on your complete devotion; in exchange she shall prove to you that her solicitude will not be lacking. . . ."[36]

Solicitude for devotion, we might also assume, left little room, if any, for union interference. In a House that was known for its repression of organizers,[37] employees were likely to think twice about joining the Chambre Syndicale if they valued their career and the pension that accompanied it.

---

[36] B.M., Speech of Alphonse Gouin to the personnel on the occasion of a *Caisse de Prévoyance* Report, 23 July 1880.

Then again, in a House that provided such extensive benefits of its own, how much compulsion could there be to protest one's conditions, or to turn to the panacea of state intervention? Bon Marché, paternalism as we shall explore more fully in the following chapter, was in fact exceptionally effective in combatting the menace of unionization and strikes.

Pension and provident funds used in this manner followed in the mainstream of the ways that similar programs had been employed by railroads, mines, and textile mills to attract, fix, and discipline their work forces. But in formulating the programs—at least the provident fund—the Boucicauts had in mind still other precedents that could go much further toward attaching the personnel to their House and their work by giving them a direct interest in the affairs of the firm. These were the early experiments in profit-sharing, of which the Maison Leclaire—a Parisian house-painting and decorating firm—set the most celebrated example in France. As early as 1842 Leclaire began to distribute profits among his workers. Later, in 1863, he created a more formalized system of parcelling gains, distributing 30 percent outright in cash to the workers and 20 percent to a mutual aid society which was incorporated and made a sleeping partner in the house. By the time of his death, in 1872, the mutual aid society held 50 percent interest in the House and the power to appoint the firm's management in the future. Leclaire's experiment was exceptional, but only in the degree to which he carried it. A number of other French firms, such as the Mulhouse textile concern of Schaeffer, Lalance (bleaching, dying, and printing of cloths), or the Chaix printing works in Paris, had also established some form of profit-sharing by the 1870s, usually through distributing part of the percentage directly to the employee, part to a fund for future payments or pensions upon his retirement.[38]

[37] Préfecture de Police, Ba 153, reports of 27 October 1892, 22 November 1900.

[38] Victor Böhmert, *La participation aux bénéfices* (Paris: Chaix, 1888), pp. 242-63, 417-25, 485-94; Nicholas Paine Gilman, *Profit Sharing Between Employer and Employee* (Boston: Houghton, Mifflin, 1889), pp. 66-105.

Profit-sharing of this sort could work in almost any establishment of some size. But its advantages to employers were especially appropriate in those firms where a bureaucratic work environment required a common sentiment of cooperation for the system to run efficiently, where a competitive and dynamic sales environment depended on the commitment of employees to the goals of the house, and where a predominantly white-collar work force would be particularly receptive to a forced savings program, with its implicit bourgeois regard for thrift and security, and would be particularly susceptible as well to the integrative implications of a program that permitted them to identify their salaried positions with more properly bourgeois capitalistic aspirations. Thus one can find profit-sharing schemes being put into effect at the Paris and Orléans railroad as early as 1844 and among a number of Parisian insurance companies in the following decade.[39]

At the Bon Marché, Boucicaut was quite obviously aware of this tradition, and where it could lead, when he structured the provident fund to grow in accordance with the profits of the house. In an inaugural address to the personnel, and in the introduction to the fund's statutes, he made his intentions eminently clear:

"In establishing the present Provident Fund we have wished to assure to each of our employees the security that a *petit capital* can bring in old age, or that, in the case of death, can be of benefit to one's family.

"We have wished, at the same time, to show in an effective way the firm solidarity that ought to unite them to the House.

"They will better understand that the vigor of their work, concern for the interest of the House, and the economical use of materials put at their disposal are so many duties which turn to the profit of everyone.

"They will become more imbued with the precepts that we never cease to prescribe to them, they will better understand,

[39] For a discussion of railroad and insurance companies see Böhmert, *La participation*, pp. 508-12, 530-39, 566-69; Gilman, *Profit Sharing*, 213-22. One insurance company, *La Nationale*, began profit-sharing in 1837.

from being more directly interested, that success depends on their efforts, their good comportment, and the attention they bring to satisfying customers: an objective to which all of us adhere."[40]

So in its most complete form the provident fund served the Boucicauts' purposes by first recreating a house community spirit and then equating this with the structure and objectives of a modern department store. Having established the means through which a paternalistic gesture could lead employees to identify their interests with those of their *patron*, the Boucicauts could propose to their personnel that they view themselves as part of a greater Bon Marché household, where all worked together for the success of the firm and, in the end, the glory of each other. The message was a powerful one. As one old employee recalled many years later:

"We will never forget that memorable evening when, all gathered together, we learned of the creation of this foundation.

"Not a discordant note could be heard. M. Boucicaut very much sensed that he had won every heart and every will and it was certainly one of the greatest joys of his life to see the enthusiasm that greeted him when he cried out: 'It is my wish that every employee be a pillar of my House.' "[41]

Pension and provident funds were only the richest issue of a still deeper paternalistic vein. Some employees—unmarried women and a number of the younger male clerks who had no family in Paris—were housed in quarters on the uppermost floors of the new building (in addition to the makeshift conditions with which a portion of the garçons were lodged in this period).[42] By 1878 there were 50 rooms for 52 women and 28 rooms for 38 young men. These accommodations included a common room with a piano for the women, a games room

---

[40] B.M., Introduction to the statutes of the *Caisse de Prévoyance*.

[41] B.M., *Hommage à Monsieur Boucicaut 1810-1877* (1912), p. 51. By 1912 Jeune, the man who made this remark, was a department head. However it is highly unlikely that he held this rank in 1876.

[42] It is likely that in the early years of the store these young clerks shared the countertop facilities with the garçons. See Paul Avenel, *Les calicots*.

with billiards tables for the men, and a library of 400 volumes apparently at the disposal of both sexes.[43] All employees, meanwhile, dined at the store twice daily. Like the living quarters, facilities for eating entered into the Boucicauts' plans for their new building, and above the sales galleries they constructed a vast kitchen and four dining rooms, the largest of which could accommodate 800 persons at a single setting. This room was used by male clerks, inspectors, and department heads, while two of the other rooms were set aside for the women—one for salesclerks and one for workers employed in the workshops. The fourth dining room was intended for garçons, coachmen, stablehands, and other employees who performed manual labor. The meals were free (although this also justified lower salaries). Boucicaut insisted that all food be "healthy and abundant," and department heads were delegated to "receive complaints that may come about."[44]

There were also programs for the education and leisure of the employees. In 1872 the Boucicauts began evening courses in English and German. The lessons were free, open to all employees, and given in the building after work by instructors especially hired for this purpose. The German class drew few students and was later dropped. But English lessons were not unpopular and each year the Boucicauts sent the best students to London for six months' additional study at House expense. Employees were further offered the opportunity to attend periodical lectures in history, science, and literature by scholars whom the Boucicauts brought in from the outside. These too were held in the evenings inside the store. At the same time, for the less cerebral (and, one suspects, the vast majority) the Boucicauts established lessons in music and fencing. The music lessons began in 1872 and included

[43] When additional space was required in the 1880s for offices and *ateliers*, the living quarters, in enlarged form, were transferred to separate buildings in the nearby rue de la Chaise and rue de Bac.

[44] *Renseignements généraux et règlement d'intérieur* (1876), Bibliothèque Nationale, WZ3266

courses in vocal and orchestral music. The house provided free instruments on loan and offered a 25 percent discount and easy terms for employees who wished to buy their own. Fencing lessons began in 1875. As usual, these courses were held in the building, in the evening after work, and under the direction of special professors, one of whom at least was permanently attached to the firm to lead the choral and orchestral groups.

Finally, there were two other programs that deserve mention. First, in the 1870s, the Boucicauts hired a doctor to give free consultations during mornings at the store, and later they set up a nearby infirmary in the rue de la Chaise. Second, the Boucicauts encouraged employees to save their earnings by offering 6 percent interest on accounts that were opened with the House. The response was far from negligible. By 1886, 927 employees had entrusted over 3,200,000 francs to the firm.[45]

The complexity of this sort of paternalism was striking. For instance, in the impulse to shape the personal character of their work force that was so clearly apparent in most of these programs, the Boucicauts once more found a felicitous interplay between their values and their needs. Catholicism and bourgeois respectability, filtered through their sentiments of responsibility and good will, could lead the Boucicauts to sponsor music and fencing lessons and even a lecture series to lure their employees out of the cabarets and music halls that young, single clerks were so prone to frequent. (How many Bon Marché employees were "saved," however, is not known. The popularity of café concerts in France in this period continued to be phenomenal.)[46] The Boucicauts' code could also lead them to set rigorous rules of behavior for those clerks who lived on the upper floors of the House. The Boucicauts dictated the regulations of the games room, outlawed card playing, and especially forbade mingling of the

[45] Archives Nationales, F12 5095. A number of these employees undoubtedly were members of the store hierarchy.

[46] Zeldin, *France*, vol. 2, p. 702.

sexes outside the library. Permission for both sexes to remain out late had to be requested in advance; rules stated that "this favor can only be rarely accorded"; and doors of the House were closed at 11:00 every night except Sunday, when they remained open until 12:30. As an administrator boasted in 1883 to a Parliamentary Committee: "There is very strict discipline . . . [the] building is watched over by a concierge whose instructions are very strict concerning infractions of the rules."[47] Yet respectability and character, as we have seen in the case of procedures and firing, were also intimately tied to the public image of the firm and to the Boucicauts' need to form a quality work force that would bring an air of gentility to a mass sales environment. So, more than indulging a personal bias, the Boucicauts again crossed into their employees' private lives—this time to cultivate gentlemanly behavior as well as to enforce it—because they saw in this a way to shape a new kind of salesclerk.[48]

Cultivating gentlemen (and gentlewomen) was merely a beginning to the ways in which these programs fitted the Boucicauts' grander scheme of things. The music classes very quickly were turned into musical societies—undoubtedly their original destination—that performed in municipal competitions throughout France, in summer concerts in the square outside the store, and in grand concerts that were held twice a year inside the building itself. In a later chapter we shall see how well these performances suited the public relations of the firm. The functional side to the Boucicauts' kitchens—their ability to feed a work force of thousands and to do so in three sequential shifts so that no more than a third of the sales force was ever off the floor at one time—should not be ignored. And it is scarcely difficult to understand why Boucicaut chose to initiate language lessons at the store (or why he did not choose to provide instruction in Latin and Greek). After the turn of the century, when trade with Latin

[47] Ministère de l'Intérieur, *Enquête de la commission extraparlementaire sur les associations ouvrières*, vol. 1 (Paris, 1883), p. 129.

[48] For a portrait of the commercial employee's life style, see Zola, *Au bonheur* and Paul Avenel, *Les calicots*.

Americans increased, the House added a course in Spanish to its repertoire.[49]

Nor is it difficult to see the spectre of control lurking just beneath the surface of these programs. If employees ate their meals at the store, then they were not likely to extend their breaks beyond the time allotted. If employees spent their evenings in the store rather than in the cabarets and music halls, then they were also not likely to stay out late at night or to arrive late for work the following morning. And if employees accepted Bon Marché authority over their private lives, then they were equally not likely to question that authority when it was exercised during working hours at the House.

More important, paternalism that encouraged thrift, that sought to broaden the employees' minds, to refine their sensibilities, and to protect their virtue fell directly in line with the great dream of all nineteenth-century employers to check the development of working-class consciousness by turning their workers into bourgeois themselves (what, after all, could be more properly bourgeois than a piano in the living room?). Admittedly the battle in department stores, where most clerks had middle-class origins and middle-class pretensions, was already half won. But it was the other half—the prospect of what might become of this identity as white-collar conditions more and more approximated those of the working-classes—that quite rightly preoccupied the Boucicauts' minds. For bourgeois culture in the late nineteenth century, one of the great dilemmas was how to continue to expand its ranks without simply creating a new enemy in its midst. This is why so many white-collar employers sought to shore up the traditional bourgeois orientations by insisting on dress codes for their employees (at the Bon Marché, men were not only expected to be properly attired, but to wear top hats upon their arrival and departure). It is also one of the

[49] The importance attached to the knowledge of a foreign language was evidenced by the notation of such skills on applications for employment. B.M., Employees Dossiers; B.M., Application booklet entitled *Vendeuses* 1909-1911.

reasons why the Boucicauts so ardently sought to cultivate gentlemanly behavior among their personnel. This too, they hoped, would affect the drift of a "vague class, floating between the worker and the bourgeoisie."[50]

Indeed, all of the Boucicauts' paternalistic programs were able to exert their draw on this drift by reinforcing a rigid distinction that existed within the House—and French society—between "employees" and "workers." The former term applied only to those persons who earned a fixed salary, and thus the men and women employed in the workshops, the individual workers like locksmiths and the several hundred women who cut catalogue samples, all of whom were paid an hourly or daily wage or perhaps were paid by piecework, were placed in the separate category of *ouvriers* or workers. The distinction was an important one, for it was strictly maintained linguistically and it suggested a separate class identity that meshed with a difference in function, even though both groups were, in reality, engaged in machine-like or semi-skilled work. But what gave the distinction particular meaning at the Bon Marché was that by limiting their paternalism to their employees alone, the Boucicauts could structurally confirm these status divisions, thereby erecting still further barriers between their employees and their workers. To be sure, the role of employees like garçons was somewhat vague here. But too much confusion between them and the clerks was avoided through such mechanisms as separate titles and separate dining rooms. And, characteristically, when a pension fund for workers was created in the 1890s, it was administered as a totally separate service.

But it was the overall implications of these programs—their catching up of the employees' lives in a larger store world where household conditions were at once reproduced and equated with the business goals of the firm—that again was most striking. By transforming the building in which one worked into the House in which one might learn and play and perhaps even live, and by structuring each of these expe-

[50] Zola, *Au bonheur*, p. 184.

riences to correspond to the objectives pursued in one's daily work patterns, the Boucicauts essentially could repeat the same kind of message they had proffered with the provident fund: that the lives of the employees and the life of the House were one and the same.

Thus the Boucicauts evolved a highly elaborate paternalism to extend and to consolidate their system of work and to provide an associational frame for integrating the employee into the firm. They established programs to respond to the functional needs confronting the formation of a department store work force and they erected mechanisms of control that could facilitate discipline and counteract a recurrence of the strike of 1869. More important, as they reaffirmed old paternal bonds and focused the life of the personnel on the store, they created a web of relationships that could identify a basically parcellized and authority-laden work situation with a sense of belonging to a new commercial household. As a result, the central symbol of the store became that of the *"grande famille"*—one big family—a symbol that also summed up the maximum possibilities for the preservation of control. "I will be happy, in placing myself at your head . . . ," wrote Boucicaut's son following the death of his father, "to perpetuate forever the memory of the man who considered himself your Father, and who worked without end for the happiness of those persons fortunate enough to belong to this *grande Famille*." Above all, as the Boucicauts structured this web to match their new commercial ends, they created conditions wherein they could propose to the employee that he too was involved in the pursuits of the store, that as a member of this household or community he too was part of making the Bon Marché what it was, and that his ultimate identity and role with the firm was in the framework of contributing in common to the growth and prosperity of the new commercial emporium. This would always be the message behind the *grand famille* image, and hence in his letter Boucicaut *fils* would also write that "the terrible misfortune that deprives us of our venerated leader cannot, under any case, arrest the progress of this great work which he founded, and today we must all join together to make it into the glorification of that man who diverted onto me and you a part of his affection and a part of his hopes."[51]

Building Organization Men: Management

The organization-man image of management has become such a commonplace in our century that we tend to forget how recent these managers really are, or what a remarkably new problem they presented to the entrepreneurs of the first bureaucratic firms. In the mid-nineteenth century middle and top management was still a rare phenomenon. Only railroads and a few industries were big enough to create something in the way of a managerial structure. For most business families, loyalty and responsibility were simply not qualities one could rely on an outsider to provide. Yet as the business world grew more bureaucratic and concentrated, delegation of authority became inescapable. Firms as large and complex as the Bon Marché developed, as we have seen, elaborate administrative structures. By the late nineteenth century, the managerial revolution had begun. In the following chapter we shall take a closer look at the managers that this revolution called forth and the values and attitudes that made up their universe. For the moment, however, we need to understand how they too were fitted into the associational frame that the Boucicauts were seeking to build. How to create a corps of middle and top managers, how to instill in them a sense of loyalty and accountability, and how to insure that they would live by and for the goals of the organization—in short, how to build the sort of organization man who a century later would be turned into a stereotype—were questions that the Boucicauts were obliged to resolve. Here again they sought the answers in a synthesis of rationalized work conditions, on the one hand, traditional household relationships, on the other.

[51] B.M., Letter of Aristide Boucicaut, *fils* to "Messieurs les Employés du Bon Marché," 1 January 1878.

Managerial salaries, for example, repeated the pattern of pegging earnings to performance. The salaries of department heads, service and office heads, and inspectors generally were listed at 3,600 to 4,200 francs, those of seconds from 2,400 to 3,600 francs. But fixed salaries were still only a fraction of total pay. Department heads received a percentage on the yearly sales increase of their departments, and thus might earn, overall, from 12,000 to perhaps 25,000 francs annually. Averages for seconds, who also received a percentage, could run from 9,000 to 12,000 francs. Even inspectors and office heads appear to have received some sort of additional compensation in line with either the Bon Marché's overall sales or overall sales increase for the year.[52]

Council members received no fixed salary. Known as *intéressés*, they were given a direct share in the profits and thus were directly involved in the success or failure of the enterprise. In part this was a reflection of the position they held. Yet it also followed from an administrative role that was expected to look beyond sales alone to the balance between income and expenses. As Zola remarked, administrators were constantly preoccupied with checking the mark-down rates of their departments. Four other persons—head cashiers and accountants—equally received a share in the profits, to guard against what a director later referred to as "the weakness of men in contact with considerable amounts of money and securities." Needless to say, *intéressés* became wealthy men. We do not have precise figures on their earnings, but Zola does refer to their counterparts at the Louvre who made 80,000 francs a year.[53]

Some stores like the Louvre or the Printemps set sales goals for their department heads and fired those who failed to keep

[52] B.M., Salary Book for Hierarchy 1896-1918; B.M., Employee Dossiers; B.M., *Conseils Généraux*; Zola, NAF10278, p. 8; D'Avenel, "Le mécanisme," p. 362. Guarantees or minimums, usually equivalent to at least the basic salary, were set for department heads, and in particularly difficult years a gratuity might also be awarded. The norm, however, was to surpass the minimum.

[53] B.M., AGE, 28 January 1888; Zola, NAF10278, p. 72. The share of the *intéressés* as a group was 12½ percent.

pace.[54] Whether this was also true of the Bon Marché simply is not known. Employee dossiers suggest that firings at this level were rare, but the sample is too small to be conclusive. However, later records indicate that the House was severe towards managers who proved disloyal or who failed to respect authority relations within the hierarchy itself. A second in mail-order was immediately sacked for independent dealings in London. Another second was dismissed for telling an inspector to keep away from the employees in his department. A department head who wished to take a few days' leave because of an injury wrote a subservient letter to his administrator.[55]

Managers, as we have noted, were recruited from the ranks.[56] Seconds were chosen from among regular employees, heads from seconds, administrators from heads. This resolved the problem of creating a chain of command for a store that had evolved into a complex and decentralized operation. How the system could work is illustrated by the career of Benoît Mugnier. Mugnier entered the Bon Marché in 1867 at the age of nineteen, apparently as a salesclerk. In 1872 he became a cashier and in 1877 was promoted to the position of second in his service. Three years later he was made head cashier. By 1885 he was a member of the council. Others might follow the career of Aleide Cormier, who entered the store as a salesclerk in 1882, became a second in the curtains department ten years later, managed to reach the position of principal second in 1894, but never climbed any higher, although he did not retire until 1911.

It is unfortunate that we do not know why the elevator worked so well for some, less well for others. Patronage undoubtedly was something of a factor in a store where so many employees entered on the reference of a member of the hierarchy, or were relatives besides. The brother of the ad-

[54] Zola, NAF10278, pp. 194-95.

[55] B.M., *Conseils Généraux*, 16 May 1895; B.M., Employee Dossiers.

[56] With the exception of two persons who had close ties to the firm prior to their entry, there is no indication of outsiders admitted to positions of authority after 1869.

ministrator Rigaud eventually became the head of his department. Mugnier himself was Madame Boucicaut's cousin,
a fact that was not exceptional. Alphonse Gouin and Louis
Morin, two more Boucicaut relatives, were to play still more
important roles in the history of the store. Indeed it is not difficult to imagine the world of clans and protégés and bureaucratic power plays that must have lain behind so much of the
Bon Marché's history. Anyone who has spent some part of
his life within an organization knows the story well. Yet it
would be a mistake to become too carried away with this pot-
boiler image. Mugnier may have made his fortune with the
store, but two other men of the same name from the same
small village area failed even to make second. Jean Theodore
Karcher, whom we shall meet momentarily, had three sons in
Bon Marché service, all of whom went nowhere.[57] More
likely advances or checks in one's career were determined by
performance and competitiveness. This, after all, was one of
the principal advantages that such a recruitment system
could bring to the Boucicauts; for by creating increasingly
lucrative and powerful positions along a hierarchical ladder,
and by making these positions available to the most successful at the immediate rung below, the Boucicauts could expect
to intensify the ambitions, drive, and output of those persons
they entrusted with authority. Continued access to the highest ranks, where power and profits were greatest, was
guaranteed through a policy that required *intéressés* to retire
at the age of fifty.

But the greatest advantage to the promotion scheme was
the sort of organization man that it was likely to produce.
Managers who worked their way up the ranks, who shared in
a common experience, and who defined their professional
lives in terms of the Bon Marché were men who could be
expected to feel deep ties to the firm and to be loyal to their
patron. They were also likely to be men highly imbued with
the traditions of the House—low prices and a high-powered
paternalism—both of which store ideology deemed essential

[57] B.M., Employee Dossiers.

to the success of the Bon Marché. In this respect the Boucicauts' recruitment policy served as a bridge between the rationalized and familial sides of the store by assuring that the hierarchy would be composed of individuals who held their positions because of their experience, their competitive abilities, and their integration into the household ambiance of the firm.

Further integration into this ambiance came through management's participation in the internal life of the House. To be a member of the hierarchy was to share in responsibilities towards the personnel as well as in power and authority; consequently, most ranking employees were involved in the Boucicauts' paternalism in one way or another. This was particularly so of the administrators who as a group were trustees of the funds. Individual *intéressés* were also in charge of programs such as housing arrangements or the music and fencing lessons, while department heads were responsible for the quality of the food service. And all of the hierarchy had the option of becoming honorary members of the performing societies, although this apparently was more of a *pro forma* expectation.[58] In this way the Boucicauts not only bound management more closely to the firm, but also reinforced the authority that managers could bring to the employees under their control.

Finally, relationships between the hierarchy and the Bon Marché were founded upon financial ties. These had originated in the practice of encouraging employees to place their money with the firm in return for 6 percent interest, but they found their most forceful expression in the *société en commandite* that Madame Boucicaut formed in 1880. By the statutes of this *société*, ownership of the store was divided into 400 shares of 50,000 francs each. Madame Boucicaut retained 250 shares and distributed the remainder to 95 employees and 1

[58] In 1891, the earliest year when information is available on honorary members, there were 157 persons bearing this title. Among them were the 3 directors and 16 administrators, 70 department and other heads, 18 inspectors, and 33 seconds.

sculptor, a friend of the family.[59] The largest shareholder among the employees was Gouin, Madame Boucicaut's relative and president of the council, who purchased 10 shares. Administrators each bought 4 shares, with the exception of one who bought only 2. Thirty-four department and office heads bought either 1 or 2 shares apiece, 7 inspectors and 17 seconds generally 1 share apiece, about 9 other members of the hierarchy from 1 to 2 shares apiece, and approximately 18 regular employees 1 share apiece.[60]

Why Madame Boucicaut chose to do this raises some questions. In a reference to the *société* Zola implied that the money the personnel had earlier placed with the firm had obliged Boucicaut's widow, heirless and wishing "to withdraw" from the house, to bring her employees into association.[61] Zola's remarks are at best vague, but there are other indications that investments may have been intertwined with authority before 1880 and thus could have played a role in the creation of the *société*. For instance the 1869 dedication of the new building was signed by Boucicaut, his son, and six "principal *intéressés*," among whom were Maillard, presumedly the man who staked Boucicaut in 1863, and Lefebvre, a man who entered the store only six weeks previous to the dedication.[62] This leads one to wonder if the council may not, at one time, have consisted of men who had invested most heavily in the House. Employee dossiers also show that a number of persons receiving shares were promoted in 1880, when the *société* was formed, again suggesting that investments could influence decisions at the Bon Marché. Still, just how deeply recruitment of the hierarchy was affected, if at all, by financial

[59] Boileau, architect of the building, would also receive the right to purchase shares in the next several years.

[60] B.M., *Société Du Bon Marché: Vve. Boucicaut & Cie* [statutes], 1880. The payment schedule was as follows: three-fifths down, one-fifth by the end of July 1880, one-fifth by the end of July 1881.

[61] Zola, NAF10278, p. 6.

[62] Georges Barral, "Une grande femme de bien," *Journal Barral* (January 1888) p. 6.

ties is debatable. Undoubtedly there must have been some controlling factor here for the highly decentralized firm to have succeeded as well as it did. It is also notable that Zola made no mention of financial interference with promotions, although this was precisely the sort of information in which he would have been interested. Nor would it be farfetched to assume that foremost members of the hierarchy were expected to place at least part of their savings with the firm. Such a policy would have been most consistent with the relationships the Boucicauts were trying to create.

Indeed, despite the bits and pieces that lend some credence to Zola's remark, it is unlikely that investments alone influenced Madame Boucicaut's decision to transform the Bon Marché into a *société en commandite*. In reality Madame Boucicaut had no intention of withdrawing from the firm, and both the choice of the *commandite* form and the manner in which the *société* was organized suggest a far broader inspiration behind its conception. This can be seen in the statutes where Madame Boucicaut reserved the right to buy back the shares of any employee who left the house, the right of preemption on any shares that a shareholder might wish to sell, the right to reject prospective buyers if she did not pick up this option, and the right to buy back shares before their transfer to heirs. She further required that all transfers of shares to non-shareholders following her death would have to be approved by major shareholders representing at least one quarter of the social capital of the firm. Moreover she reserved for herself the right to name directors who would succeed her upon her death and required future directors to be major shareholders—in effect, to be persons intimately associated with the firm. Finally, she stated in the statutes that it was her intention to sell her remaining shares, as much as possible, to employees of the house.[63]

What seems clear, then, is that Madame Boucicaut made her decision in 1880 not as an act of convenience, but rather as one of sentiment. By transforming the Bon Marché into a

[63] By her death she had ceded, in sum, 214 of the 400 shares.

closed commercial company, with access to ownership and control primarily limited to past and present employees, she evidently was seeking to assure that the Bon Marché would in the future be run by men who in large measure had been her husband's associates and who were deeply immersed in the traditions of the firm. To an aging woman, without an heir, whose adult life had been caught up in the building of the greatest store that Paris had ever seen, a store that existed as an extension of the Boucicaut household, and a store whose success, moreover, was largely predicated on these household relationships, this solution was clearly the only means of preserving beyond her death the Bon Marché as she and her husband had known it and wished it to be. Very simply, it was stated at the beginning of the statutes that "Madame Boucicaut, wishing to render tribute to the memory of her husband, founder of the Bon Marché, has decided to bring into partnership her *intéressés* and various employees of the House." In more expressive terms, Boileau, architect, friend, and shareholder, later poetically lauded her for assuring the unity and solidity of a "new Alexander's empire."[64]

Thus the *société* completed the process of integration that the Boucicauts had begun with the base and sought to extend to their managers as well. This is not to say that the distribution of shares was without its impact on the regular employee. Over the years more and more of their number would be permitted to buy shares, a substantial reinforcement of the *grande famille* image. Yet, by and large the *société* was oriented towards relationships with the hierarchy and represented a sentiment that those persons to whom authority was delegated should belong, and did belong, to the firm in an integral way. Like the paternal relations at the base, it suggested a restructuring of the old pattern of succession in the small shops where the loyal assistant might marry the *patron's* daughter and become heir to the boutique. Now the heirs were assistants who had placed their hopes and savings with the store and its dynamic intentions, who had been re-

[64] B.M., *Fête de Madame Boucicaut*, 19 July 1886.

cruited for both their talent and their loyalty, their competitiveness and their understanding of House traditions, and who in general shared in an internal life of the firm that was deemed necessary to its success as a *grand magasin*. In effect, the Boucicauts were again creating conditions, this time on the managerial level, that could lead their employees to see their relationship with the Bon Marché as one of participation in an organizational and active commercial household.

How this spirit could be reflected in the mind of the hierarchy is illustrated by a set of letters that Jean Theodore Karcher, the Bon Marché secretary, wrote Madame Boucicaut during her frequent absences from Paris after 1880. Karcher, who had entered the Bon Marché in 1865 as an interpreter and who had worked his way up to mail-order second and then to store secretary in 1875, wrote of his store and his *patronne* in a way that personified the organization man the Boucicauts wished to create. On one hand, his letters were filled with personal remarks, were written in the tone of a devoted family servant, and expressed an absolute loyalty to Madame Boucicaut. They tended to combine store and owner within the same thought and might, for example, herald the success of a sale as "it is worthy of you, Madame." Similarly they often referred to the personnel in household terms—"your people" Karcher wrote on one occasion and "the Bon Marché family" on several others. Yet Karcher's letters were also replete with the imagery of an active and successful department store, and the world they depicted was one of departments and bureaus, a myriad of different employees, and sales figures in the millions. They revealed a loyalty not only to Madame Boucicaut but to the Bon Marché and what it represented, and their author gloried in the store's triumphs, identifying wholeheartedly with the organizational and competitive character of the firm. Frequently Karcher used military images, portraying the great commercial bureaucracy as a great army and its great exposition days as great battles, so that on the morrow of one such sale he could write:

"Yesterday was truly a success. Never has the crowd been so considerable and never, either, has our sales volume been so colossal. 1,520,485.20 francs! It makes me proud to march in the ranks of a peaceful army that knows how to reap such victories."[65]

In his more intense moments he could even produce his own poetry of modern activity, as on the occasion of the 1883 white sale when he wrote:

"From eight in the morning the house filled with buyers milling about our white displays. As always the store was marvelously adorned, her banisters lined with white calico and flowing with pillow lace, her columns wrapped with white muslin. . . .

"The sight was fairy-like, but it was no time to be an idle spectator. Everyone, in effect, is thrown into the melee, all our supporters are convoked, and mail-order or bureaucrats, firemen, gasmen, workers or cutters, all improvise as sellers, or at least as *débiteurs*.

"And truly the battle heats up, the crowd presses forward, engulfs the doors, masses and crushes about the cashiers, assaults the stairways. . . .

"The sales figure, moreover, is of an eloquence beyond comment."[66]

So in this bureaucrat's sentiments for his firm and his celebration of its boundless energy, we can once again see how intimately the Boucicauts were able to wed their rationalized world to household traditions, and, consequently, how effectively they could succeed in molding and integrating a new kind of employee.

RITUALIZATION

In *The Elementary Forms of the Religious Life*, Durkheim remarked how closely the things that communities hold sacred are dependent upon the rituals that commemorate them, and that, in fact, the sacred "attains . . . [its] greatest intensity at the moment when the men are assembled together and are in

[65] B.M., Karcher Letters, 8 February 1887.
[66] *Ibid.*, 13 February 1883.

immediate relations with one another, when they all partake of the same idea and the same sentiments." Thus rituals, Durkheim went on to note, were the most forceful affirmation of those bonds that hold collectivities together.[67] At the Bon Marché, where an inner world ambiance was cultivated through store gatherings, celebrations, and ceremonies, ritualization served much the same purpose. At no moment was the *grande famille* image so vividly projected, the collective spirit so intensely summoned, the cohesion of a store community so dramatically manifest as during the special rites of the House. It is a side to the Bon Marché that expresses more than any other the internal relationships that the Boucicauts founded at the firm, and as such it is a side that merits examination.

House ceremonies, like rationalization, could take many forms. Some were merely festive occasions, opportunities to gather together in ways that would accentuate a sense of community while masking daily bureaucratic realities. There were periodical summer picnics such as the 1886 outing to Madame Boucicaut's suburban estate at Fontenay-aux-Roses. There were annual Christmas parties within the store itself. At times the music societies performed in *"soirées intimes"* for their honorary members (perhaps including the remainder of the personnel). All of these were innocent affairs, although the Boucicauts did not hesitate to cloak them in an aura of fantasy, much as they would with their public relations. Thus magical scenes of a Disneyesque Bon Marché, Dumas-like scenes of moonlight and sword play covered the programs of in-House concerts or those of the *Assauts d'Escrime* that the store held annually.[68]

[67] Emile Durkheim, *The Elementary Forms of the Religious Life* (London: George Allen and Unwin, 1915), pp. 344-50, 375-78.

[68] The *Assauts d'Escrime* were the final fencing competitions that the Fencing Society (these lessons too had shortly given way to a more formalized organization) held each year. The audience for these competitions is difficult to determine. Certainly honorary members (i.e., the store hierarchy) came, and very possibly they brought wives or guests. Some clients or other public persons might also have been invited. Some regular employees may have been honorary members and perhaps other employees as well were invited

Yet, as with paternalism, gatherings and festivities and the community life they projected were rarely separated from a context of dynamism or control. This was especially so of the annual grand concerts that were prominent in the public relations of the House. Store-wide affairs where attending managers and employees seconded the performance of the hundred or so participants, these spectacles were transformed on an internal plane into celebrations of House unity and the effort in common to promote store success. There was a ritualistic side, as well, to the inauguration of paternalism, exemplified in the evening that Boucicaut collected the personnel together to announce and explain his founding of the provident fund. Annual gatherings of this nature would continue at least into the 1880s. The pension fund, too, began with an evening gathering of the personnel. Karcher, in his enthusiastic way, has left us a glimpse of Bon Marché mastery over the collective event:

"The personnel were massed before and about the platform, the women lining the upper galleries, and I must say that it would have been difficult to find a more attractive location or a more attentive and rapt crowd.

"At eight o'clock the administrators take their place on the platform. . . .

"M. Weber acts as spokesman and in an extremely remarkable speech retraces the philanthropic work to which you have added your name alongside that of the late M. Boucicaut.

"He relates your constant concern for the humble, the inferior, for those who are not able to rise to positions that offer an interest on sales or profits. He recalls the provident fund founded for them and then, to the applause of everyone, he announces the new foundation whose statutes he will read.

"The reading proceeds amidst a profound silence. Everyone followed line by line the text read by M. Weber, so well that at

---

to attend. But is not likely that these were as grand a spectacle as the concerts held within the store. Still, program covers from later years suggest these were something of a special, and elegant, event, and it was customary for the house chorale to perform.

the end of each page one could hear a great, brief rustling: three thousand sheets turning simultaneously. . . .

"M. Weber concludes by announcing that he will carry back to you the applause of your personnel and finishes by saying: Mme. Boucicaut gives you a million; yet she promised you nothing. Imitate her example and in turn, without promising her anything, give her what is in your power, your devotion and concern that you owe to the interests of this great Bon Marché family—this is at least the sense of his speech if not the precise text."[69]

It was, however, with the passing of the Boucicauts that the most profound ritualization of Bon Marché household relationships occurred. When Aristide died, a funeral of great pageantry took place in which all employees of the Bon Marché participated. The procession from the small church of St. Thomas Aquinas to Montparnasse cemetery was headed by his nearest relatives (although his son was too ill to attend), followed by the principal members of the hierarchy, each of whom carried a wreath of camelias, violets, lilacs, and roses. Immediately behind the hearse marched four clerks carrying two immense wreaths with the inscription "To M. Boucicaut—the employees." Then came the remainder of the personnel, the Boucicauts' domestic servants, and friends of the family, including the heads of other great Parisian stores and many provincial manufacturers with whom the Bon Marché did business. Estimates of the size of the cortege ranged from 4,000 to 8,000 persons. An observer tells us that as the coffin was removed from the church several employees, contrary to law, attempted to take it from the undertaker's personnel and to carry it themselves. At the burial there was an oration by the chief of the silk department, who proclaimed that Boucicaut's memory would remain not only among "those of us who have the good fortune to belong to this family, but among those too, near and far, who have followed and admired progress." He then recalled to the assemblage, primarily composed of employees, that Boucicaut

[69] B.M., Karcher Letters, 31 July 1885.

had left "a widow and a son who have always been associated with his generous thoughts and to whom we must transfer all the affection and all the respect that we have had for the person just departed from us." The Bon Marché remained closed for two days following the funeral, and it was closed again for half a day the following year so that the entire personnel could attend the commemoration service for the first anniversary of Boucicaut's death. At this service, as if to emphasize the fealty relationships that were being expressed, the garçons, in full uniform, formed a guard of honor and the House chorale sang the mass.[70]

Ten years later a similar scene occurred with the passing of Boucicaut's widow. Over 12,000 death announcements were mailed out, listing among the bereaved: "Messieurs the Directors, Administrators, and Employees of the Bon Marché." Echoing this sentiment, cards and letters of condolence were sent to the Bon Marché and its personnel. One retired notary offered to "Messieurs the members of the Council of Administrators and Messieurs the employees of the Bon Marché . . . keenest and most sincere condolences . . . for the recent loss of their revered *mother*, the worthy and charitable Madame Boucicaut." On the day of the funeral another ceremony of great pomp took place. Again all of the employees attended, with an honor guard of department heads surrounding the hearse and a larger guard of honor formed among garçons who marched along both sides of the cortege. According to police estimates, 8,000 persons took part in the official ceremony while 20,000 onlookers surrounded or entered the cemetery.[71]

Once more funeral orations mingled commemoration with ideology. Plassard, Madame Boucicaut's close friend and designated head director, spoke first. He lauded her generosity and declared that: "Continuators of her work, by the fact of

[70] Préfecture de Police, Ba 967, reports of 28 December 1877 and 23 December 1878; "Fortunes," *London Society; Le Soir*, 29 December 1877; *Le Rappel*, 28 December 1877.

[71] Préfecture de Police, Ba 967, report of 12 December 1887. There is also a sketch of funeral arrangements among Karcher's letters.

her wishes . . . we will try to imitate her wisdom, her stead-fastness, her justice, her goodness, and contribute thus to the prosperity of this great establishment whose destiny has been confided to us." Next spoke Monsieur Jeune, in the name of the personnel, who recalled the "immense stupor that seized this great Bon Marché family" on the news of Madame Boucicaut's death, regretted that the personnel could no longer dedicate to her their "filial gratitude," and finished with the message that: "A final hope shines for us, my friends, that of continuing to devote ourselves to the work [oeuvre] that she bequeaths us and to the chiefs entrusted by her in the past, who have received from her the mission of being our benevolent and enlightened guides in the future."[72] Among those who gave orations after Jeune were Fontenay, another representative of the personnel, Bonnefous, representative of former Bon Marché employees, and Boileau.[73]

That Madame Boucicaut's passing could evoke such an outpouring of sentiment stemmed from a recognition of the good deeds that had marked her life, particularly since the death of her husband. Admittedly she was a wealthy woman, without immediate heirs, who enjoyed dispensing her gifts through dramatic gestures—like the time she presented Louis Pasteur with an 100,000-franc check.[74] Yet she was also a woman who had never forgotten her simple origins, and, like her husband who also had been known for his philanthropy, she contributed readily to most needy causes. If her relationships with her employees were linked to the need for integration and control, they were also expressions of deeply felt ties and responsibilities; in large measure her creation of a pension program and the société can be seen as the gesture of a woman who had come to regard her employees as an adopted family. It was fitting, then, that, honored so in her death, she bestowed with her passing her most remarkable of

---

[72] Whether Jeune was by this time a member of the hierarchy is not known. Cf. note. No. 41.

[73] B.M., Testament de Madame Boucicaut.

charitable deeds and maternal acts, for she left practically all her fortune to benevolent institutions or her employees.

A document of some thirty-seven pages, her will provided for sizeable donations to associations for artists, teachers, and destitute journalists, Catholic programs for young workers, and religious groups of all denominations. There were allocations for the foundation of retirement homes at Fontenay and Bellême, the foundation of a Catholic hospital in Paris, and, because she had never known her own father, the foundation of three homes to provide temporary refuge and medical care for young girls "who have experienced for the first time the misfortune of being seduced." But above all, and in keeping with the traditions of the House, her thoughts turned to her personnel, to "those who are my devoted collaborators, whatever rank they may occupy in this great House which my husband and I have, with them, brought to this present level of esteem and prosperity." To these men and women she bequeathed more than 13,000,000 francs, to be distributed in proportion to time of service and with distinctions between employees and *ouvriers*. In addition, individual grants to numerous employees, past and present, figured prominently among gifts to family and friends. So as with most households, it was especially in death that the idea of one big family filled the air.[75]

Entrepreneurial Roles and Business Change

We need to consider one final question in this chapter. We have noted the closeness between business and family in nineteenth-century France and we have seen that the Boucicauts were no exception. In a variety of ways the Bon

[74] Pasteur had come to her residence seeking a contribution for his research. See Dasquet, *Le Bon Marché*. The story may be apocryphal.

[75] B.M., *Testament de Madame Boucicaut*. To employees with less than three years service she left 1,000 francs apiece. Employees with three to five years' service received 3,000 francs. Those with six to nine years received 6,000 francs and employees with ten or more years were left 10,000 francs each. Legacies to *ouvriers* and *ouvrières* ranged from 100 francs to 1,000 francs.

Marché could have passed for the quintessential French family firm. Relationships at the Bon Marché were enveloped in a deep household ambiance, as if the firm were merely an extension of the family to whom it belonged. The Boucicauts preserved and cultivated a sense of fiefdom. The store was their creation, their status, their lives, never merely a financial end in itself. Indeed if Madame Boucicaut turned the Bon Marché into a *société en commandite*, this was to assure that the firm would remain a family enterprise of sorts following her death. Nor did the Boucicauts tend to look beyond themselves, or their retainers, for financial support. And yet, although we are told that these attributes were essentially conservative and inward-looking,[76] the Bon Marché became the greatest retail success that Paris, and perhaps the world, had ever known. Why, then, did the Boucicauts find the traditions of the French business community no impediment to building a large-scale, dynamic, and bureaucratic business enterprise?

The answer again lies in the special relationships that the Boucicauts established at the Bon Marché and in the fact that change in a society may come through a restructuring of traditions and values to fit new conditions. Once we recognize that paternalism was also a response to the Boucicauts' *own* needs to acclimate to their new business roles, it becomes clear that the French family firm was a far more flexible instrument than the conclusions of David Landes and others would tend to allow. Evidently what was critical in determining entrepreneurial roles in a culture where family values and family proprietorship were especially stressed was not whether an enterprise remained a closed family firm founded on household relationships but rather the structure and orientation that were given to these relationships. For the Boucicauts, the way around the problems of expansion that could haunt other French businessmen was to create a new kind of household that would permit them to reconcile the traditional value system with dynamic business change.

[76] Cf. Introduction.

Thus, precisely because of the relationships they established with their hierarchy, the Boucicauts were able to accept growth and the delegation of authority that ineluctably came with it, even though they were no more inclined to relinquish customary family control than any other French businessman.

Much the same might be said of the Boucicauts' ability to reconcile conflicting views of themselves. If the Boucicauts, in the traditional manner, did not wish to make business an end in itself, if they preferred to carve for themselves a niche beyond their daily routine of profits and losses, if their goal was to retain a sense of their firm as a personal expression of themselves, then their paternalism enabled them to play out these roles. And yet, if they equally wished to push back the frontiers of commercial innovation, if they equally wished to build a remarkably dynamic French business enterprise and bask in the renown that this endeavor could bring, then their paternalism, as it was structured, permitted them to play out these roles as well. Indeed what was so striking about Boucicaut paternalism from this point of view was not only that one role could be assumed without interfering with the other, but that the qualities of the former could so readily be turned to the account of the latter.

In the end, all of the Boucicauts' associational structure came to endow the Bon Marché with an institutionalized character. Increasingly the Bon Marché was referred to as an *oeuvre*, an image that fittingly assimilated the extensive paternalistic environment with the magnitude of the store's commercial success. Pictorial images, poetical allusions to old and new empires, celebrations and rituals, attributed an exceptional status to the House. There was the sensation that the Bon Marché was something profound, something extraordinary, a great adventure upon which all its members had embarked. Most of all, there was the *grande famille* image, the central theme in the creation of a new idea of the firm, and a concept that permitted the Boucicauts to anchor themselves in the traditional value system, while they again redefined these values for their own, and new, purposes.

THE DIRECTORS

THE TWO AND A HALF DECADES following Madame Boucicaut's death witnessed little change in the relationships that the Boucicauts had established at the Bon Marché. Directors saw little reason to tamper with an associational frame so suitable to a bureaucratic context. But the very sameness of these years was in itself significant, pointing to the persistence of household relationships in a period of increasing managerial control. In the directors we can see not only a reflection of a managerial revolution that was coming to pass in the French business world, but also a reflection of how bourgeois France was to experience this revolution without fully abandoning those values and traditions it especially held dear, and that served it so well. The repetitious side to these years is equally notable because it has left us with a far more articulate record of the ideology, motivations, and responses of those persons with whom we are concerned.

FAITHFUL CONTINUATORS

The passing of Madame Boucicaut did of course bring changes at the highest levels of power and authority in the House. Immediately following her death, and in accordance with the statutes of 1880, two new governing bodies came into being. The first of these, the Ordinary General Assembly (*Assemblée Générale Ordinaire*), served, in the main, as an annual report to the shareholders. The second, the Special General Assembly (*Assemblée Générale Extraordinaire*), had a more diverse role. Liable to summons at any time, its purpose was to deliberate on such matters as modifications of the statutes, the election of directors, or the acquisition or construction of new buildings.[1]

Each of these bodies was compact and closed. Only those persons who held four shares or more—that is those persons who had invested at least 200,000 francs in the *société*—had the right to attend either assembly. At least one-third of all shares held, however, had to be represented at ordinary assemblies for these meetings to be valid, and the requirement for special assemblies was raised to one-half.[2] Attendance figures indicate how small these meetings were. In 1889, 1892, and 1897, when there were at least several hundred shareholders, only 19, 27, and 24 persons, respectively, participated or were represented in the ordinary assemblies. For the same years the figures for special assemblies were 20, 59, and 58 respectively. In 1900 persons with two shares were permitted to sit at ordinary assemblies. But not until 1910, when the thirty-year tenure of the statutes came to a close and a major review preceded their renewal, did a significant change in the number of persons attending these meetings take place. After this date, individuals holding what was then the equivalent of one-half share could participate in the assemblies, although quorum requirements were now raised to four-fifths of those persons possessing one-half share or more. Thus for most of the prewar period these assemblies were elite affairs. To complete the correlation between shareholding and power, voting was in proportion to the number of shares held, although a maximum of twenty votes was allowed any single individual and a decision to modify the

[1] In French legal terms, the Bon Marché was transformed at Madame Boucicaut's death from a *société en commandite simple* into a *société en commandite par actions*.

[2] It should also be noted that provisions were made in case a quorum could not be achieved. Originally the statutes simply required that in this instance a new assembly should be called within no less than eight days, this assembly valid no matter how few persons attended. By 1890, however, a more complex system prevailed. If a quorum was not achieved on a given day, shareholders in descending order of importance would be convoked until the one-third or one-half quorum was arrived at. But if still no quorum could be achieved on that day, then the same provisions for a new assembly as in 1888 would be applicable.

statutes required a three-fourths majority. Other issues were decided by a simple majority.

Real power, however, resided not with the assemblies but with a third new governing body—the *gérance*—whose three directors presided over the council of administrators (*intéressés* in charge of individual store sectors) and supervised the day-to-day affairs of the House. The authority of these men was far more extensive than that of the designated directors who had preceded them under Boucicaut's widow and son. In the earlier period, designated directors were known simply as president and vice-president of the council, and their relationship with that body had been a strongly reciprocal one.[3] This relationship persisted for the first five years after the transition, perhaps because the first senior director was a man of limited commercial experience, perhaps because several major shareholders continued to sit on the council. But by 1893 control of the council, and hence of the daily affairs of the House, had passed into the hands of the directors. The shift is recorded by the council minutes of the post-1887 period. Before 1893, *intéressés* continued to play a strong leadership role at their meetings, often initiating discussions, while all decisions were made in the name of the council. After 1893 few discussions were initiated by the administrators. References to the council as a body were now generally limited to its consultation on matters presented by the directors, and all decisions were authorized either anonymously or by "*MM. les Gérants.*"

Power relationships between the directors and the assemblies were far more complex, though, in the end, no more constraining on the directors' control. As bodies of ownership, assemblies elected the directors, set the terms of their pay (and percentages on profits), held the final word on matters of fundamental importance, and generally held the *gérance* accountable for the course of affairs. Moreover, assemblies, at least in the early years, brought together men who had been associates of the now apotheosized Boucicauts, and hence men who understood as well the workings

[3] B.M., AGE, 14 January 1888.

of a major department store. Consequently, they expressed a sense of competence when deliberating on issues and a sense of authority when criticizing the directorship.

Still, if directors were subject to certain controls and were ultimately responsible to the wishes of the shareholders, they nevertheless met with little difficulty in establishing their leadership over the assemblies. In part this followed from the limits of the assemblies in their checks over them. Elections of directors occurred on a regular basis—terms were for five years—with no provisions for immediate recall aside from the case of prolonged illness.[4] A surveillance council, charged by the ordinary assembly with reporting on the books, was content to operate as a rubber stamp. The assemblies further lacked any control over day-to-day matters, including the promotion or firing of managers at all levels of the hierarchy (administrators seem to have been chosen within the council itself). In turn, then, the directors came to the assemblies with immense management authority. They also came with a good share of institutional authority, for French law required that the *gérants* of a *société en commandite* assume financial responsibility and that their names be stated in the title of the firm. In 1888, for instance, the House was formally known as Au Bon Marché: Maison Aristide Boucicaut *and* as Plassard, Morin, Fillot & Cie. Finally, directors came as shareholders in their own right, often major ones, and thus enjoyed a dual role in the assemblies.

The directors' authority also emanated from their control over the assemblies' discussions. On the surface these were meetings between the owners and their managers. In reality they were something far different. At ordinary assemblies shareholders listened to a report from the senior director, who set the agenda and tone for the gathering. At the more

[4] By the terms of the original statutes, no limits were set on the tenure of the men to be designated by Madame Boucicaut as directors. In the first AGE, however, it was decided that limitations would be set, staggered at five, six, and seven years so that in the future only one director would be up for election. This system of staggering elections in itself added to the power of the directors, as a complete housecleaning at a single AGE could never be envisioned.

important special assemblies, directors were in the habit of presenting major projects for consideration only after they had first worked out the details within the council or perhaps among themselves. If the assembly chose to appoint a study commission, directors had the power to be named to this if they wished. Generally, however, they preferred a pretense of neutrality, exerting their influence behind the scenes.[5] As for proposals initiated by individual shareholders, these immediately became subject to comment by the directors. The directors were, then, at both the ordinary and special assemblies the focal points, and generally the initiators, of all discussions. Not surprisingly, it was rare that they lost a vote.

In theory the three directors were equal in their powers. Each man's signature carried equal authority, proposals and decisions were jointly authorized, and directors shared a common office. But the position of senior director quickly became a preeminent one. The senior director occupied the center desk in the common office, his name appeared first in the title of the company, and, while each of the three men received three percent of the profits, the senior director's salary was 48,000 francs compared to 36,000 for the other two.[6] More important, Jules Plassard, who had been president of the council since 1885 and who was the first senior director, immediately assumed in 1888 the role of spokesman for the three. The precedent was set, and after his departure the senior director continued to be the dominant presence at the council and at the assemblies. Just what the relationship was between the three men in the less perceptible world of bureaucratic in-fighting is difficult to determine. Distribution of responsibility appears to have been largely a function of realms of expertise. Yet a man like Narcisse Fillot, who had been a close associate of the Boucicauts and who was re-elected several times, could enjoy an undisputed authority

[5] With one minor exception in 1888 (regarding percentages on the profits for the chief cashiers and accountants), at no time do commission reports appear to have been contrary to the directors' wishes. See B.M., AGE, 28 January 1888.

[6] B.M., Statutes, *Société du Bon Marché*; B.M., AGE, 28 January 1888.

among his co-directors during his tenure as senior *gérant* from 1899 to 1912.

As individuals, the directors appear to have led successful but uncolorful lives. The heroic years of the Bon Marché died with the Boucicauts, and the era of the directors is tinged with that greyness one has come to expect of prosperous bureaucratic regimes. These were not men to inspire passionate or dramatic (and certainly not humorous) biographies, and there is little likelihood that they will ever abandon their semi-anonymous corner of posterity. Most were simply career bureaucrats, organization men who made it to the top, men concerned with sales and balance sheet figures, with keeping a steady course, and with running their operations as efficiently as possible. In this respect they fit our image of the new managers who were beginning to dominate the business scene, our image of the passing of the business setting from an entrepreneurial to a managerial stage.

But the circumspection and respectability with which they led their public lives, their devotion to their families at the expense of greater glamour, and that *parvenu* quality that these *commerçants* could never entirely shake, especially when they built their *hôtels particuliers*, placed them firmly within the nineteenth-century bourgeois mold as well. We must be careful not to place too much distance between these men and the society from which they arose; indeed it is the element of continuity as much as the element of change that needs to be stressed. And nowhere is this clearer than in their continuation of the Boucicaut synthesis that wed the traditional world of household to the emerging world of bureaucracy.

All directors were individuals with deep associations to the firm as the Boucicauts had built it. Two of them, Emile Morin, who was senior director from 1893 to 1899, and his successor, Fillot, were men whose professional lives were set within the history of the Bon Marché itself. Morin had entered as a clerk in 1856 and Fillot had entered under the same conditions five years later. Of the other six directors in the prewar period, four—Ernest Ricois (entered 1871; director 1893-1910), Ernest

Lucet (entered 1871; director 1899-1912), Anselme Caslot (entered ?; director 1910-1920), and Chambeau (entered 1878; director 1912-1915)—were equally men who had begun their career at the base under the Boucicauts and who had worked their way up the ranks. The remaining two, Jules Plassard and Auguste Dru (entered 1899; director 1912-1920) were exceptions to this rule, although they were each individuals whose lives had been caught up with the Boucicauts or their legacy. Plassard was a solicitor by profession, but he was also a close personal friend and counselor of Madame Boucicaut. In 1885 he became president of the council following the departure of Gouin, and then senior director following Madame Boucicaut's death. Dru had initially been the principal clerk of Madame Boucicaut's notary. He began his career at the Bon Marché at the rank of general secretary because of his intimate knowledge of the firm's institutional affairs.[7]

For each of these men, then, the familial environment of the Bon Marché was a part of their lives, and something of value to preserve. Structurally, they sought to retain an internal cohesiveness within the store by reinforcing the restrictions on share transfers to outsiders. In this they were aided by arrangements that Madame Boucicaut had made for the sale of shares in her possession at the time of her death to persons already associated with the firm (many of the shares going to current major shareholders).[8] But the directors and

[7] On Morin and Ricois, see Archives Nationales, F12 5218, F12 5253. On Fillot's career, see especially B.M., *Livre d'Or*. Information on Lucet and Plassard has been drawn from private interviews: Monsieur and Madame Philippe [granddaughter of Lucet], private interview held in Paris, 1974; François Gibault [great-grandson of Plassard], private interview held in Paris, 1973-74. Lucet, who in other times might have succeeded his father as a tailor in Jouilly, was obliged to come to Paris and seek work when the *collège* at Jouilly, one of his father's major clients, placed its order for uniforms at the Belle Jardinière for a lower price. Ironically, then, the new merchandising that practically ruined his father's trade was to provide the younger Lucet with hitherto unimaginable opportunities for wealth and success. Chambeau's date of entry is listed on an untitled paper in the B.M. containing several names and dates of entry. On Dru see B.M., M. Dru, Victor Auguste, February 1919. The reasons for Gouin's departure are not known.

[8] B.M., Will and Succession of Madame Boucicaut. Before her death

the assemblies further restricted future transfers by requiring a majority of the special assembly to approve prospective sales when its sanction was required. In the case of refusal, a shareholder could place his share(s) up for auction; but only current shareholders and members of the hierarchy could bid.[9]

Yet the problem of liquidation was not so easily resolved. Shares that had sold at 50,000 francs in 1880 increased enormously in value, selling for 360,000 francs in 1893 and for a staggering 600,000 francs by 1898.[10] But as long as severe limitations on share transfers existed, it was difficult to convert one's paper fortune into hard currency. Throughout the period directors and the assemblies were confronted with shareholder pressure to relax the restraints. Their response was to ease employee access to shareholding, first by dividing shares into eighths, later into thirty-seconds, still later in 1910 into 64,000 shares valued at 312.50 francs each, and then again in 1912 into 128,000 shares at 156.25 francs apiece. In 1900 the special assembly further agreed to the sale of shares to employees of two years' service or more, simply upon approval by the directors and the surveillance council. At the same time, these employees were granted access to the bidding on share auctions. Still, if standards for share transfer were considerably relaxed, the assemblies steadfastly refused to authorize sales to outsiders. Not until the very end of the prewar period would open sales come about.

Thus, even after the passing of the Boucicauts, the Bon Marché remained a closed family firm of sorts, and this spirit carried over as well into the personal lives of the directors, their associates, and the principal shareholders. Intermar-

---

Madame Boucicaut had also set up a *société civile* which appears to have been the mechanism (and perhaps tax shelter) by which this transfer was guaranteed. The *société civile* was also to act as the institutional guarantor of the retirement fund. B.M., Statutes, *Société Civile du Bon Marché*. A number of names listed in the share transfers are not identifiable, so their association with the firm is not verifiable. But most definitely were members of the firm, and all large transfers went to such persons.

[9] B.M., Statutes, *Société en Commandite Par Actions*, 1890.

[10] D'Avenel, "Le mécanisme," p. 338; B.M., Employee Dossiers.

riage does not appear to have been uncommon. Fillot married the sister of a colleague. Dr. Louis Lucet, son of the director, married the daughter of Zoegger, a member of the council. Joseph Plassard, son of Jules and a major shareholder who was so wealthy that although a lawyer he never had a client, married the divorced wife of Emile Morin. Later, after her death, he made a second marriage to the daughter of Mougel, head of the *blanc* department.[11]

Perhaps marriage patterns of this sort were simply accidental. More likely, however, they followed from the tendency of directors and administrators to introduce the world of the Bon Marché into their family lives and to raise their children with a sentiment of personal attachment to the firm and its traditions. The social life of families like the Lucets or the Zédets (an *intéressé* at the turn of the century) was largely circumscribed within the world of Bon Marché acquaintances. In the Plassard family visits to the store tended to be a daily occurrence. In the Mougel family a copy of Madame Boucicaut's will was kept for all to read.[12] Indeed one may speak of a cult of the Bon Marché that was handed down from generation to generation, so that even today the great-grandson of Jules Plassard displays the pictures of Aristide and Marguerite Boucicaut in his salon, while the descendants of still other important figures retain a strong interest in the current and past affairs of the House. Perhaps the most striking expression of continued ties among children was the case of Madame Gigon, daughter of the first head of mail-order, who bequeathed 100,000 francs to the Bon Marché's paternalistic funds. At a commemorative ceremony attended by a delegation of Bon Marché employees, her widower explained her reasons: "Madame Gigon had . . . a debt of gratitude to the Bon Marché, not only to your directors and your chiefs who . . . made the Bon Marché prosperous and preserved its good name, but also to you, ladies and gentlemen, and to your colleagues who are, in part, the modest artisans of an

[11] B.M., *Livre d'Or*; Monsieur and Madame Philippe; François Gibault.

[12] Monsieur and Madame Philippe; François Gibault; Monsieur Zédet [son of the administrator], private interview held in Paris, 1974.

affluence that has permitted us to do a little good in this world."[13]

But it was especially in the images to which these men so readily turned, the roles they so consciously prescribed, that we can see the linking of Boucicaut relationships to the post-Boucicaut era; the appropriateness of these relationships to the directors' own needs to fix their business identity, set their authority, and secure loyalty to themselves and the House; and finally a more articulate expression than the Boucicauts themselves have left of how these relationships had come to be defined. In speeches at assembly and council meetings or on special occasions, directors were fond of intermingling calls for continued growth and prosperity with references to "our beloved Bon Marché," thereby retaining that blend of dynamism and household that the Boucicauts had so carefully laid as the basis for their idea of the firm. On retiring, Emile Morin declared that "in leaving this House where I have passed the best years of my life and come upon friendships that are dear to me, I am at least satisfied, my dear friends, to remark that we have brought our beloved Bon Marché to a degree of prosperity that places her in the first rank." Even in the mundane matter of new construction Fillot introduced his plans "with the profound conviction that they will contribute to the growth of our beloved House in the future."[14]

In effect the directors sought in their speeches to portray the Bon Marché as a continued family firm and social institution, entrusted by the Boucicauts to a second generation of directors and shareholders. Authority itself became dependent on a certification of historical descent, respect for Boucicaut traditions, and commercial prowess that added to the glory of the House. At the election of a director in 1898,

[13] B.M., Employee Dossier of Charles Guillemont [Madame Gigon's father]. Madame Gigon died in 1922. Continued ties did not, however, prevent second and third generation shareholders from pressing for relaxation of restrictions on share sales. Joseph Plassard, for example, was to be a constant force in this regard.

[14] B.M., AGE, 11 April 1899; AGO, 26 August 1910.

Morin charged the special assembly to consider "only the interests of the *Société* and the desire to assure the future and
prosperity of this House that Monsieur and Madame
Boucicaut have handed down to us and which, for this reason, must be for us doubly dear."[15] At the important special
assembly in 1909, when a commission was to be chosen to review the statutes before their renewal, Fillot opened the ses-
sion with a long discourse on the past and future of the Bon
Marché.

The address itself is worth reviewing. Beginning with the
remark that "a return to the past can be for each of us
the source of valuable lessons," Fillot first turned to the
Boucicauts. He reminded the assembly that "the name of the
Bon Marché is so intimately bound to that of its founder that
we cannot consider the future of the House without conjur-
ing up the memory of M. Boucicaut, the man of great genius
who laid [the store's] foundations and who left upon it his
imprint in such a vigorous and strong way that it preserves
and will preserve for a long time this deep impression." He
also recalled that after the death of her husband "Madame
Boucicaut had but one thought, to consolidate the *oeuvre*
founded by the husband she missed; and with this thought in
mind she associated her principal collaborators and employees in order to form the present *Société*,"[16] succeeding so
well that at her death "she left the Bon Marché prosperous
and the plans of her husband near realization." Then, continuing in this vein, Fillot turned to the achievements of the
directors. He noted first that "our efforts . . . have always
been inspired by the principles, the traditions that M. and
Mme. Boucicaut passed on to us: to develop and perfect
without arrest the marvelous organism whose direction was

[15] B.M., AGE, 18 July 1898.
[16] These words were in keeping with a further institutionalization of store
ideology. After Madame Boucicaut's death, the introduction to the statutes of
the *société* was modified to read: "Madame Boucicaut, wishing to render tribute to the memory of her husband, founder of the Bon Marché, and to consolidate his *oeuvre*, has believed it useful to associate her collaborators and
various employees. . . ."

confided to us while endeavouring to increase the well-being of the personnel." Next he proceeded to give a roll call of sales figures from 1852 to 1909. And only then, after he had firmly impressed upon his listeners the image of a store whose unparalleled success was integrally tied to its founders and to the traditions they had bequeathed, testifying in the process to the directors' custodianship of the Boucicauts' *oeuvre*, did Fillot arrive at the cause of his speech—the election of a commission of review.[17]

Qualities of leadership were defined in much the same way. Directors and administrators were presumed to be a commercial elite, and initiations into the council might require a pledge "to work for the grandeur and the success of the House." Proficiency in management was clearly expected. But no new managerial ethos evolved in contradistinction to nineteenth-century bourgeois standards. As men of *"intelligence"* and *"activité,"* directors remained imbedded in the bourgeois clichés of the times. They continued to preach devotion and loyalty as essential virtues and responsibilities. Administrators were initiated into their first council meeting with a pledge of complete devotion to the Bon Marché. A similar rite became *pro forma* following the election or reelection of directors. Infidelity was in fact the greatest of sins in the language of the House,[18] and praise for one's devotion was rarely missing from tributes to individual directors.

Above all, store ideology defined the ideal leader as the "faithful continuator" or the "worthy successor" of the founders of the firm, again dwelling on an idea of custodianship that wove together images of familism, dynamism, and continuity. Fillot lauded Lucet, on his departure from the *gérance*, for having "totally dedicated yourself to your mission, delighted to see your efforts contribute to the ever-increasing prosperity of our beloved House." On a similar occasion he paid Ricois the tribute of having given "body and soul to this

[17] B.M., AGE, 14 December 1909.
[18] A department head guilty of receiving kickbacks from suppliers was rebuked as *"cet acheteur infidelè."* B.M., *Conseils Généraux*, 28 January 1895.

House so winning and so dear" and of having contributed to
the Bon Marché's "premier rank in world commerce."[19]

Fillot himself, who had the deepest ties to the Boucicauts
and was most eminent among their successors, became the
model continuator of the founding family's work. Events
such as his fiftieth anniversary with the firm or his retirement
from the directorship were marked with long speeches in
which the Boucicauts figured prominently and in which Fillot's life was personally and inextricably linked to that of the
House, its traditions, and its commercial success. On one
such occasion Lucet remarked that Boucicaut knew how to
make the best of his employees into his collaborators "in
order to continue, develop, and immortalize his *oeuvre*"; that
he had quickly recognized Fillot's talents and had made of
him his intimate confidant; and that for these reasons there
was no one better than Fillot to "continue, enlarge, expand,
and make prosperous the work of genius and philanthropy
created by M. Boucicaut and continued by his venerated
companion whose memory will always be blessed."[20]

At another occasion Caslot noted that: "If the Bon Marché
occupies a predominant place in world commerce, if the lot of
our employees, of our workers, has been made better, these
results are in large part due to Monsieur Fillot. He has shown
himself to be the worthy successor of the founder of the Bon
Marché, inspired by their principles and their sense of justice,
having always in mind a greater House, a happier personnel."[21] And at his funeral Ricois summed up the man as: "the
most devoted collaborator of his illustrious *patron*, the confidant of his thoughts and his views, the most enlightened continuator of the work that Monsieur and Madame Boucicaut
have bequeathed us . . . in one word . . . the soul of this
grande maison du Bon Marché."[22]

Thus the directors of the Bon Marché set the roles of managerial leadership in a post-Boucicaut era by institutionalizing

[19] B.M., AGO, 29 August 1912, 26 August 1910.
[20] Speech by Lucet at Fillot's *Cinquentenaire*, 1911.
[21] Speech by Caslot on Fillot's retirement, 11 September 1913.
[22] Speech by Ricois at Fillot's funeral, 24 November 1920.

the relationships of their predecessors. They created an image of a continued family firm, and they endowed with the quality of sacredness the personal sentiments, ideals, aims, and practices of the founding family. In this way they were able to transfer into a period of increased bureaucratization the same relationships of integration and dynamism among managers that had contributed to the enormous success of the store under the Boucicauts and to legitimize their own authority within the new hierarchy. At the same time they were able to assure for themselves the continuity of a commercial enterprise whose household traditions were very dear to them and whose continued existence, institutionalized character, and pre-eminent commercial ranking most likely provided their lives with much of their meaning. Directors were the finest example of the kind of organization men whom the Boucicauts had wished to form. In the choices they made on their own identity and on that of the firm they illustrate, as had the Boucicauts, how closely knit together managerial and family values could be.

MEMBERS OF A SINGLE FAMILY

It is clear, as one reads through the speeches of the *gérance*, that the thoughts of the directors rarely strayed from the paternalism of the Boucicauts. The philanthropy of the founders, the social dimensions of their *oeuvre*, the directors' own contributions to the employees' welfare are images that recur with a remarkable frequency. Respect for paternalistic traditions was, in the minds of the directors, an inescapable part of the Bon Marché heritage, an inseparable part of the household relationships that they wished to preserve.

For many, undoubtedly, continued stress on paternalism was the gateway to social respect, to justification, and to that legitimate niche in the French business world that would permit them to share, as had the Boucicauts, in the dual dimensions of traditionalism and dynamism that underlay the social programs of the House. For some, like Fillot, it was also an obligation, a responsibility, a recognition that the origins of the *société* had "entailed a sort of moral mortgage in favor of the employees."[23] But for all, unquestionably, there was the realization that paternalism had been crucial to the success of the store, and that leadership roles would have to be set in this mold if the prosperity of the firm was to be maintained.

Indeed, as Fillot reminded those shareholders who called for open sales, "Monsieur and Madame Boucicaut considered their employees as members of a single family grouped around them, and all their actions bore witness to the interest they took in their employees." This, Fillot went on, explained why Madame Boucicaut had endowed the *société* with a *"caractère familial."* As long as shares remained in the possession of employees or former employees or "their representatives," the well-being of the House and its personnel could be assured. Outsiders could not be expected to show the same generosity as those men schooled in the Boucicaut traditions, and, as Fillot cautioned in his most telling remark, in a House where "prosperity is intimately tied to the interest of our employees, any blow to their privileges could have repercussions whose seriousness would be difficult to measure."[24] Thus if directors clung tightly to the family tradition of the Bon Marché, it was largely because they believed that the fortunes of the store were bound in the end to employee relations that only a household environment could secure.

Fillot's speech, mixing respect for the Boucicauts' paternalism with dire warnings lest these traditions go unheeded, was not uncommon for the period. There was an intense quality to the paternalistic image running through the speeches of these years, betraying in the directors a persistent and thinly veiled fear that a break in the paternalistic structure might bring the whole magnificent venture tumbling

[23] B.M., AGE, 10 January 1914.

[24] *Ibid.*, 12 July 1912. Caslot repeated this argument in 1914 when he remarked that open sales would mean an end to the "perfect harmony" between capital and labor at the Bon Marché, and that the House would be "deprived of those advantages that can be drawn from this particular situation." *Ibid.*, 10 January 1914.

down. Why this heightened sensitivity? In part, the bureaucratization of control in a firm that projected an ambiance of
household was to blame. But developments at the Bon
Marché and growing pressures from the outside were also responsible for the tenor of concern among House leadership.

The work system remained one problem. Directors did not
alter the conditions of work significantly, but they did add to
their tensions with such innovations as the widespread use of
auxiliary employees. Auxiliaries were men and women who
were paid by the hour and who served an apprenticeship,
primarily in the offices, before becoming *titulaires* or regular
employees.[25] Some may have grumbled over their station.
Most desperately wished to regularize their position, and
probably kept their frustrations to themselves. As a group,
auxiliaries were not much of a threat to management. Yet
their situation reflected a still greater foreclosure on middle-
class opportunities and a growing insecurity that was coming
to envelop middle-class lives, and few regular employees
were likely to pass an auxiliary without occasionally recogniz-
ing their own circumstances as well. Moreover, the sheer
growth of the firm brought an influx of new personnel, while
more sales and departments meant more offices and bureaucracy. And as bureaucratization grew, so too did rationalization,[26] again creating possibilities for employee discontent.

At the same time, Bon Marché work conditions were increasingly subjected to outside criticism and to pressure for

[25] Very likely the use of auxiliaries followed from increased taxes on department stores that were a consequence of the anti-department store
movement and that were allocated largely on the basis of the number of regular employees at a given store. See Chapter VI. Auxiliaries were primarily
relegated small but necessary chores, such as aiding in the preparation of
publicity.

[26] Increased rationalization can be seen, for example, in a clearer definition
of salary schedules (which were also, for a while, lowered). The greater care
given to recording and completing dossiers in this period and repeated recommendations by directors that no employee be admitted without a fully
processed dossier or that applicants be required to undergo a brief writing
examination also attest to an increased concern for formalism, efficiency, and
performance under the directorship.

change. A league of small shopkeepers, organized in 1888, initiated a scathing attack on department store work as the embodiment of the decline in lower-middle-class careers.[27] The end of the 1880s also saw a resurgence of the commercial employees' union that had lain in torpor for nearly two decades following the failure of 1869. Throughout the 1870s and most of the 1880s, the Chambre Syndicale had distinguished itself primarily by the pettiness of its movement. Internal squabbles were frequent, membership rarely surpassed a few hundred at most, and at one point the president absconded with part of the union treasury.[28] The history of the labor movement is not always one of heroic struggle and tough-minded resiliency in the face of repression (which was nevertheless very real).[29]

But by the late 1880s, as more and more Frenchmen in general, more and more workingmen in particular, were beginning to organize, the fortunes of the movement began to turn about. By December of 1888 membership had risen to almost 3,000, and over the next decade there was a steady increase until by 1903 the Chambre Syndicale claimed 12,000 adherents.[30] Its program was not revolutionary, but it did present a long list of grievances, from shorter hours and Sunday rest to better work conditions to the right to participate in the *conseils des prud'hommes*.[31] Meanwhile in 1887 another union, the

[27] See for example "Guerre Aux Bazars," *La Revendication*, 26 July 1888.

[28] Préfecture de Police, Ba 1422 and Ba 152; Artaud, *La question*, pp. 127-31; Office du Travail, *Associations*, pp. 621-36. In 1881 the Chambre Syndicale appears briefly to have organized 1800 members of whom 1400 were reportedly either from the Louvre or the Bon Marché. Office du Travail, *Associations*, pp. 630-31. But police reports indicate that in 1882 the Chambre had split, the combined membership of both groups now totalling a mere 150 persons. Préfecture de Police, Ba 152, report of 30 March 1882.

[29] Préfecture de Police, Ba 1422, report of 12 October 1874.

[30] Préfecture de Police, Ba 153, report of 8 August 1891; Artaud, *La question*, p. 137. Artaud suggests, however, that the latter figure was inflated. How many members were employees of the Bon Marché is unknown.

[31] Préfecture de Police, Ba 152, report of 12 October 1907; Ba 153, report of 20 January 1894, 8 April 1900; Artaud, *La question*, p. 133; Office du Travail, *Associations*, pp. 639, 650; Pierre Delon, *Les employés* (Paris: Editions Sociales, 1969), pp. 53-54; *La Petite République*, 11 May 1900.

Syndicat des Employés du Commerce et de l'Industrie, was formed; it numbered 2,000 members by the turn of the century, nearly 8,000 on the eve of the First World War. Catholic in its origins and its membership, the SECI nevertheless steered clear of yellow unionism and pushed for a program roughly equivalent to that of the Chambre Syndicale.[32]

By absolute standards these numbers still represented a small minority of the commercial employees of Paris. But, relatively speaking, the union movement had come a long way since the 1870s and 1880s, and, along with groups like the small shopkeepers' league, they were able to exert constant pressure on both stores and legislators to better working conditions, pressure that was not without results. In 1900 the *"loi des sièges"* (the seat law) gave women clerks the right to sit down when not waiting on customers. In 1903 the government extended laws on hygiene and safety requirements to commercial establishments. In 1906 a six-day work week became law. In 1907 commercial employees won the right to participate in the *conseils des prud'hommes*. Meanwhile, demands for shorter hours and for the right of employees to dine with their families led many stores to shorten their business hours. In 1901 the Bon Marché began closing its doors at seven in the evening.[33]

There were also strikes, one at the Magasins Dufayel[34] in 1905 and another at the Galeries Lafayette in 1909. Neither of these was successful, but they were symptomatic of an increased militancy among all employees. Even the Bon

---

[32] T. B. Caldwell, "The Syndicat des Employés du Commerce et de l'Industrie (1888-1919): A Pioneer French Catholic Trade Union of White Collar Workers," *International Review of Social History* (1966); Artaud, *La question*, p. 143; Joseph Boisgontier, *Le syndicat des employés du commerce et de l'industrie* (Paris: Jouve, 1920).

[33] Employees were asked if they wished to continue dining at the store in the evening. The majority said no and received a small daily sum to pay for their meals. Those who preferred to eat at the store apparently continued to do so, although employees lodged by the store and preferring to eat out were "invited" to give up their rooms.

[34] This was a department store catering primarily to the lower classes. See Chapter V.

Marché, whose representatives had boasted before a parliamentary committee that "strikes are impossible in our House,"[35] experienced a brief flare-up in 1900.

The incident began among the garçons, then spread to the rest of the personnel, who held meetings to express their grievances. The immediate cause of the affair seems to have been a heavy demand on overtime as the store strained to prepare for the coming world's fair and for a partial move into a new annex. But it was also likely that behind these meetings lay the increased agitation of the Chambre Syndicale. Since 1897 the union's *Journal des Employés* had attacked the Bon Marché in a series of extravagant articles. These focused in particular on health conditions, likened the store to a prison camp, and, most seriously, accused the directors of betraying the traditions of the Boucicauts. The directors' response was as might be expected. They assured the employees that overtime would not be abused in the future. They posted a note that read: "the Directors of the Bon Marché remind the personnel that their greatest wish is to preserve in the House the familial character intended for it by Monsieur and Madame Boucicaut." And they dismissed several employee leaders and refused to discuss matters further. The affair fizzled out, although it did set off further agitation in other Parisian department stores.[36]

So the uneasiness of Fillot and his colleagues in these years was not without foundation. And the stress that their adversaries could equally place on the continuity of the Boucicaut tradition, albeit with a different interpretation, underscored

---

[35] Ministère de l'Intérieur, *Enquête*, p. 128. The purpose of this commission was an inquiry into profit sharing at various firms, and the remark on the impossibility of strikes was primarily in reference to a discussion of the provident fund.

[36] "Au Bon Marché," *Journal des Employés*, 1-15 April 1900; B.M., *Conseils Généraux*, 20 March 1900; Préfecture de Police, Ba 153, reports of 21 March 1900, 8 April 1900, 9 April 1900; "Les employés de magasins," *La Petite République*, 2 April 1900; *Le Soir*, 11 April 1900. For articles in the *Journal des Employés* attacking the Bon Marché, see especially the series "La vérité sur le Bon Marché" in the May-October issues, 1897. Whether all the personnel or simply part of the personnel were involved in this incident is uncertain.

1. The frontispiece of the 1911 *agenda*. At the top: Aristide and Marguerite Boucicaut. Below: views of the store in 1863, 1873, and 1910.

2. The monster exposition hall, dwarfing the city skyline. (From the frontispiece of the 1896 *agenda*.)

VUE GÉNÉRALE DES MAGASINS DU BON MARCHÉ

3. The colossus, wings outstretched, crowds crushing along the doors, a flurry of activity in the foreground. (From the frontispiece of the 1887 *agenda*.)

VUE GÉNÉRALE DES MAGASINS DU BON MARCHÉ

4. View of building with *gemeinschaftlich* foreground. (From the frontispiece of the 1888 *agenda*.)

5. The ribbons gallery (1886 *agenda*).

6. The rue de Sèvres entrance
(1888 *agenda*).

7. The rue de Sèvres staircase,
during the *blanc* (1887 *agenda*).

8. The central staircase (1898 *agenda*).

9. The silk gallery (1879 *agenda*).

10. Winter concert in the store (1887 *agenda*).

11. Madame Boucicaut's funeral.

12. The directors and council members posing for the *livre d'or*. Seated at the head of the table, from l. to r., are Ricois, Fillot, and Lucet.

13. *Demoiselles (livre d'or)*.

14. Umbrella salesmen (*livre d'or*).

15. English lessons at night in the reading room (1887 *agenda*).

16. Fencing lessons (1887 *agenda*).

17. The reading room (1907 *agenda*).

18. Homage to Boucicaut (1900 fencing program).

19. The kitchen and main dining hall for employees (1901 *agenda*).

20. Clown suspended above the Bon Marché (illustrated card).

21. and 22. Scenes in the life of a *Parisienne*. (left) High fashion shopping at the Bon Marché. (right) An evening at the Opera (Ghent exposition pamphlet, 1913).

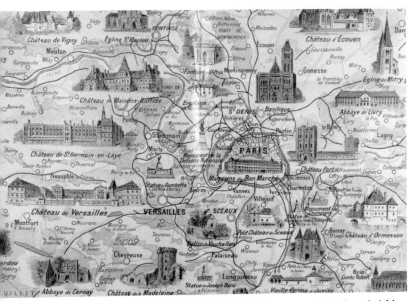

23. Monuments of the Paris region, with the Bon Marché representing Paris (*agenda* fold-out).

24. Toy French and Russian soldiers saluting as the two nations approach alliance (1892 catalogue).

25. Catalogue covers for the 1903 *blanc* sale (l., Paris catalogue; r., provincial catalogue).

26. Hand-sewn lacework to be sold at the Bon Marché (illustrated card).

27. Taking the omnibus home after a trip to the Bon Marché (illustrated card).

28. Mail-order service. In the background, packages are being classified by rail depots (1887 *agenda*).

29. Three delivery wagon scenes. (top left) The delivery wagon depot.
(top right) A visit to the stables (decorative lamps and ceilings appear in an earlier view).
(bottom) Delivery wagons begin their outward-bound procession.

30. The *petit* Parisian's vacation (illustrated card).

31. Cover of the glove and lace catalogue, 1912.

32. Cover of the *blanc* catalogue, 1914.

33. From the summer season catalogue, 1883.

34. From the house linens catalogue, 1907.

36. The Bon Marché expedition to the Sultan of Morocco (illustrated card).

37. Bathing suits / Bon Marché designs (1880 *agenda*).

35. Halley's comet flying over the Bon Marché.

the directors' own recognition of the pull that paternalism exerted on the work force. Even after the war, when authority relationships in France had all but disintegrated, and when the Bon Marché was hit by a major and violent strike, the leaders of the employees would feel compelled to gather their strikers around the statue of Madame Boucicaut in the square before the store and to declare that the current direction no longer followed her "way of doing things." Two days later, two thousand employees marched to Montparnasse cemetery to place a wreath on the Boucicauts' tomb.[37]

As best they could, then, directors were careful to preserve the paternalistic legacy the Boucicauts had bequeathed them and to add to it as well. In 1892 they created a pension plan for *ouvriers*. At the turn of the century they began to operate a separate and expanded program of relief for widows or orphans of former employees.[38] This program was paid for almost entirely out of personal contributions from the directors and administrators. Ricois gave 30,000 francs in 1904 and 20,000 more upon his retirement in 1910. In 1907 the administrators Colledeboeuf, Laporte, Picard, and Zoegger gave among them over 22,000 francs. Fillot was by far the largest benefactor, contributing more than 400,000 francs in his lifetime and another 200,000 in his will. In 1910 the fund formally became known as the Fillot Foundation. Two years later, following a suggestion of Fillot, the Foundation added a system of family allowances for employees with three or more children—an inspiration whose growth-oriented overtones were in the best traditions of the House.[39]

The philanthropic side to these donations must not be ignored. Contributions were steady and they were substantial. They represented the finest spirit of benevolence and duty that the Boucicauts had been able to pass on to their successors. But the pattern in which contributions were made—

[37] Préfecture de Police, Ba 1389, reports of 25 October 1919, 27 October 1919.

[38] The new program replaced the previous provisions for aid to widows and orphans contained in the pension fund.

[39] These allowances were put into effect in 1913.

donations often came upon retirement, upon election to the Legion of Honor, or following election to the *gérance*—and the tendency of the fund to become *the* recipient of individual philanthropic gestures, suggest as well that contributions followed from set role expectations. In effect the fund became another means by which social responsibilities and a personal commitment to the House could be institutionalized, assuring in turn that the Boucicaut paternalistic tradition would carry through to a new generation of managers.

But the directors fixed their greatest energies on the provident and retirement funds. Developments with the latter during these years reveal much about the importance and uses of this fund in particular, and much about the manner in which employee-store relationships were perceived by the directors in general. As the number and stability of the personnel steadily increased, and as the original endowment grew less and less sufficient, the directors were obliged to call a major review of the program at the turn of the century. Morin first brought the matter to the attention of the special assembly in 1897 with the warning that:

"We must not forget, messieurs, that the fund has rendered us . . . numerous and conspicuous services, but that it has also created for us pressing obligations from which we cannot withdraw. The principle of the right to a pension has been established in the House, it is counted upon by all the employees, and we cannot be indifferent to this issue today without incurring the gravest liabilities and jeopardizing the prosperity and future of the house."[40]

Morin then proposed, and the assembly accepted, that the House deduct seven percent of the profits each year to shore up the existing fund.

Four years later, however, the assembly appointed two commissions to consider whether the increasing financial burden of the program did not require an overall revision of the fund itself. The first, appointed from within the council, was concerned primarily with a potential merger of the re-

[40] B.M., AGE, 12 February 1897.

tirement and provident funds, although it finally advised against this proposal.[41] The second commission, appointed from within the special assembly, made a more extensive survey of possible changes. It first looked at the Samaritaine's retirement plan, where the store and employees made matching contributions to the fund. But it rejected this plan because, so it said, employees with families, who could not contribute much to the fund, would be penalized with lower pensions. Nor did the commission look with favor on a program that would force the Bon Marché to admit that its pensions were insufficient or that it was unable to provide for the personnel's security through its own means. This was closer to the mark. What the commission feared most was any change in the fund that would dilute House authority or the fullest advantages the present plan offered for attaching the personnel to the firm.

This point of view became more explicit as the commission reviewed and rejected the Louvre's plan, which placed 1,000 francs in an employee's account after five years and added 200 more francs each succeeding year. This plan, admitted Fillot, who communicated the commission's report, had the advantage of defining from the start the financial burden that the firm would be obliged to undertake. "But to create and maintain a retirement fund can only be understood on the condition that the advantages received from it are in keeping with the enormous sacrifice that it imposes," and this, claimed Fillot, the Louvre plan did not do. By fixing definite amounts, he explained, it could not create among the employees the same sense of obligation towards the house as existed at the Bon Marché.

Most telling, however, were the arguments for rejecting the retirement plan of the Compagnie d'Orléans (presumably the Paris and Orléans railroad), where an annual sum was placed with either the National Retirement Fund or with an insurance company. Again there were advantages to this scheme, foremost of which was the possibility of dismissing

[41] *Ibid.*, 9 July 1901.

older employees without incurring recriminations for wishing to revoke their pensions. But, as Fillot noted, such a
scheme would also "alter completely the institution as it was
conceived by Mme. Boucicaut. . . . [For] if this solution gives
complete liberty to the House, it gives it equally to the
employee, destroying the bonds that exist between him and
the House and that are so useful. . . . [And] if difficult or
troubled times occurred, we might bitterly regret having deprived ourselves of a means of action which would at least
oblige employees nearing retirement to abide by their duty,
allowing us to reconstitute a personnel without too much
harm." Fillot and the commission further feared, among
other things, that the Orléans program might lead to the
"meddling" of employees in discussions regarding the sums
to be allocated. "That is a possibility that appears to us difficult to reconcile with the discipline that is necessary in a
great House like ours."

It seems clear, then, that the commission had little desire to
tamper either with the advantages for control or with the
spirit of what was now known as the *Fondation Boucicaut*, the
review serving primarily as an occasion to exorcise doubts
and to reaffirm traditions. As Fillot stated at the beginning of
the report: "The result of the comparative investigation
which we have undertaken has been . . . the deep conviction
that [the program] in operation at the Bon Marché responds
better than any other to the aspirations of our personnel and
to the hope that we must sustain of seeing them attached
more and more to the future and the prosperity of our
house."[42]

Institutionalized paternalism was the major concern in
these years, but it was not the only means by which directors
could legitimize their authority as the continuators of the
Boucicauts or simply keep before the personnel the Boucicaut
image and the traditional relationships associated with it. In
1889 a curious letter was sent to the directors that may have
been a spontaneous gesture but more likely originated in

[42] B.M., AGO, 17 January 1902.

the upper levels of the hierarchy. Signed by a number of employees, the document—and it was drawn up as such—thanked the directors for their scrupulous execution of Madame Boucicaut's will "that permits us to blend into a single sentiment of gratitude and respect our lost benefactress Madame Boucicaut and you, Messieurs, who have known how to carry out with firmness, with wisdom, the final wishes that she could not have confided to better hands than yours. . . . We have incurred towards you, Messieurs, a debt of gratitude that we do not believe can be better discharged than by continuing to bring the fullest devotion to the exercise of our duties, permitting us to contribute, too modestly in our opinion, to the greatness and prosperity of the Magasins du Bon Marché."[43]

Pictures, a favorite medium of Bon Marché image making, were also brought into play. In 1900 the program cover for the *Assaut d'Escrime* offered an extraordinary scene that would have warmed the heart of any bourgeois employer: several employees in fencing attire presenting themselves to a bust of Boucicaut under the rubric "Homage to M. Boucicaut, XXVth Anniversary of the Foundation of the Fencing Course." Directors also posted a portrait of Boucicaut in the eating halls and offered to sell copies to the employees at one franc apiece.[44]

Paternalistic relations remained imbedded in the daily affairs of the firm. At council meetings it was not unusual for directors and administrators to pass on individual requests for aid or even to initiate such requests themselves. At a meeting in November 1892, for example, the council decided to grant 100 francs to an *ouvrier*, Gregoire Gregoiroff, who was sick and had a wife and child to support. At the 21 December 1891 meeting the *intéressé* Laborie brought to the council's attention the death of a former employee who had left behind him three young children and two old parents. The council again voted a grant of 100 francs. Moreover, the

[43] B.M., "A Messieurs des exécuteurs testamentaires de Madame Boucicaut," 9 July 1889.
[44] B.M., *Conseils Généraux*, 17 April 1893.

middle levels of the hierarchy, as under the Boucicauts, were personally drawn into the paternalistic structure. In April 1902 the council decided that inspectors should pass each week at the Hôpital Boucicaut,[45] where the store reserved beds for its personnel. Perhaps this was mostly to check up on slackers. But the inspectors were also expected to inquire about the needs of their patients and "to give them . . . an indication of the concern that is felt for them." Later in the same year the council decided that a delegation of four employees and perhaps a second should be sent to the funerals of all deceased employees, the second to be drawn from the deceased's service or department.

Altogether, what directors were after was to retain the idea of a greater Bon Marché household as the Boucicauts had conceived it. Employees and managers, it was hoped, would assume not only that the continuity of the firm remained unbroken at the top, but that they too continued to share in the past, present, and future of the House, that along with the directors they formed a single community working together for the continued growth and prosperity of a great business and social institution. It had been in this vein that directors had organized Madame Boucicaut's funeral, and in the following years they continued to see to it that employees at every level participated in events that touched on the life of the firm.

When Plassard died in 1909, Fillot, Ricois, several administrators, and a garçon corporal and two uniformed garçons attended the funeral as an official delegation, while arrangements were made to permit all other employees who so wished to attend as well. The House made similar arrangements, including a change in dinner hours, to accommodate all those who wished to attend the funeral of Fillot's wife in 1900.[46] Employees were also expected to share in the responsibility of keeping up the Boucicauts' graves. On All Saints Day in 1893, for instance, employees contributed over 400

---

[45] This was the hospital provided for in Madame Boucicaut's will.
[46] B.M., *Conseils Généraux*, 9 June 1909, 20 April 1900.

francs for flowers, one-third of the total expense.[47] But not all events were so gloomy. In 1890 a delegation of directors, other managers, clerks, garçons, and the store chorale was sent to Madame Boucicaut's native village to attend the inauguration of a bridge that she had endowed in her will. The delegation left the store on a Saturday morning and returned the following Monday evening, a vacation for many, no doubt, but most likely also a memorable experience.[48] In 1912 a similar delegation, this time including large numbers of former employees, set off for Bellême to attend commemorative festivities in honor of Boucicaut. For those unable to attend, a pamphlet was printed recounting the events and the speeches of the day.[49]

Just how deeply did these sentiments penetrate the personnel—a question that in retrospect might also be asked of the Boucicaut years as well? On the broad statistical level there was of course the steady increase in employee stability throughout the entire prewar period. There were also few cracks in store-employee relations after 1869. True, an incident did occur in 1900, but this was a brief, relatively uneventful episode, and as the largest commercial employer in Paris the Bon Marché remained remarkably free of the problems that other stores encountered. Not only were there no strikes, but there is no evidence that a Chambre Syndicale section was ever set up at the Bon Marché as it was at the Printemps, the Samaritaine, and elsewhere.[50] Even the articles of the *Journal des Employés* and the events of the strike of 1919, in their own way, attest to the powerful influence of Bon Marché paternalism.

But what of the inclinations, attitudes, and emotions of individual employees, beyond the anonymity of collective

[47] B.M., "Dépense de la Toussaint pour la tombe de Madame Boucicaut" (handwritten note).

[48] There is a description of the outing in B.M., *Inauguration du Pont Marguerite Boucicaut . . . Programme*, 24 August 1890.

[49] B.M., *Hommage à Monsieur Boucicaut*.

[50] Office du Travail, *Associations*, pp. 657-58; Artaud, *La question*, pp. 275-77.

statistics and group actions? Did these in truth correspond to
the values, roles, and very personal bonds that management
was trying to instill? There are, to be sure, no employee records comparable to the assemblies, council meetings, and
ceremonial addresses which permit us to enter into the motivations, and often the minds, of the directors and their associates. But we can, in the employee dossiers, occasionally
glimpse the individual thoughts of clerks, garçons, and some
managers as well, thoughts, moreover, that tend to confirm
what the statistics suggest.[51]

We can see, for instance, that employees were clearly
aware of the demands and relationships expected of them.
One applicant in 1898 wrote that "the fine reputation of your
store concerning relations with your employees is my principal reason for wishing to enter the Bon Marché. . . . I am
ready to send you references which will prove that wherever
I have passed I have never been rebellious nor lacking in my
loyauté or candor." Auxiliaries who wished to become *titulaires*
(with rights to paternalistic programs) were equally careful to
phrase their applications within the catchwords of the House.
"I will do everything I can to fulfill my duties zealously and in
a manner that will satisfy my chiefs with my behavior and my
devotion," wrote one, while another wrote that "I will endeavor to continue to fulfill my duties as best I can in order to
retain the good will of my chiefs and for the prosperity of the
Bon Marché." At the same time employees who were retiring
were prudent to *request* the pensions and provident monies
due them, and to wrap these requests in reminders of their
devotion and expressions of their gratitude for the generosity
of the House.

We can also see how readily employees could embrace the
household ambiance of the firm, especially with the hope that
favors might be forthcoming. An auxiliary garçon who had
just entered the House thanked his administrator for "your
kindness and your exalted protection that you have wished to

[51] The following references are taken from the post-Boucicaut period when
dossiers were more completely maintained than in the earlier years.

accord me. . . . I hope that M. Périllat will never forget me because I have confidence in your goodness and exalted protection" (garçons were not hired for the breadth of their vocabulary). A cashier second, beset by difficulties since his retirement, requested a grant "by virtue of the instinctive sentiment that causes a suffering child to extend his arms towards his mother, because I have always looked upon the house of the Bon Marché as a *grande famille.*" Indeed the frequent requests for aid during and following one's employment were in themselves a significant commentary on the effect of the relationships the store was seeking to foster.

But, even more important, we can see genuine personal ties that had developed among these men and women, genuine familial sentiments and a sense of personal trust in the firm and its management. "I will be grateful if you will extend to my daughter the benevolence that you always had for me; it is a request that I address to you now that she is separated from her parents [for] she still needs the good counsel that I can no longer give her," wrote a retired employee to one of his chiefs upon his daughter's entry into the store. "I have learned with great pleasure . . . of the generous gift that you have had the kindness to offer me. I am even more grateful to you during these difficult hours when one feels very close to his own and to those who, from afar, are wholeheartedly with their servants defending the soil of the homeland" wrote another employee in the first year of the war. The letter ended with the preposterous but nevertheless evocative statement that "I will do everything within my weak means to throw back the invader for the honor of France and the Grands Magasins du Bon Marché." The war stirred another employee, who had entered in 1900, to write one of his managers, asking him to convey to the directors "the very sincere wishes I have for them personally and for our beloved Bon Marché; please thank them too for the good deeds that they have lavished on their mobilized employees since the beginning of the war and inform them of my great gratitude."

And as with all families, real or artificial, death became an occasion when bonds and personal sentiments were re-affirmed. An administrator telegraphed from Versailles that his son had died and requested a list of names and addresses of the shareholders and the personnel of the store. The widow of a former employee wrote the *gérance* to thank them for the presence of the administrator Barat at her husband's funeral. She added that during his final days all her hus-band's thoughts and words had been "of the Bon Marché, so that one might say that he died not in his home but in the House that he loved so much and that he was so loath to leave." Most of all, the *grande famille* image became a reality in those moments when past and present employees placed an-nouncements (and invitations) of the weddings or deaths of their children, parents, grandparents, or even in-laws in en-velopes and mailed these off to the Bon Marché directors.[52]

Perhaps nothing captures better those things that I have tried to express in these two chapters than an event which oc-curred in the spring of 1907. The occasion was the presenta-tion of a *livre d'or* or golden book from the personnel to Fillot in honor of his promotion in the Legion of Honor, a promo-tion that had come following the Bon Marché's prize-winning role at the world's fairs of St. Louis and Liège. Already the award had been celebrated in a number of ways. On the very evening that the promotion had been announced, the council had gathered together to congratulate Fillot, Ricois declaring that "you are, my dear friend, the soul of this great House and the most enlightened continuator of the *oeuvre* that was bequeathed us by M. amd Mme. Boucicaut with everyone's trust."[53] And Fillot in turn had responded by donating 45,000 francs to the employee funds, and by offering a series of banquets—"familial banquets" as they became known—for the entire personnel of the House. Now the employees in

[52] Invitations and announcements of this sort can most frequently be found among the dossiers of employees who had spent a fair amount of time at the Bon Marché (and among the dossiers of members of the hierarchy).

[53] B.M., Speech by Ricois, *Promotion de Monsieur Fillot: Allocations*, 12 Oc-tober 1906.

their turn, led by their junior directors and administrators who had planned and edited the book, were commemorating the event in the form of a superbly laid-out volume that contained the photographs and signatures of the more than seven thousand men and women under Fillot's direction.[54]

The *livre d'or* began simply with a frontispiece that read: "The Personnel of the Bon Marché to Monsieur Fillot," followed by a one-page "Tribute to M. Fillot" that explained the purpose of the book in the familiar rhetoric of the house:

"United in a common thought, the members of the *grande famille du* Bon Marché express their joy at the news of the eminent award with which the state has so justly honored you. . . .

"Mixed with this joy is the legitimate satisfaction of having done our share and of having contributed with all our force to the prosperity of the enterprise which you head. . . .

"We have seen you at work; we have appreciated, in light of the obtained results, the difficulties of your task, and we know how to render tribute to the untiring energy with which you love the workers placed under your command.

"Thus the bonds of esteem and affection which have attached us to you for a long time are tightened, and we have wished to offer you a lasting memory of this event.

"In this '*Livre d'Or*' you will find grouped the portraits and signatures of those who have been, according to their means, your devoted collaborators.

"We do not doubt that until the end of a life that we hope will be as long and as happy as it has been hardworking and upright, you will enjoy reviewing again this assembly of men and women who, under your firm and paternal direction, endeavoured to imitate the great example you set, an example for which they are profoundly grateful."

Next came the portraits of the Boucicauts, followed by a brief text that recounted the transfer of the store from Madame Boucicaut to the directorship and that was headed

[54] The original *livre d'or* is in the possession of Madame Cotillon, daughter of Narcisse Fillot. A copy, without signatures and less ornate, exists in B.M.

by two views of the House, one in 1863, and the other in 1906. This in turn was followed by the photos of the five men who had held the post of *gérant*. Then again came a text, this time a longer one, that recounted the life and virtues of Fillot, affirmed his place in store ideology, and provided all readers with a model of the organization man who, through his intelligence, hard work, devotion, and complete comprehension of the Boucicauts' traditions, had arrived at the pinnacle of store leadership. Then there were two more pictures, the first a photo of the current directors in their office, the second a photo of directors and administrators gathered at the council table under the portraits of the Boucicauts. So the introduction provided a visual review, as it were, of the metamorphosis of the firm into a bureaucratic household. Finally there came the great Bon Marché family itself, a striking, seemingly unending succession of portrait clusters arranged by the function each group performed, 7,000 faces, 88 separate categories, and 144 pages in all.

In producing the *livre d'or*, the directors and their associates thus were creating a compendium of store relationships since 1869. As an honor to Fillot—a man who had entered the store as a simple clerk in 1861; a man who through his talents and loyalties had rapidly worked his way up the hierarchy to chief cashier in 1864, administrator in 1874, and eventually chief director; a man who had been Boucicaut's principal collaborator in the 1870s, entrusted with working out the details to the provident fund; a man who as director had been the most conscientious guardian of the traditions of the Boucicauts, preserving and expanding their paternalism, defending zealously the familial character of store ownership; a man who as director had also presided over years of great expansion and unprecedented sales; a man who thus by 1907 had become more synonymous with the Bon Marché than any other individual aside from the Boucicauts—they were, in effect, offering a tribute to the history of the House itself, its successes, its traditions, and its values. And, like the "familial banquets" upon which it followed, the *livre d'or* was clearly conceived by them to confirm, this time from base level up, what a carefully cultivated store ideology had long been asserting: that the Bon Marché was the sum of the common and active participation of all its members in an extraordinary and momentous commercial adventure. Finally, and above all, through this family album that was produced in recognition of the store's preeminent status in the French business world, the directors and their associates were offering to Fillot, to themselves, and to the rest of the firm, a consummate symbol of the new commercial community, dynamic and bureaucratic in nature, that they and their predecessors had ceaselessly sought to create. At bottom the *livre d'or* was a compendium not only of Bon Marché history, but of the reconciliation between traditional bourgeois values and the coming of the modern business firm.

PART THREE

Public Relations

V SELLING CONSUMPTION

AMONG THOSE PHRASES so readily associated with the new department stores, and so loosely turned to as though their very mention was sufficient to raise the tone of the discussion to a plane of significance, was the "democratization of luxury." The term itself is a superficial one, and in some ways misleading. Although mass retailing gave way to stores expressly directed at a lower-class clientele, the principal firms like the Bon Marché remained middle-class institutions. The bourgeoisie more so than the working classes were the chief beneficiaries of the revolution in marketing before the First World War.

But "democratized luxury," the puffery and misguided notions aside, did stand for something in the minds of men who were grasping for some means of expressing, conveniently and compellingly, the implications of *grands magasins* selling vast quantities of merchandise to vast numbers of people at considerably lower prices than ever before. It stood for a market that was now prepared to turn practically any retail article into a mass-consumer good. And thus, at a more fundamental level, it stood for the realization that bourgeois culture was coming more and more to mean a consumer culture, that the two were, in fact, becoming interchangeable.

The department store alone did not lead to the appearance of a consumer society, but it did stand at the center of this phenomenon. As an economic mechanism it made that society possible, and as an institution with a large provincial trade it made the culture of consumption a national one. Above all, as a business enterprise predicated upon mass retailing, it played an active role in cultivating consumption as a way of life among the French bourgeoisie.

This promotion of a consumer culture was to raise issues as vital as those of the bureaucratization of careers and the transformation of entrepreneurial roles. In the following chapter we shall see how these issues fit into a larger complex of social concerns that once again obliged the *grands magasins* to seek an accommodation between tradition and change. For the moment, however, we must consider how the Bon Marché set about selling not only merchandise, but consumption itself.

AN EIGHTH WONDER

In one respect, selling consumption inherently followed from the new merchandising practices that differentiated the department store from the traditional small shop. The concentration of services, integration of operations, and especially the stress on rapid turnover expanded markets by lowering prices.[1] Deliveries, returns, and conscientious service made shopping a pleasurable experience. Fixed prices decreased consumer suspicions and quickened the pace of shopping.

Yet these were only the preconditions upon which a consumer culture could be built. More than price and service in-

[1] How much lower prices were in department stores was a matter of debate. Small shopkeepers contended that only leader items were sold at advantageous prices, and Zola once noted that while leader items were offered at 20 percent less than similar goods in small shops, other articles were sold at prices similar to those of the boutiques. However, in another note, Zola reversed himself, maintaining that "there is at least an 18 percent margin between the prices of the *petit commerce* and those of the *grands magasins*." Other commentators offered comparative mark-up rates for department stores and small shops of 14 and 41 percent respectively in one case and 12 and 36 percent in another. Altogether, the consensus among contemporaries, department store critics aside, was that better buys could be had at the new stores than ever before; and, given the stores' organization and marketing philosophy, it is difficult to believe that this was not the case. Zola, NAF10278, pp. 75, 201; A. de Foville, "Les causes générales des variations des prix au XIX siècle," *L'Economiste Français* (1 June 1878), pp. 684-85; G. Michel, "Le commerce en grands magasins," *Revue des Deux Mondes* (1 January 1892).

centives, mass marketing demanded a wizardry that could stir unrealized appetites, provoke overpowering urges, create new states of mind. Selling consumption was a matter of seduction and showmanship, and in these Boucicaut excelled, enveloping his marketplace in an aura of fascination that turned buying into a special and irresistible occasion. Dazzling and sensuous, the Bon Marché became a permanent fair, an institution, a fantasy world, a spectacle of extraordinary proportions, so that going to the store became an event and an adventure. One came now less to purchase a particular article than simply to visit, buying in the process because it was part of the excitement, part of an experience that added another dimension to life. This ambiance, in conjunction with the powerful temptation of vast, open displays,[2] was to be the great luring feature of the Bon Marché.

The new building itself was designed for this effect. Provided with a stately façade of stone and topped with cupolas, the exterior belied the commercial machine within. This was particularly true of the main gateway on the rue de Sèvres. Monumental and ornate, it rose the entire height of the building and was seated under a cupola, crowned with a pediment, conceived as an archway for the first two stories, and decorated with caryatids and reclining statues of the gods. The impression was that of entering a theatre, or perhaps even a temple.

Inside, the monumental and theatrical effects continued. The iron columns and expanse of glass provided a sense of space, openness, and light. Immense gallery opened upon immense gallery, and along the upper floors ran balconies from which one could view, as a spectator, the crowds and activity below. Three grand staircases, elegant and sweeping, conveyed the public to these floors as if they were climbing to

[2] The role of the open displays themselves cannot be minimized. Zola wrote that "women are thus dazzled by the accumulation of merchandise. This is what has made the success of the *grands magasins*." Later d'Avenel noted that "it seems that one sale begets another and that the most dissimilar goods, juxtaposed, mutually support each other." Zola, NAF10278, p. 201; D'Avenel, "Le mécanisme," p. 356.

loges at the opera, while on the second floor could be found a reading room with the major newspapers and journals of the day, and a great hall in which the paintings of contemporaries (second-rate artists, Zola tells us) were exhibited for free. Later the two rooms were merged into a single salon, twenty meters long and eight meters high, and conceived in the grand style of a Louvre Museum gallery. Nearby was a buffet, a room whose fine furnishings, curtains, and palm leaves made it not unlike the lounge of a theatre.[3]

Part opera, part theatre, part museum, Boucicaut's eclectic extravaganza did not disappoint those who came for a show. Merchandise heaped upon merchandise was a sight all its own. Bargain counters outside entryways produced a crush at the doors that attracted still larger crowds, thus creating for all the sensation of a happening without and within. Inside, the spectacle of flowing crowds intensified, orchestrated by barred passages, by cheap, tempting goods on the first floor that brought still another crush to the store's most observable arena, and by a false disorder that forced shoppers to travel the breadth of the House.[4] The oft-frenzied actions of thousands of employees, the din of calls about the cashiers, and the comings and goings of garçons in bright livery were the tumultuous accompaniment of a sensational proceeding.

Everywhere merchandise formed a decorative motif conveying an exceptional quality to the goods themselves. Silks cascaded from the walls of the silk gallery, ribbons were strung above the hall of ribbons, umbrellas were draped full blown in a parade of hues and designs. Oriental rugs, rich and textural, hung from balconies for the spectators below.[5] Particularly on great sales days, when crowds and passions

[3] Garçons in the buffet served Bordeaux and Madeira wine to adults, syrups to children.

[4] Boucicaut was, for example, fond of placing women's dresses in one section of the store, coats and ready-to-wear in another. Zola, NAF10278, pp. 59-61.

[5] In an observation that may have been taken from the Bon Marché, Zola remarked in *Au bonheur des dames* that Mouret primarily was concerned with their decorative and exotic appeal, selling his rugs practically at cost. Zola, *Au bonheur,* pp. 290-91.

were most intense, goods and decor blended one into another to dazzle the senses and to make of the store a great fair and fantasy land of colors, sensations, and dreams. White sales, especially, were famous affairs. On these occasions the entire store was adorned in white: white sheets, white towels, white curtains, white flowers, *ad infinitum*, all forming a single *blanc* motif that covered even stairways and balconies.[6] Later, Christmas displays became equally spectacular. In 1893 there was a display of toys representing an ice-skating scene in the Bois de Boulogne. In 1909 plans included a North Pole scene in the rue du Bac section, a Joan of Arc display in the rue de Babylone area, and an airplane "with turning propellor and luminous toys" above the rue de Sèvres staircase.[7]

So the store, monumental, theatrical, fantastical, became an attraction in its own right to entice the public to visit the displays and to make of their trip an extraordinary experience. As early as 1872 Boucicaut was billing the Bon Marché as "one of the sights of Paris." Soon after he offered daily tours of the House. Each day at three o'clock shoppers, or mere visitors, were invited to assemble in the reading room. From there a guide conducted them throughout the building, visiting behind-the-scenes activities and passing through the great galleries and their displays of merchandise.

It is in this role of impresario that we must also see Boucicaut's inauguration of House concerts within and without the store. The very inspiration was suggestive of the directions in which bourgeois society was moving—and being moved. The presentation of concerts as regularly scheduled public events was itself of recent date, developing rapidly along these lines only in the second quarter of the nineteenth century. But their growing proliferation under middle-class sponsorship for predominantly middle-class audiences pointed to the extent to which an enterprising bourgeoisie, cognizant of a growing bourgeois demand, was coming to or-

[6] Recall Karcher's reaction in Chapter III.
[7] B.M., *Conseils Généraux*, 18 October 1909.

ganize the nation's leisure and arts, as well as its industrial output, into marketable commodities. The scale remained limited, but the tendency was undeniable: middle-class culture, even in the narrowest definition of its artistic pursuits, was assuming a consumer mentality. Still, the step from promoting entertainment events as a consumer event in themselves to exploiting them for substantially wider commercial purposes was a considerable one, and it is here that Boucicaut's productions take on significance, standing as it were on the threshold of modern marketing techniques.[8]

The implications of these concerts were staggering. Music and shows had a long history as come-ons, but never had the connections been quite so sweeping. Now anything partaking of middle-class identities and middle-class tastes, or even simply of public fads, could become a means to a totally unintended and disassociated end: the promotion of a consumer society. If music could be sold to the middle classes either because there was a market that wished it aesthetically or that wished it socially as a sign of refinement—one of those ways by which the upper levels of the bourgeoisie sought to distinguish themselves from the lower orders, thereby setting the tone by which the lower bourgeois strata would just as eagerly seek to assert *their* distinction and hence *their* claim to middle-class status—then it could also be sold to the middle classes as an inducement to consumption of a very different sort. And if formal choral societies had equally become a widespread phenomenon over the past forty years, to be found largely among artisans and clerks but encouraged by middle-class audiences who warmed to this exhibition of solidarity with their own image of themselves (a side that did not escape the Boucicauts), then these societies too could be turned to the mass marketer's account, selling far more than good cheer and bad music.[9]

[8] On the evolution of concerts, their sponsorship and their audience in the first half of the nineteenth century, see William Weber, *Music and the Middle Class* (New York: Holmes and Meier, 1975).

[9] On choral societies, see *ibid.*, pp. 100-08; Zeldin, *France*, vol. 2, pp. 483-85.

Thus Boucicaut began his series of concerts. The first performance within the store was held in 1873, and until the death of Madame Boucicaut there would generally be one or two such events a year, usually in November and January. Saturday evening summer concerts in the square outside the Bon Marché began in the same year. Until the First World War these took place weekly, from June to September, except when the House societies were performing outside of Paris, or during inventory or Assumption.

The productions were grand and well-planned affairs. For the summer concerts, open to the general public, the House printed about 1,600 programs in advance. These were distributed at the cashiers, at entry ways, or in the reading room. Winter concerts—far more lavish in their conception, attended by invitation only, and apparently something of a society event—[10] played to as many as 7,000 persons (of whom several thousand were employees). Rehearsals, for which performers were released early from work, were scheduled several times a week. Later, in the 1880s, well-known singers, including several from the opera, were added to the program. On the nights of the concerts themselves, large numbers of counters were dismantled, seats and special decorations set in place. Expenses ran into the thousands of francs.

As another of Boucicaut's showcase orchestrations, Bon Marché concerts played a dual role. On one level, they were presentations to the public of a new kind of employee: disciplined, cultivated, gentlemanly. This was important, because retail clerks in the past had acquired a disreputable image. Referred to by the derogatory term of "calicot," a title that had stuck from an unflattering portrait in a play by Scribe,

---

[10] Invitation lists reveal large numbers of addresses from the fashionable districts of Paris. Deputies, military officers, and occasionally barons also received invitations. At the same time the House was careful to invite the heads of railway stations and officials well-placed in the post office, all of whom could be of considerable importance to a store with such a large mail-order trade. Invitations were also sent regularly to the press. B.M., Concert Materials.

clerks were notorious for their disorderly behavior, their un-
trustworthiness, and their claims to a status they did not
have.[11] Such an image could be acceptable in a small shop
where neither service, nor ambiance, nor even necessarily
trust was critical to a sale. But in a retail world that now
stressed shopping as a pleasure in itself, the image had to
change, and to this end House concerts provided a promotional device that displayed for once not the salesgoods, but
the sellers themselves.[12]

But it was again the ability to make of the store something it
was not that was most important here. As one reviewer
remarked:

"When one leaves a concert given by the Bon Marché, it is
truly difficult to gather together all of one's impressions, the
program having undertaken all that is possible, and even
the impossible.

"The lights, flowers, and splendors heaped beneath the
eyes of the guests, the eminent artists one has applauded, all
in the end shimmer, sound, and run together in the memory
of someone the least distracted, and one remains dazzled,
dazed for some time while trying to recover the necessary
stability to arrive at some sort of judgment.

"Let us speak first of the hall. In less than an hour the
store, glutted with merchandise, abandoned to a world of
gnomes or genies, is rapidly transformed, as in a fairyland,
into a bewitching palace, dazzling with its lights, filled with
flowers and exotic bushes whose effect is splendid. Everywhere carpets and silk tapestries from the Orient are flung
and hung in abundance, forming charming salons, hallways,
and retreats, all embellished by the good taste of the tapestry-

[11] In "Le Combat des Montagnes ou La Folie-Beaujon," M. Calicot (named
for a type of muslin) is an employee masquerading as a veteran of the *Grande
Armée*. The play was first presented in 1817. See Avenel, *Les calicots*, pp.
15-16; J. Valmy-Baisse, *Les grands magasins* (Paris: Gallimard, 1927), p. 145.
According to Zola, it was said that *"le calicot est bon à tout et propre à rien."*
Zola, NAF10278, p. 213. See also "Le calicot," *Gil Blas*, 26 November 1881.

[12] Press reaction was not oblivious to this side of the concerts. See for
example *L'Orphéon*, 5 December 1887.

workers. Immense departments, earlier filled with customers, soon will serve as an altar to the cult of music. . . ."[13]

It was, then, on concert evenings that image and reality at
last blended into one. Merchandise counters gave way to a
stage, salesclerks transformed themselves into performers,
the building became a deluxe concert hall. So ready to portray
his emporium as a theatre, or the opera, or a land of enchantment, Boucicaut had found the supreme effect. Spectacle and entertainment, on the one hand, the world of consumption, on the other, were now truly indistinguishable.

In still other ways the Bon Marché sought to call attention
to itself and to create about it a special air. To present itself as
a city and national institution while simultaneously display-
ing to mass audiences the best of its wares, the House participated in all major international fairs, including those of
Chicago and St. Louis. At the 1900 world's fair in Paris, it had
its own pavillion. The store was equally fond of publishing
descriptions of itself and its wonders. At first the firm relied
upon the national press, which has never been known for its
high standard of ethics. Articles on the Bon Marché, most
likely prepared in the offices of the same, appeared in *L'Illustration* and *Le Monde Illustré* throughout the 1870s and early
1880s.[14] Later in the 1890s, the House began to publish its
own pamphlets, in foreign languages as well as in French,

[13] *L'Orphéon*, 5 January 1886.

[14] See the following: "Les nouveaux magasins du Bon Marché," *Le Monde
Illustré*, 23 March 1872; *L'Illustration*, 23 March 1872; "Les nouveaux magasins
du Bon Marché," *Le Monde Illustré*, 30 March 1872; *L'Illustration*, 30 March
1872; *L'Illustration*, 10 October 1874; "Magasins du Bon Marché," *L'Illustration*, 6 March 1875; "Le Bon Marché," *Le Monde Illustré*, 13 March 1875; "Les
agrandissements du Bon Marché," *L'Illustration*, 2 October 1880; "Les agrandissements du Bon Marché," *Le Monde Illustré*, 2 October 1880; "Les agrandissements du Bon Marché," *Le Monde Illustré*, 9 October 1880; "Les agrandissements du Bon Marché," *L'Illustration*, 9 October 1880. Suspicions about the
origins of these articles are raised by the fact that: (1) articles in both journals
were often the same; (2) the articles frequently were filled with blatant advertising content; (3) handwritten copies of the articles exist in the Bon Marché
Archives. For a further discussion of collusion between the Bon Marché and
the press, see Chapter VI.

usually under the rubric of *An Historical Account of the Bon Marché* or *A Visit to the Bon Marché*.

Printed in the thousands and passed out to House visitors, particularly to persons who took the House tour, these pamphlets, along with the articles, were written in a tone of fascination with the store and its workings. The Bon Marché was an "establishment without parallel," the "most unique establishment in the world," a "monument," a "commercial institution," a "palace." White sales were a "féerie," the opening of a perfume department "the great attraction of the season" (how the public relations men must have choked over that one). One article, recounting a sale of Oriental rugs and porcelain, exclaimed that "all artistic Paris gathered at the Bon Marché that day, and the store offered the sight of a vast Oriental museum . . . transporting the imagination to the sunny land of a thousand and one nights."

Everything about the store was "immense," "vast," "gigantic." In particular, articles and pamphlets delighted in accounts of the size and scope of behind-the-scenes operations and projected an image of an incredible commercial machine that could impress the wildest of imaginations. Basements were a "veritable labyrinth." Giant electrical machines producing light for thousands of lamps were described in meticulous detail. Statistics abounded on the hundreds of employees in various services or on the thousands of letters the store received daily. And always there were descriptions of the kitchens, of their enormous equipment that could roast 800 beefsteaks at a single time, or that could prepare more than 5,000 meals in a single day. "It is necessary, if one wishes a comparison, to return to the descriptions of Homer who recounted in the Iliad how warriors roasted entire cows," remarked one pamphlet of a store never restrained in its analogies.

Perhaps more than anything else the Bon Marché conducted its self-promotion campaign through the immediacy of pictures. In House pamphlets, House *agendas* (calendar books), House catalogues, free picture cards passed out to children in the hundreds of thousands[15] in sets or series (so that cards became collectors' items and return visits were obligatory), or even simply in children's games, the Bon Marché used the medium of pictures to play up the monumental and spectacular side of its image. There were pictures of the entrances and reading rooms that accentuated their splendor. There were pictures of behind-the-scenes operations, vast kitchens, and the sliding chutes down which packages were sent spiralling. There were maps of the Paris region, with a picture of the Bon Marché in the circle of Paris. There were centerpiece foldouts in *agendas* entitled "Monuments of the Paris Region" or "Paris/Picturesque and Monumental," the one a colored map of churches, bridges, and chateaux outside Paris, with the capital itself represented solely by the store, the other a set of colored postcards of the Opera, the Hôtel de Ville, Notre Dame, and the Bon Marché. A children's game from the turn of the century consisted of a maze of the city, winding from the Bon Marché to the Arc de Triomphe.

The role of illustrated cards here was especially interesting. At least as far back as the sixteenth century, peddlers had passed from village to village selling cheap images of royal personnages, famous villains, customs, costumes, and a multitude of other subjects. In particular they sold images of religious scenes, pictures of saints to hang on one's wall or to carry on one's person.[16] These were the distractions of an earlier time, the medium for transporting oneself beyond the realm of the ordinary, the paraphernalia of a child's magical world. In the mid-nineteenth century the trade grew enormously,[17] again, as with the concerts, to be appropriated by

[15] These figures are from the mid-1890s on. Distribution figures for illustrated cards before this time are not available.

[16] John Grand-Carteret, *Vieux papiers, vieilles images* (Paris: A Storck, 1902), p. 42; Eugen Weber, *Peasants into Frenchmen* (Stanford: Stanford University Press, 1976), pp. 455-59.

[17] Two firms alone from Epinal—the center of such illustrated productions—may have turned out as many as 17,000,000 cards during the Second Empire. Weber, *Peasants*, p. 457.

those with wider commercial interests.[18] But there was more. To present these now with pictures of the Bon Marché on the back, or as a series of scenes of sights of Paris that included a view of the Left Bank emporium, or simply to change the subject to scenes of middle-class life in which the Bon Marché might figure prominently (a theme we shall return to shortly) was to create a whole new enchanted world of association. For the bourgeois child growing up in late-nineteenth-century France, the magical, the exotic, the fantastic, and the extraordinary were still the stuff of legendary figures, fairy-tales, and heroes of the French nation; but they had also become the stuff of department stores as well.[19]

Indeed fantasy and the Bon Marché could be entirely interwoven. One series portrayed a shipment of Bon Marché toys by desert caravan to Morocco. Another told of the return of Halley's comet, featuring a tour of modern wonders created over the past seventy-five years.[20] Pictured as a fairy queen on cards of deep purples, blues, and reds, the comet was led to the Eiffel Tower, the Opera, and finally to an immense, glowing Bon Marché from an airplane overhead. A similar theme, appearing on a Christmas catalogue, pictured a clown suspended in mid-air, a magical Bon Marché below. In a triumph of silliness (by the laws of human nature customarily all the more effective), a combination picture series and narrative produced the story of "The Wonder." This was a tale of a sultan in the Indies whose three sons all love the same cousin. Endowed with great wisdom, the sultan decides that her hand will go to whoever can show her "the latest and most useful wonder of the world." One brother brings a magic carpet. Another brings a magic apple that

[18] Department stores were not the only ones to seize on the idea. Practically any company with something to advertise began to distribute similar cards.

[19] Although the Bon Marché continued to distribute cards with traditional themes, religious subjects were no longer among these. The Boucicauts were not politically naive. But then this too was reflective of the transfer of magic to secular, indeed commercial, concerns.

[20] This series appeared in 1910, when the comet was to make its most recent appearance.

cures all maladies and eventually saves the girl's life. But the third brings a telescope through which she can glimpse the Bon Marché and its treasures. Dazzled by the sight, the heroine cries "yes . . . this is the wonder." So the third brother wins a wife, and together they set off on an elephant to visit the store's coming white sale.

Above all, the spectre of a modern wonder was to be found in the ubiquitous pictures of the building. Everywhere the Bon Marché was to be seen—on the backs of cards and catalogues, the frontispiece of *agendas*, the headings of store stationery, store order forms, and store invoices—rising from the ground as the most colossal and fabulous of palaces, wings stretched nearly to the horizon, crowds crushing along its window displays, carriages, omnibuses, and delivery wagons creating a flurry of activity on the streets before it. Or, viewed from above, its vast dimensions given full exposure, the Bon Marché was like a monster exposition hall, engorging crowds through its entry ways, dwarfing the city skyline as the great cathedrals had dominated Paris in earlier days. Indeed pictorially the Bon Marché was a cathedral of another sort, charismatically beckoning of its own world of entrancement.

And ultimately the store did become a new church. Dubuisson, an authority on kleptomania, remarked that "the *grand magasin* finishes . . . by exercising upon certain temperaments an attraction entirely comparable to that the Church exercises on others."[21] Zola noted that: ". . . the department store tends to replace the church. It marches to the religion of the cash desk, of beauty, of coquetery, and fashion. [Women] go there to pass the hours as they used to go to church: an occupation, a place of enthusiasm where they struggle between their passion for clothes and the thrift of their husbands; in the end all the drama of life with the hereafter of beauty."[22]

[21] Paul Dubuisson, *Les voleuses de grands magasins* (Paris: A. Storck, 1902), p. 42.
[22] Zola, NAF10278, pp. 88-89. In his novel Zola wrote of his imaginary store: "It was the cathedral of modern commerce, solid and light, made for a people of clients." Zola, *Au bonheur*, p. 275.

For increasingly large numbers of women, a new, irresistible cult of consumption had been created.

A WAY OF LIFE

The Bon Marché opened its doors to everyone, but most often it was the bourgeoisie who passed through them. A working-class clientele undoubtedly existed, but its numbers were limited by the cash-only policy. Indeed, alongside the Bon Marché, the Louvre, and other major houses, there grew up a whole subculture of department stores that specialized in credit sales for the working-class trade.[23] There was, in fact, something distinctively *respectable* about the Bon Marché that could make it forbidding to those who lacked middle-class pretensions, let alone middle-class means. The store drew its tone from the quarter that enveloped it, one that was known for its affluence, its Catholic orders, and its *bien-pensant* ways. As a specialty the Bon Marché catered to the religious trade,[24] an accent on propriety characteristic of the store's custom as a whole. Fashionable but reserved, the House drew heavily among visiting provincials, while the fastest circles in Paris were likely to go elsewhere.[25] Yet

[23] The principal of these was the Magasins Dufayel located in the eighteenth arrondissement near the outskirts of Paris and claiming a sales volume of about 70,000,000 francs at the end of the century. For details see *Administration et Grands Magasins Dufayel*, 1898, Archives du Département de la Seine, D 17z; Saint-Martin, Les grands magasins (Paris: 1900), pp. 36-37, 90-95, 123-24; Georges d'Avenel, *Le mécanisme de la vie moderne* (Paris: A. Colin, 1900-1905), vol. 4, pp. 376-83.

[24] The Bon Marché always maintained stocks of religious articles and, later, religious uniforms. Catholics themselves, the Boucicauts during the early years of the store relied on nuns of the quarter to aid them in their paternalism. See Petition, Le Gouriéric. So close was the identification between the Bon Marché and this clientele that rumor-mongers suggested that the House and the Church were linked to one another. Belief in this *canard* extended even to the police. One agent reported at the time of Boucicaut's funeral: ". . . no ecclesiastics were seen at the burial, even though several persons have said that the Company of Jesus had confided great sums of money to the deceased." Préfecture de Police, Ba 967, report of 28 December 1877.

[25] Zola, NAF10278, p. 209.

the common thread running through the clientele was less one of temperament than of identity. The Bon Marché sold its wares to all those who shared, or wished to share, in the middle-class way of life. Stalking grounds of both upper and lower bourgeoisie, the Bon Marché swept through its portals not only those lured by irresistible prices or by an irresistible event, but also those who saw in the emporium an irresistible linkage with their life style or their dreams. This too was to have its role in the selling of consumption.[26]

To leaf through the catalogues, the *agendas,* and the illustrated cards of the Bon Marché is to come upon the world of French bourgeois culture before the First World War in a way that perhaps no other medium can so vividly convey.[27] It is not a comprehensive picture that these lists and illustrations offer us. There is no hint of the failings of middle-class mar-

[26] In addition to the fact that the Bon Marché sold for cash only, the bourgeois character (petite bourgeoisie included) of the Bon Marché's clientele can also be seen in Zola's list of prospective clients for *Au bonheur des dames,* containing types drawn nearly completely from the bourgeoisie (it is to be remembered that Zola's notes were based largely on his visits to the Bon Marché and to the Louvre). In another note, Zola refers to the attraction of the petite bourgeoisie to the new stores. Zola, NAF10278, pp. 164-72, 202. For a more direct statement on the predominance of the bourgeoisie at the major stores, see Giffard, *Grands bazars,* p. 269. In undated minutes from assembly meetings in the early 1920s, Colledeboeuf, a man who had been with the Bon Marché for many years, remarked that "the Bon Marché clientele is principally bourgeois." B.M., Undated *Assemblées Générales,* 1920s. When the Bon Marché absorbed the Magasins Dufayel in 1924, there were complaints from shareholders that this would harm the reputation and standards of the Bon Marché, since the two stores were completely unlike, including their clientele (the heads of the Bon Marché in turn promised that the sole connection between the two stores would be a financial one). *Le Petit Economiste,* 12 December 1924; *La Vie Financière,* 24 December 1924. Finally, pictures in catalogues and agendas leave no doubt that this was a store selling, for the most part, to a bourgeois clientele. In fact not until the end of the prewar period did work clothes appear in Bon Marché catalogues, and even then these were primarily of the genre of uniforms for grooms, chauffeurs, valets, and bell boys, that is uniforms most likely bought by their bourgeois employers.

[27] On catalogues: The Bon Marché printed semi-comprehensive catalogues such as a *General Catalogue for Summer,* but it also mailed out other catalogues throughout the year. Many were issued by departments and most were printed in conjunction with a sale. They might be simply reviews of new or traditional stocks or they might be devoted completely to specialty items.

riages, no sign of the pressures or anxieties that could weigh upon middle-class lives. It is an idealized view that one gets, but then one that for this very reason is capable of imparting the self-image of that culture. How the bourgeoisie liked to conceive of their lives, what they expected of their lives, the minimum baggage they felt they could carry along with them in their lives all come into focus in the pages and pictures of the Bon Marché. Nor are we dealing here with merely a surface phenomenon. The images and accoutrements bespeak a reality all their own. It is through them that we begin to understand what we mean when we refer to the respectability or to the solidity or the certainty of prewar bourgeois life. And it is thus through them that we encounter a substantial part of the way the bourgeoisie did live their lives.

In this dense world of sensations and impressions there are images that especially seem to capture the culture that they were intended to portray. There are the covers of *blanc* catalogues that itemize the details of a proper bourgeois household: the richness of collections, the richness of embroidery, the solidity of storage chests, the very indispensability of linen to the bourgeois way of life. There were certain things, these scenes remind one, that a bourgeois home could not do without. There had to be too many sheets. There had to be curtains on the windows. There had to be tablecloths on the dining table (the dining room itself being another bourgeois requisite).[28] The setting of the table—a frequent cover scene—recalls still other bourgeois basics. The household had to be equipped to entertain in the proper fashion. And it had to have servants, at least one or two.

There is the precision with which the bourgeoisie defined their lives. Women did not wear just coats, but coats for visit, coats for travel, coats for ball, or coats for the theatre. When they went to town they wore a dress for the city and at night a dress for dinner. In times of mourning one dressed in mourning,[29] a fact no different than that men had their shirts for the

[28] Tablecloths seem to have been the most recurrent motif on the covers of these catalogues.

[29] Mourning garb, in its own way, was something of a fashion item. Catalogues often carried several pages of selections.

day and their shirts for evening dress, their outfits for sport and their outfits for travel. This was a carefully patterned society where appearance was always, to a point, a function of occasion, a badge that one understood what was correct and adhered to it rigorously.

The occasions themselves reveal the bourgeoisie's world. This was also a civil, leisurely, and gregarious society, an image equally conveyed in *agenda* events and catalogue pictures. It was a society of sociable visits or days of reception. It was a society that ate well and that held large dinners. It was a society that patronized theatres as a social event. And it was a society that traveled and played a great deal. In the summer one always seemed to be at the seashore or on a trip to the countryside. There were always badminton games and tennis games or bicycle rides or hunting forays. This was a very active society. By the turn of the century the Bon Marché was selling gymnastic equipment for the entire family. But it was also a very relaxed society. An 1880 summer clothing catalogue carried the following scenes: women sitting on a bench in a garden, women in a park, women holding parasols or fans, women painting, girls chasing butterflies, girls looking at chickens on a farm. For children it was a playful and carefree society. Children in illustrated cards or catalogue scenes were well-fed and well-dressed (boys almost invariably in sailor suits). In Paris they visited zoos, played in the Tuileries, or went to circuses. In wintertime they attended their own fancy-dress balls, and in summer they followed their parents to the ocean or to the provinces. There were whole series devoted to vacations at the seashore or adventures in the country. Life, these pictures tell us, was warm and secure, its pleasures a thing to be taken for granted.

There are the images of family life in the bourgeois manner. This was a culture where children were visible, well-scrubbed, and cared for. At the turn of the century the Bon Marché employed 80 people in its baby clothes department, 55 in knitted goods for children. In Bon Marché scenes children played among themselves, but they were as frequently accompanied by their parents, especially their mother, whose role was to be with her children. Children shared their own

182   PUBLIC RELATIONS

world, but they were part of their parents' world too. Family occasions were a fundamental part of bourgeois life. There were ordinary moments like family dinners (although *blanc* catalogues suggest a certain ritualization here), and there were special moments, as when children got married to begin a household of their own. In 1907 there were over 100 employees attached to the Bon Marche's trousseaux department.[30]

Family life also meant family expectations, a final image that these pictures convey. Children were expected to be *bien élevés*, a concept that ranged from proper bearing to learning the social graces. Bon Marché catalogues carried back braces "recommended as a support for persons having a tendency to stoop" and support collars "to prevent children from lowering their heads." Catalogue scenes showed that gentlemen always shook hands. Illustrated cards showed that children learned how to dance and that they dressed correctly just as their parents. Most of all being well-raised meant, as the articles and clothing for school and university and later the bar make clear, preparing oneself for a proper station in life. This, along with private property, was the *sine qua non* of being bourgeois.

As a reproduction of bourgeois life in these years, the Bon Marché catalogues, *agendas*, and illustrated cards thus offer a glimpse of a world and its values that has rarely been replicated. Yet there is a good deal to be found in these materials beyond simply the reflection of a class' self-image. Far more than a mirror of bourgeois culture in France, the Bon Marché gave shape and definition to the very meaning of the concept of a bourgeois way of life.

The picture of the proper household, the correct attire, the bourgeois good life were all, to a degree, Bon Marché creations. They were the way many middle-class people did live their lives, largely because middle-class institutions like the department store told them that this was the way they *should*

---

[30] Figures on employees are drawn from the *livre d'or*. Very likely these numbers included individuals attached to workshops or the reserves in the basement.

live their lives. Institutions like the Bon Marché made bourgeois life palpable. They produced a vision of a bourgeois life style that became a model for others to follow. The relationship between the Bon Marché and its culture was therefore a symbiotic one, with implications that were several and profound.

In one respect the Bon Marché came to serve essentially the same role as the Republican school system, at least for those of middle-class means or middle-class aspirations. It became a bourgeois instrument of social homogenization, a means for disseminating the values and life style of the Parisian upper middle-class to French middle-class society as a whole. It did this by so lowering prices that the former's possessions became mass-consumer items. But it also did this by becoming a kind of cultural primer. The Bon Marché showed people how they should dress, how they should furnish their home, and how they should spend their leisure time. It defined the ideals and goals for French society. It illustrated how successful people or people who wished to be successful or people on their way to becoming successful lived their lives. All this it did in ways that fit the upper-middle-class mold. In its pictures and in its displays the Bon Marché became a medium for the creation of a national middle-class culture.

Thus, through the Bon Marché, Paris and the countryside became more alike. The millions of catalogues mailed from the center to the provinces carried the message of a set way of life, much as the textbooks the Ministry of Public Instruction sent to the communes carried a set vision of society. Bon Marché catalogues brought Parisian fashions, and the values and expectations underlying them, more directly into the homes of middle-class people in Limoges or Nîmes or the small country towns of the Touraine. Provincials who shopped by mail-order or who travelled to Paris to buy directly from the store (and these must have numbered in the tens of thousands or more every year) shared in a common culture, whether they lived in the large towns of Normandy or in the small villages of Auvergne. This was not something new that the department stores initiated. But it was a process that the *grands magasins* reinforced and accentuated in the course of creating a national clientele.

Perhaps more important, the Bon Marché spread bourgeois culture to the new white-collar workers, steering these floaters toward middle-class shores. The Bon Marché offered these people, whose formidable growth toward the end of the century was largely a product of the *grands magasins* themselves, a way of life to imitate and the access and identification that would enable them to do so. It was the latter of these proposals that was especially significant. Through the department store, middle-class pretensions could find satisfaction because images and material goods were coming to constitute life style itself. Bon Marché goods were so interwoven with perceptions of the bourgeois way of life that a purchase of a Bon Marché tablecloth or a coat for the theatre became a purchase of bourgeois status too. One could imagine that one was bourgeois by wearing the uniforms that the Bon Marché prescribed or by simply buying a tennis racket or clothes for the seashore. One could feel relatively secure that one's children would share in bourgeois advantages if one dressed them in sailor suits or bought them trousseaux. It was the old concept of *l'habit fait le moine* raised to a far vaster scale than ever before imaginable. Becoming bourgeois had always, to a point, been a matter of consumption, but never so clearly, never so extensively, and never at prices that made its attainment so comparatively easy.

This meant something else again. As bourgeois culture became a purchasable commodity, so too did *it* become a mere matter of consumption. Bourgeois culture could be sold in the marketplace because over the course of the century it was coming to be more and more a culture of consumption. This also was a process the department store had not initiated, but one that it had accentuated to such a degree that the very scope of quantitative change made it qualitative as well. It was the department store that was largely responsible for lowering prices and for creating overpowering urges to consume. Even more, the department store turned the bourgeois model in a likeminded direction. The very definition of bourgeois that appeared in the pages and displays of the Bon Marché was no longer sharing a certain life style but rather buying certain goods in order to live that way of life. By Bon Marché standards, identity was to be found in the things one possessed. Consumption itself became a substitute for being bourgeois. All of which implied that the principal medium of consumption—the department store—now became the arbiter of bourgeois identity, defining it accordingly with what the House had to sell.

Here lies the fullest meaning of the idea that the Bon Marché shaped the bourgeois way of life. The images the Bon Marché spread to the middle-class masses were not simply drawn from the values and habits of the Parisian *haute* bourgeoisie. They were also a Bon Marché creation that translated those values and habits into marketable goods. In Bon Marché pictures and on Bon Marché counters the concepts of a proper household or proper dress or being a leisure class were transformed into so many linens, so many dresses, and so many sporting goods. At the same time, new needs were created almost systematically, so that the definition of life style was kept fluid and open in accordance with changes in the consumer goods available. Fashions were the clearest example of this. It was not simply that clothing styles varied from year to year or that complete changes occurred, as in the early years of this century. There were also entirely new kinds of clothing to fit entirely new kinds of wants. By the 1890s the Bon Marché was selling cyclist apparel for both men and women. A decade later it was carrying coats for the automobile. By 1913 the House carried the trend further, mailing out a fifty-page catalogue entitled "Clothing and Goods for Travel and the Automobile, Bicycles and assorted accessories, Games for Open Air, Sports." Any craze, or even any event, became an occasion for consumption. As Franco-Russian relations drew closer together, Russian toy soldiers began to appear on Bon Marché counters. In 1892 a Bon Marché gift catalogue pictured French and Russian soldiers saluting each other, thus placing bourgeois consumption at the service of public policy, and public policy at the service of bourgeois consumption. Later, in 1905, there were special offerings of Russian and Japanese toy soldiers, and in 1913 there were toy soldiers from the Italo-Turk War. Or new consumer needs might mean simply a replacement of the old with the coming of the new. In 1910 the Bon Marché advertised "complete installations for modern kitchens," perhaps one of the first instances in the creation of what was to become the most powerful urge behind the culture of consumption—the belief that new meant better, and hence indispensable.

But there was still more. To sell a consumer culture, the Bon Marché sold itself as an integral part of bourgeois life in France. Much like the theatre, whose image the Bon Marché was always ready to assume, the House offered itself as a bourgeois social fixture, a meeting ground and a place to be seen as well as a place of entertainment. This was why the Bon Marché provided a reading room with newspapers and writing paper, and a buffet with wines and syrups. Shopping, as the Bon Marché presented it, was now a full-time preoccupation. Shoppers were expected to spend their day at the store; and if they needed a place to leave aged parents or restless children, a place to meet friends or to arrange rendezvous, or simply a place to repose and prepare themselves for a return to the galleries, the House was willing to provide for these needs.

The conjunction of consumption, life style, and the life of the store could also be found in the special sales and the promotions that came in their wake. Yearly rhythms, the Bon Marché suggested, were now structured in the sequence of Bon Marché events. Months were no longer consequential, and even seasons lost much of their former meaning. Instead, the year now progressed from a clearance sale in early January to the Christmas and New Year's sale in December. Along the way were the *blanc* (late January or early February), a sale of gloves, flowers, lace, and perfume (late February), season's novelties (March), a summer clearance sale, and a special sale of carpets and furniture (September). Summer fashions sales took place in April or early May, winter fashions

sales in October. Like the Revolutionaries of 1793, the Bon
Marché created a calendar all its own. Winter was a time
when white goods and New Year's gifts were bought, spring
and fall a time when old fashions were discarded and new
styles adopted. For all those persons who read newspapers or
received catalogues or in some way or other were exposed to
the sales, it was not difficult to conceive of the year as a continual scheduled visit to the store on the Left Bank.

Cards for children served much the same function. Just as
pictures of the store were integrated into sets on the institutions of Paris, so too were there series that portrayed a visit to
the House as part of a child's daily adventures. There were
cards that pictured buying trips at the Bon Marché and cards
that showed children and their mothers riding omnibuses
and carrying bundles with Bon Marché labels. One series,
devoted to the end-of-the-year sale, showed children hawk-
ing signs of the coming exposition. Other cards portrayed
Bon Marché delivery boys bringing Bon Marché packages, or
even children receiving cards as they left the Bon Marché.
Cards of this sort, along with those of visits to the Tuileries or
trips to the seashore, were all of the same genre. Each depicted a side to growing up in France, each was a device to
shape a bourgeois child's image of his world.

Most interesting of all, in this vein, were the *agendas*. Like
illustrated cards, these too were deeply rooted in the popular
culture of France, having as forerunners the almanacs of earlier days. Almanacs as simple calendars, listing the days of
the year, the phases of the moon, and church holidays can be
traced as far back as Roman times.[31] Almanacs in book form,
published annually and containing diverse information in
addition to calendars, date from the end of the fifteenth century. In 1679 the first *Almanach Royal* appeared, offering pre-
dictions for the year's weather and information on the phases
of the moon, mail service, palace holidays, and the principal
fairs of the kingdom. By 1697 it was also listing state dig-

[31] Outside Western civilization, still earlier calendars were produced by
the Egyptians and the Chinese.

nitaries and important civil servants. The *Almanach Gotha*, dating from the eighteenth century, was still more diverse. Here one could find statistics on various countries, advice on personal hygiene, articles on the human body, and details on the peoples of the world. For the semi-literate and beyond, there was a whole genre of almanacs, largely astrological and sensational, but also offering advice on health, farming, and cooking. During the reign of Louis XV, almanacs, doubling as calendars or books for noting dates and expenses, became a phenomenon of enormous proportions. There were prophecy almanacs, astronomical almanacs, medical almanacs, almanacs of fashion, of songs, of religious holidays, and so on, until practically every subject became the excuse, or the material, for another almanac.

Almanacs were probably the most widely read of publications, often the only literary contact for great numbers of individuals. Their popularity led propagandists, as well as publishers, to issue almanacs in abundance. In earlier days state decrees had forbade political use of the medium. But by the nineteenth century the restrictions had gone, and political almanacs were once again common. Another form of propaganda was commercial. This took two directions. First, there were professional almanacs, listing the merchants of a particular profession along with the usual almanac offerings. The *Livre Commode* began this tradition as early as 1691 and was later succeeded by the *Almanach du Commerce de Paris* and then the *Didot-Bottin*. Second, some individual merchants issued their own almanacs, like La Faye the perfumer, who in 1772 published a combination catalogue-almanac, or Bresson, who sold designs to be sewn on screens and furniture, and who published an almanac containing information about his work.[32]

Bon Marché *agendas* emanated from this second strain.

---

[32] Emile Mermet, *La publicité en France, histoire et jurisprudence* (Paris: 1879), pp. 125-45; Victor Champier, *Les anciens almanachs illustrés* (Paris: Bibliothèque des Deux Mondes, 1886), pp. 46-47; John Grand-Carteret, *Les almanachs français* (Paris: J. Alisie, 1896); Geneviève Bollème, *Les almanachs populaires aux XVII et XVIII siècles* (Paris: Mouton, 1969).

Perhaps the first of their kind offered by the new *grands maga-sins*, the *agendas* basically were calendar books with space to jot down daily engagements. Like earlier almanacs they con-tained a range of information and amusing diversions. There were cartoons, menus, and extracts of articles and engravings from encyclopedias or other books. There were also theatre plans and lists and information on the postal system, *lycées*, museums, churches, hospitals, police commissariats, and oc-casionally notaries. In the 1890s, centerfold texts with colored pictures on "The Cries of Paris" or on world affairs or on co-lonial possessions became a standard feature. And there were also publicity and information about the Bon Marché, a good deal in fact. Pictures of the store with House slogans were common. So too were full-page announcements of sales dates, information on mail-order, details on deliveries, and directions for omnibus lines leading to the Bon Marché.

In one sense, then, Bon Marché *agendas* were a brilliant ve-hicle for store self-promotion. Trading on the popularity of almanacs in France, and serving a variety of functions, they were assured of a market that would swallow them whole and accept the information they offered on store and city life. But, in a still larger sense, they were another means of iden-tifying the Bon Marché with the bourgeois way of life. By placing store news alongside details on churches, theatres, *lycées*, and notaries, *agendas* implied that the Bon Marché was another bourgeois social institution of Paris. And by placing pictures of the House and reminders of special sales along-side "Reception Day" pages and monthly dinner menus, *agendas* further suggested that a visit to the Bon Marché was another part of the bourgeois social calendar. Indeed, by creating an image in which bourgeois society could not be conceived of apart from the Bon Marché, these calendar books proposed that a trip to the store was simply another of one's daily comings and goings. Like catalogues, sales, and picture cards, *agendas* told their readers that the life of the bourgeois and the life of the department store had become one and the same.

VI SELLING THE STORE

Ambivalence and Hostility

For Zola the great success of the *grands magasins*, their seduction of the middle-class masses, and their turning of consumption into a way of life were all part of the poetry of modern activity. He too was dazzled by the new emporia, and he wrote most powerfully of the spectacle of their displays and the flow of their crowds, reflecting constantly a personal fascination with the size and scope of their vast operations. Yet the portrait that emerged in *Au bonheur des dames* encompassed another, less alluring, side to the department store world. To the store's fashionable shoppers was added *"la foule,"* the masses of women whose identity was captive to the goods they could buy. To the magnificence of displays was added the decline in standards, old Bourras' carefully crafted umbrellas failing dismally beside the cheaper wares of Mouret. To Mouret's brilliance and success was added the broken community of small shopkeepers, driven from their livelihood in pathetic fashion. To the energy and immensity of the organization was added the image of a steam engine, where employees were atomized, where old ties were discarded, and where everything was ruled by a struggle for existence. In Zola's vision there was an awareness that a way of life was passing, that with the department store was emerging a society more impersonal, more uniform, more machine-like, more mass-like. And, for all his fascination, for all his desire to "go with the century, to express the century which is a century of action and conquest . . . to show the joy of action and the pleasure of existence," Zola could not escape lingering, with an air of uncertainty, on what was to be lost in the wake of this path.[1]

Zola's reaction was not uncommon. Aside from polemicists, most contemporary observers expressed an ambivalence of sorts about the new stores. Generally the attitude was favorable, as in the studies of Henri Garrigues and Léon Duclos, two doctoral students who regarded the *grands magasins* as a great step towards progress. Yet Garrigues regretted that employees were "nothing but cogs in a vast machine," and he saw in mass production and mass distribution the creation of a uniformity "without thought, without character." Similarly, Duclos observed that the new stores had a pernicious influence on craftsmanship, that beneath the appearance of luxury was a decline in quality.[2]

Other critics were less certain that the good outweighed the evil. The author of an article in the *Figaro* declared himself "an excited witness to the works of the century! I see in the great bazars above all the interest of consumers . . . the interest of households of average means. The great bazar is . . . a beautiful and a good creation of our age." But this was only an introduction to a far more pessimistic view:

"However, I must confess that the great bazar, by creating a uniformity of clothing and furniture in these little households, wounds certain undying feelings in me. . . . We have arrived at a day when precut clothes are less expensive than uncut cloth. . . . In the past a dress a woman made was like

---

[1] The quotation is from Zola's introduction to the manuscript that he was about to write. Further on, he wrote that he had no intention of "crying" over the ruin of small shopkeepers. Still, a sense of pathos is conveyed in the novel, and his observations were later used by department store critics to support their arguments. Zola, NAF10277, pp. 2, 6.

[2] Henri Garrigues, *Les grands magasins de nouveautés et le petit commerce de détail* (Paris: Librairie Nouvelle de Droit et de Jurisprudence, 1898), pp. 74, 132-36; Léon Duclos, *Des transformations du commerce de détail en France au XIX ème siècle* (Paris: L. Boyer, 1902), pp. 137-38. Garrigues' objections were softened, however, by the belief that the levelling of standards would not be forever. At some point in the future, Garrigues was certain, people would be saturated with such products and production would then return to a more artistic level.

her biography. Now . . . the same design and the same cut of clothing cover women who certainly are not of the same upbringing, that is to say, of the same soul. . . .

"Yes! These great bazars are, at this time a social good—but they are the premonitory symptoms of an immense phalanstery the twentieth century is preparing. For truly the first time I am happy that I am no longer young and I hope that I will not see these enormous things of the future. I am one of those who prefers the individual ownership of a pot of flowers rather than the . . . collective ownership of the Tuileries Gardens."[3]

Pierre Giffard's Les grands bazars of 1882 carried this sense of ambivalence a step further. Like Zola, Giffard was fascinated with his subject. Department stores, as he presented them, were more readily seen as "colossuses," "gargantuas," "giant fairs," "towers of Babel," and "fairytale palaces." They were a glittering, spectacular world and, what is more, a transforming world whose significance Giffard grasped and accepted. But in Giffard's mind they were also an immoral world, a world where one could find:

"The husband who has driven his wife to the great bazar, who leaves her for long hours as prey to the seductions of lace, who leaves her to go on and on in the wonderful storehouse of attractions where she empties her purse, her eyes on fire, her face reddened, her hand shivering, placed on that of a gloves salesman, while he goes off during this time with shady women to the furnished hotels of the eighteenth rank."[4]

In this world, beyond the glitter, or indeed as part of the spectacle, passions were unleashed, illicit love affairs rampant, perversions not unknown. Female clerks were a "group of women who inevitably become depraved or deprave others," women who gave their love freely for love or for profit. Female clients had their own affairs, occasionally seduced by clerks, or, more often, using the reading rooms to

write letters to their lovers. Worse still, they were seduced by
the stores and driven to a frenzy of buying and stealing.
Meanwhile through the stores circulated men known as
"*frotteurs*"—"the maniacs who follow the crowds in order to
rub up against them," while outside the store were "the
hideous pustules of the *grands bazars*," hawkers of all sorts,
including prostitutes who waited in prey for the passing
throngs.[5]

Much of this was of course right out of Giffard's imagination. Shivering hands and depraved *demoiselles* are the stuff of
which bestsellers are made, and Giffard was a master of titil-
lation. Still, his portrait was more symptomatic than unreal.
Other more sober writers were equally alarmed that the
grands magasins were loosening the bourgeois community's
moral fiber. They too raised questions about the super-
charged atmosphere of these emporia, questions that further
suggested an uneasiness with the mass, bureaucratic environment that the department stores brought with them. In
particular they tended to focus on two of the problems Giffard had raised—the situation of female clerks and rampant
kleptomania—each of which requires some discussion.

The attention fixed upon the *demoiselles de magasin* was far
out of proportion to their representation of the work force.
Before their role as strikebreakers in 1869, women had not
been commonly employed in the *magasins de nouveautés*. After
the strike they tended to infiltrate a number of departments
catering specifically to women's needs, although at the time
of Zola's visit in 1882 there were only 152 women clerks
among the store's 2,500 employees. There were, in addition,
several hundred women who cut cloth samples for catalogues
and who answered correspondence, plus a number of
women who worked in *ateliers*. But none of these was considered an *employée*. Even after the turn of the century, when
women were employed in greater numbers, it would appear
that they never made up more than one-sixth of the *employé*
work force. Just how these statistics compare with those of

[5] *Ibid.*, pp. 105, 116, 288-90.

the other big stores is uncertain, although there is no suggestion that the Bon Marché was an exception to the rule. Yet,
regardless of these figures, nearly every discussion of
employees tended to dwell at some length on female clerks, a
dissertation on female employees was produced in 1911,[6] and
Zola chose a *demoiselle* as the central figure of his novel.

For most writers this attention was never far removed from
a more prurient interest in the personal lives of the *demoiselles*, an interest in the lives of petit bourgeois girls living
away from home, making their own living, and concentrated
in large stores, where they were in constant contact with
young men and exposed to high-pressured dealings with all
levels of the public. The concern, moreover, was not without
foundation. If Giffard's remarks about depravity and his
statistics that 10 percent married, 10 percent remained "hon-
orable girls," 10 percent lived in concubinage with male
clerks, and 70 percent spent their evenings in riotous living[7]
were simply the salivations of an overexcited misogynist,
there was a general consensus that the lives of *demoiselles*
were not a model for other young French women.

In certain respects this was a product of confusion. At some
lesser stores, where salaries were very low and lodgings and
meals not provided, women employees could live in desperate straits. Prostitution was not unknown, and this reputation spread to the profession as a whole. More of a factor,
however, was the general looseness in the personal lives of
women employees. Taking a lover was common and acceptable, and Sunday picnics or introductions by friends made it
difficult for fresh arrivals from the provinces to escape seduction for long. Such an outlook could also condone seeking a
lover as a means of raising one's station in life. Affairs with
store executives occurred occasionally, and Hériot, cofounder of the Louvre, was reputed to have kept a salesgirl as
a mistress. Most likely, liaisons with clients occurred as well,
although probably not in any great number. But licentious-
ness never became an end in itself. Marriage remained the

[6] Lainé, *Les demoiselles*.   [7] Giffard, *Grands bazars*, p. 107.

goal of practically all *demoiselles* and those who succeeded often left their jobs. As a result the majority of working women were under thirty-five years of age and single, thereby further contributing to the image of the *demoiselles* as a distinct social set.[8]

Yet immorality among female clerks, for all the discussion it provoked, was never more than a partial issue. The implications of sexual behavior extended far beyond a mere vicarious probing into the personal habits of young working girls. *Demoiselles* captured the bourgeois public's attention because they were so unlike other working women. Most came from middle-class origins—albeit at the bottom of the scale—and most, because of their work and the salaries they earned, were drawn closer to the center of French middle-class culture.[9]

Or, rather, most came to resemble that center much as a good, but imperfect, forgery resembles its original. Women clerks were not quite full-fledged bourgeoises, but they were not quite working class either, and, if the nature of their

[8] Zola, NAF10278, pp. 177-80, 206, 232; Lainé, *Les demoiselles*, p. 104; Saint-Martin, *Grands magasins*, pp. 209-10; B.M., Employee Dossiers; V. Mataja, "Les grands magasins et le petit commerce," *Revue d'Economie Politique* (May-June 1891), p. 476; Françoise Parent-Lardeur, *Les demoiselles de magasin* (Paris: Les Editions Ouvrières, 1970). It was not unusual, however, for women clerks at the Bon Marché who married fellow employees to remain with the firm.

[9] In general, women clerks may have earned less than the men, but there is no indication from Bon Marché records that a clearcut policy to discriminate existed at that store. Commissions, in any case, were most likely the same, so that women clerks probably earned on the average more than 3,000 francs in a year. This was more than twice as much as even the best salaries to be found in the small shops. It was not unusual for women to come to the Bon Marché from positions paying only several hundred francs a year (whether there was also a commission is uncertain, although if there were, it could not have been very large). B.M., Employee Dossiers; Paul Leroy-Beaulieu, *Le travail des femmes au XIX ème siècle* (Paris: Charpentier, 1873), pp. 109-10. On the other hand, only a handful of women rose to department head and no woman employee ever sat on the council. For example, the original shareholders of the *société* included only three women—two department heads and one second. Women with more schooling than was customary might also begin work as sample cutters. B.M., Employee Dossiers.

work placed them close to the latter, the nature of their life style approximated the former. They were part of a new breed, a new middle-class stratum with entertainments and circles in many ways their own, yet never too far removed from the bourgeois above them. In their manners and their dress *demoiselles* could appear almost indistinguishable from more proper bourgeois women. They might frequent restaurants and cabarets catering especially to them, but they also spent their leisure time and money on the same sorts of pursuits as other middle-class people.[10] *Demoiselles* and the ladies they waited on were not all that far apart.

This is what made the question of dissoluteness far more disturbing than the standard Sodom and Gomorrah tales emanating from the factories.[11] Debaucheries among working-class women were one thing, among middle-class women something else again. This is also why discussions of *demoiselles* as working women were such a fascinating subject, and why, in turn, these discussions tended to merge with more general considerations on department store work. In a way the women were simply the most conspicuous subjects for an assessment of the lives of white-collar people who were becoming so numerous and for what this implied for middle-class culture as a whole. Discussions—and more often critiques—of working conditions in the *grands magasins* by their very nature raised the question of the spread of bureaucratization to middle-class careers. They questioned what it was like to do parcellized work in large, anonymous firms and, as with the concern over sex, they questioned how such work affected one's home and family life. In another sense they questioned the spread of bureaucratization to bourgeois culture itself. The working lives of white-collar people and the institutional framework within which bourgeois people spent *their* daily lives were scarcely in-

[10] For remarks on the leisure lives of these people and lower-middle-class culture, see Theresa M. McBride, "A Woman's World: Department Stores and the Evolution of Women's Employment, 1870-1920," *French Historical Studies* (Fall 1978), pp. 680-81.

[11] See, for example, Leroy-Beaulieu, *Le travail*, pp. 230-44.

separable. And, finally, they questioned where all this might be leading. Lurking behind even the breeziest accounts was always the fear of whether these people might not, after all, be lost to the working classes. Whether white-collar work simply posed a problem for bourgeois values and promises, or whether it posed, in the end, a far greater threat to bourgeois order and control was something that these writers could never quite determine. [12]

The image of department stores as dens of iniquity took a still sharper turn over the issue of shoplifting. As department stores grew, so too did the number of thefts committed by customers. Zola estimated that each day seven to eight thefts occurred at the Bon Marché. In 1893 the Bon Marché took 662 thefts to the courts, the Louvre 467, [13] and this was most likely only a fraction of the number of thefts committed in that year. So concerned were the stores that they obliged inspectors to divide their duties between disciplining employees and policing the clientele. By the 1890s the situation had gotten so out of hand that the Bon Marché was offering employees a ten-franc bonus and two evenings off for signalling to an inspector that a theft was taking place. [14] Much of this stealing was done by professionals or by common shoplifters. Some women came to the store with dresses specially designed for hiding merchandise. Others prepared special acts with their children to distract observers from the thefts they committed. But it was particularly the dramatic increase in the occurrence of kleptomania that aroused the most attention and fears.

Early studies of kleptomania had focused primarily on two themes. First, there was the question of how to define and to explain it as a medical phenomenon. Second, there was the question of legal responsibility: should kleptomaniacs be punished for the crimes they committed? In each respect the

[12] One need only read the admiring accounts of Bon Marché discipline to appreciate the degree of this uneasiness. See below, pp. 226-28.

[13] D'Avenel, "Le mécanisme," p. 359.

[14] B.M., *Conseils Généraux*, 2 December 1891. This decision was made after two persons, one with 1,224 francs worth of goods, the other with 1,155 francs worth of goods, had been arrested the previous day.

issue formed part of broader considerations. Behind the first question lay the study of a whole range of abnormal actions, all of which were obsessive or pathologically impulsive in character. Behind the second lay a medical reform movement that sought to place such obsessive or irresistible behavior beyond the definition of criminal liability.

How the two came together can be seen in the work of C.C.H. Marc, whose *On Madness Considered in Its Relationship to Questions of Forensic Medicine* of 1840 offered one of the first lengthy explorations into the cases of kleptomaniacs. Marc borrowed heavily from the earlier work of Philippe Pinel and especially Jean-Etienne Esquirol. Writing at the turn of the nineteenth century, Pinel had developed the concept of what he called *"folie raisonnante"* (reasoning insanity) or the condition of insane behavior coupled with normal thinking processes. Esquirol had then expanded this idea, developing the much broader category of monomania or partial delirium. Under monomania, individuals might become so obsessed with a certain idea that they would be led to behave deliriously, although in all other instances they would remain rational. In other situations the reasoning faculties of monomaniacs might remain intact, justifying or rationalizing extravagant behavior. Or, monomaniacs might be subject to a lesion of the will. In this case the monomaniac would be led to commit acts that "neither reason nor sentiment determine, that conscience rejects, and which the will can no longer repress; the actions are involuntary, instinctive, irresistible." Monomania, then, became a catchall phrase for all sorts of obsessive or partially delirious behavior, and it was within this conceptual framework that Marc explained kleptomania. To Marc the disease was "monomania of theft," "an instinctive, irresistible propensity to steal," "a monomania without foundations in reasoning, residing instead in a lesion upon . . . the will."[15]

[15] C.C.H. Marc, *De la folie considérée dans ses rapports avec les questions médico-judiciaires* (Paris: J.-B. Baillière, 1840), vol. 1, pp. 221-25, 239-40, 244-45, vol. 2, pp. 247, 253, 302; E. Esquirol, *Des maladies mentales* (Paris: J.-B. Bail-

Marc's writings on kleptomania, however, were never separated from the issue of medical jurisprudence, which was, after all, the subject of his book. If kleptomaniacs were monomaniacs, then the principal question remained whether they were criminally accountable for their actions. Along with Esquirol and other disciples like Georget, Marc believed that monomaniacs should be regarded as mentally ill. But his book also reflected the arguments of those who looked upon the concept of monomania as too vague and too open to abuse, and who strenuously opposed its introduction into the criminal code on the mentally insane. Marc insisted that the first priority of the psychiatrist in cases of theft was to ascertain whether kleptomania was real or apparent. The psychiatrist must examine the nature of the theft, the possibility of motive, and the personal and medical history of the patient. Only when he was satisfied on all of these counts that a monomania existed beyond any doubt could he proclaim the accused a kleptomaniac and thus a victim of mental disorders.[16]

Over the next several decades the number of writings on kleptomania increased. Most often these were case histories, descriptions of bizarre circumstances surrounding a theft and investigations into the perpetrator's medical past. Thinking on the subject evolved in certain ways. There were suggestions that kleptomania rarely occurred independent of other mental disorders. Kleptomania was a form of epilepsy or a form of hysteria, another open-ended concept coming into favor among French psychiatrists. There were attacks on the validity of the monomania concept. There was greater stress placed on heredity, a symptom of somaticist adherence to Darwinism. By and large, however, the thematic context in

---

lière, 1838), vol. 2, pp. 1-2; Erwin H. Ackerknecht, *A Short History of Psychiatry* (New York: Hafner, 1959), pp. 36-42.

[16] Marc, *De la folie*, vol. 2, pp. 247-303. See especially pp. 258-59, 273-74, 276; Raymond de Saussure, "The Influence of the Concept of Monomania on French Medico-Legal Psychiatry (from 1825 to 1840)," *Journal of the History of Medicine* (1946), pp. 365-97.

which kleptomania was discussed changed little. There was still the concern over legal responsibility. There was still the search for medical reasons to explain why kleptomaniacs behaved as they did.[17]

But by the end of the century kleptomania suddenly began to appear in a new light. Whereas in the past the focus had been on the pathology of the individual, psychiatrists now began to emphasize the social milieu in which kleptomania occurred. No longer a mere function of personal eccentricities, kleptomania was now seen to be shaped and determined by forces of cultural change. The reason for this shift was the rise of the department store and the sharp increase in kleptomania-like behavior that seemed to accompany it.

Beginning with an article by Charles Lasègue in 1879, psychiatrists began to draw a connection between impulsive stealing and the *grands magasins*. In 1883 Dr. Legrand du Saulle, who claimed to have been studying the problem since 1868, coined the term "department store thefts," and this quickly entered the language of analysis. By the turn of the century the concept had so evolved that another psychiatrist, Paul Dubuisson, wrote a book entitled *Department Store Thieves (Les voleuses de grands magasins)*.[18]

[17] M. H. Girard, "Kleptomanie," *Gazette Médicale de Paris* (15 November 1845), pp. 735-37; L. Lunier, review of "Observations de folie instantanée chez des personnes inculpées de vol" by Boys de Loury, in *Annales Médico-Psychologiques* (July 1848), pp. 130-32; M. Baillarger, "Quelques observations pour servir à l'histoire de la médecine légale psychologique," *Annales Médico-Psychologiques* (April 1853), pp. 479-81; E. Renaudin, "Journaux allemands," *Annales Médico-Psychologiques* (April 1855), pp. 233-42; Brierre de Boismont, "Journaux italiens," *Annales Médico-Psychologiques* (July 1868), pp. 146-51; P. Juquelier and Jean Vinchon, "L'Histoire de la kleptomanie," *Revue de Psychiatrie et de Psychologie Experimentale* (1914), pp. 47-64; Ackerknecht, *History*, Chapter VII.

[18] Charles Lasègue, "Le vol aux étalages," *L'Union Médicale* (23 December 1879), pp. 989-95; Legrand du Saulle, *Les hystériques* (Paris: J.-B. Baillière et Fils, 1883), pp. 435-56; Dubuisson, *Voleuses*. See also: M. Letulle, "Voleuses honnêtes," *Gazette Médicale de Paris* (1 October 1887), pp. 469-71; A. Lacassagne, "Les vols à l'étalage et dans les grands magasins," *Revue de l'Hypnotisme et de la Psychologie Physiologique* (September 1896), pp. 76-82; Roger

The break between these men and earlier writers was not a complete one. All agreed, to varying degrees, that the kleptomaniacs they studied suffered from more complicated disorders. Some were hysterics, some neurasthenics, some more critically mentally ill. All wrote of department store thefts as simply an addition to traditional kleptomaniac behavior, and few devoted their analyses exclusively to the former. All continued to pursue the medical classification of the phenomenon, distinguishing between a variety of symptoms and conditions. All remained concerned with legal implications.

Yet what particularly struck this generation of psychiatrists was both the sheer number of kleptomaniacs arrested in department stores and the fact that so few of these were incited to steal elsewhere. At the beginning of his article Lasègue noted that "since the transformation our *grands magasins* have undergone, thefts have multiplied under conditions peculiar and uniform enough to provoke some surprise." Legrand du Saulle wrote that "department store thefts . . . constitute a Parisian happening truly and completely contemporary, since they only date from the recent foundation and opening of the *grands magasins* themselves." A Dr. Lacassagne wrote that "department store thefts have assumed in our day a real importance because of their growing number, the value and variety of goods stolen, [and] the quality of the persons committing these thefts." Later he remarked that "most of these kleptomaniacs are only arrested in the department stores. They steal there and nowhere else." Describing the case of a kleptomaniac habitually arrested at the Bon Marché and the Louvre, two doctors added: "Never, she told us, had she been driven to steal in *les petits magasins*."[19]

Dupouy, "De la kleptomanie," *Journal de Psychologie Normale et Pathologique* (1905), pp. 404-26.

[19] Lasègue, "Vol," p. 989; Legrand du Saulle, *Hystériques*, pp. 436-37; Lacassagne, "Vols," pp. 76, 77; F. Boissier and G. Lachaux, "Contribution à l'étude de la kleptomanie," *Annales Médico-Psychologiques* (January 1894), pp. 42-54.

It was observations of this sort that led to the new emphasis on social setting. If kleptomaniacs committed so many thefts in department stores, then it was not only because they were predisposed to steal but because the department stores created conditions that incited them to do so. Almost as if they were auditioning for writing school (or perhaps giving way to their own pathological impulses), the psychiatrists vied to produce the most lurid account of department store temptations. Giffard would not have been prouder of the results. Lacassagne wrote of *"excitants*[20] of the social order that might be called the *apéritifs du crime."* Dubuisson wrote of seductions and cults, remarking that when it came to temptations "Satan could not have done better." Legrand du Saulle's essay is worth quoting at length:

"These immense galleries, as freely accessible to the idle in search of distractions or adventures as to serious shoppers, enclose and expose . . . the richest cloths, the most luxurious dress articles, the most seductive superfluities. Women of all sorts, drawn to these elegant surroundings by instincts native to their sex, fascinated by so many rash provocations, dazzled by the abundance of trinkets and lace, find themselves overtaken by a sudden, unpremeditated, almost savage impulse. They place a clumsy if furtive hand on a display and *voilà*, with one unthinking stroke, they wipe out the most respectable past, improvise as shoplifters, and render themselves criminal; soon they will have to explain themselves before the authorities and justice."[21]

The victims themselves were no less evocative. The following is an account taken from Dubuisson's investigations:

"Once plunged into the sensuous atmosphere of the *grand magasin*, as told to us by a very respectable provincial lady recently arrived in Paris and whose first outing had been a double visit to the Bon Marché and the Louvre, I felt myself

[20] There is a sexual overtone to the French word *exciter* and its variations such as *excitants* that is not fully conveyed by the usual meaning of the English term "to excite."

[21] Lacassagne, "Vols," p. 78; Dubuisson, *Voleuses*, pp. 39-40, 42-43; Legrand du Saulle, *Hystériques*, p. 437.

overcome little by little by a disorder that can only be compared to that of drunkenness, with the dizziness and *excitation* that are peculiar to it. I saw things as if through a cloud, everything stimulated my desire and assumed, for me, an extraordinary attraction. I felt myself swept along towards them and I grabbed hold of things without any outside and superior consideration intervening to hold me back. Moreover I took things at random, useless and worthless articles as well as useful and expensive articles. It was like a monomania of possession."[22]

Indeed the spell of the stores was so strong that women who were caught often expressed "a sort of relief: they claim that the *grand magasin* in the long run had become for them an obsession, a nightmare, and they are conscious of finally being delivered from it." For others the reaction was just the contrary, a desolation at the thought that "they will henceforth be deprived of the *grands magasins* which had become for them everything in their life."[23]

The implications of all this were not lost on the department stores, who did their best to hush up these thefts. Women who were apprehended, particularly the well-to-do, were taken to an office where they were invited to make a contribution to the welfare of the poor. Still, the fact of rampant kleptomania became a matter of public knowledge. It was a subject that again evoked a mixture of fascination and reprobation for reasons that are not difficult to understand, especially if we return to two more themes in the writings of psychiatrists on department store thefts.

For all their concern over the maladies of their patients, men who wrote of *excitants*, Satan, and seductions were never able to draw a clear line between disease and dissolution, mental abandonment and sin. In the pathology of kleptomania there was always a tinge of moral excess, or at least of the carnal side of things. This could be seen in the frequent analogies to intoxicated behavior, the recurrent refrains of "my head was spinning," "I lost my head," or "I felt com-

[22] Dubuisson, *Voleuses*, p. 53.　　　[23] *Ibid.*, p. 52.

pletely dizzy."[24] It could be seen even more so in the deep relationship between kleptomania and sex. Lasègue drew comparisons between the impulse to kleptomania and that of exhibitionists.[25] Others saw in kleptomaniacs the same perverted behavior of fetischistic collectors:

"When I can grab some silk, then I am just as if I were drunk. I tremble, although not from fear because the sordidness of what I have just done does not occur to me at all; I only think of one thing: to go into a corner where I can rustle it at my ease, which gives me voluptuous sensations even stronger than those I feel with the father of my children."[26]

Legrand du Saulle went to great lengths to refute a popular belief that hysterics—a category into which large numbers of kleptomaniacs were placed—were primarily women frustrated in their sexual drive.[27] Even at the most innocuous level, kleptomania was constantly being linked to the female sexual and reproductive organs. In case after case, kleptomaniacs were pregnant women, women undergoing their menstrual period, women whose period was overdue, or women beginning to undergo menopause.

In themselves these facts were troubling, but what made them still more shocking was the nature of the individuals identified with them. It was not simply that so many kleptomaniacs arrested in department stores were female—women were, after all, the major clientele of the stores—[28] nor that so many whose sex, as Legrand du Saulle put it, was entrusted with "a noble mission in society,"[29] turned out to have a darker side to their character. Women and sin was never a topic totally relegated to the closet of nineteenth-century society. But department stores were the playground

---

[24] *Ibid.*, p. 188.   [25] Lasègue, "Vol," p. 992.

[26] Dupouy, "De la kleptomanie," p. 413.

[27] Legrand du Saulle, *Hystériques*, pp. 1-14.

[28] One psychiatrist, Charles Lunier, did make an effort to point out that a fair number of kleptomaniacs were men. But even he was obliged to admit that most thefts of this sort committed in department stores were carried out by women. Charles Lunier, "Des vols aux étalages," *Annales Médico-Psychologique* (September 1880), pp. 201-42.

[29] Legrand du Saulle, *Hystériques*, p. 23.

of a particular class of women, and it was this, coupled with the above revelations, that struck such a raw nerve in bourgeois sensibilities. What made department store thefts such an irresistible subject to the psychiatrists studying them and such an alarming subject to those who read about them was that so many of these women came from thoroughly respectable bourgeois backgrounds, women "belonging to the comfortable, even the affluent classes . . . women well bred, whose life outside the department stores is beyond reproach,"[30] women stealing things of little or no consequence that they could easily afford. From Lasègue to Legrand du Saulle to Dubuisson this was a motif that appeared over and over again, always with the same sentiment of astonishment and concern, always with the feeling that the question of criminal responsibility was shifting from the individuals to the stores. Dubuisson remarked that "women find there [department stores] a milieu where whatever they possess in the way of moral staying power can no longer protect them, whereas they defend themselves successfully in all other settings."[31] Lacassagne warned: "the department stores make great profits. . . . However the prosperity of these colossal enterprises must not take place at the expense of public morality."[32]

In the end, department store kleptomania remained a limited problem. Despite the horror it aroused, few took seriously the prospect of a mass criminalization of French middle-class women. France did not become a nation half Jekyll, half Hyde. Still, there was something in the whole affair to torment the middle-class soul. Bourgeois institutions were expected to uphold the moral order, not threaten it, and yet this did not seem to be the rule in the case of the department store. Indeed it no longer mattered whether one stole or not—in the eyes of inspectors and employees all shoppers already possessed criminal-like status.[33] All of which pointed to something still further: that the pathological frenzy to

[30] Dubuisson, *Voleuses*, p. 2.   [31] *Ibid.*, p. 187.
[32] Lacassagne, "Vols," p. 82.
[33] Parent-Lardeur, *Demoiselles*, pp. 80-83.

which some women were driven had become simply the seamier side of the new consumer society, where the old virtues of thrift and self control were giving way to a culture of gratification. Looking at kleptomania from the bourgeois point of view was like seeing one's reflection in an El Greco painting—distorted, taken to extremes, and yet possessing an underlying, recognizable reality.

Forebodings over department stores came from still one other quarter, one that was to evoke the deepest anxieties, the fiercest opposition, and, unlike the others, absolutely no ambivalence. This was the quarter of all those who individually and collectively saw themselves as the casualties of the rationalization of the marketplace. Like the questions of *demoiselles* and kleptomania, it too requires a certain amount of attention.

Professional grievances against the *grands magasins* came from a number of sources. Artisans like cabinet-makers complained bitterly that department stores were cornering the market in their trade and were contracting their work out to lesser skilled craftsmen under demeaning conditions, thereby destroying both their work and their community.[34] Factory agents and other intermediaries between production and distribution complained that their professions were being outright annihilated. Even factory owners had their complaints. For some the increased orders of department stores were accompanied by an all but titular control of production. "Today," Zola noted, "the Bon Marché and the Louvre make the law." For others the department stores could be unscrupulous business associates, as in the case of those stores that bought 50 out of 300 pieces at 2 francs each, sold then at 1 franc 50 to depreciate the article, then bought the remaining

[34] "We wish to reduce to ruin, if necessary, those scoundrels who force work at sixteen hours a day for onerous prices, disorganizing our faubourg in order to transfer it beyond Montreuil, Bagnolet, etc. to supply and make the fortune of the commission agents and the bazars, like the Louvre, Bon Marché, etc. where the product of our unremunerated work is shamelessly displayed." Préfecture de Police, Ba 1422, Chambre Syndicale ébenistes/ meubles sculptés call for meeting, 31 August 1892.

250 pieces for practically nothing, only to sell them subsequently at 3 francs apiece. It was circumstances like this that explained why a linen manufacturer was willing to supply an employees' cooperative during the 1869 strike.[35]

Foremost among those with a grievance, however, were the small shopkeepers, many of whom simply could not compete with the *grands magasins*. Just how sharply the new stores ate into their trade was a question no one seemed able to answer conclusively. But if defenders of department stores were forever pointing out that the total number of merchants had not diminished over the last decades of the century and that the *grands magasins* never represented more than ten percent of the market, there was, nevertheless, a more depressing side to the statistics.[36]

The economist Charles Gide, for instance, noted that only those shops that were not in direct competition with the new stores had held their own or had augmented their numbers. The rest were driven to relying on what he saw as the deplorable (pathetic might be a better word) tactics of kickbacks to servants, extension of credit, and gifts to shoppers who bought a certain amount of merchandise.[37] Joseph Bernard, who wrote a dissertation on the problem of small shopkeepers, agreed that their numbers had not decreased, but remarked that "the crisis is no less the bitter for it. Far from

[35] Zola, NAF10278, pp. 197-98, 224; Artaud, *La question*, p. 255.

[36] According to André Sayous, shops with more than one employee had grown in number, while those without employees had tended to *"diminuer dans le commerce."* Sayous also maintained that specialty chain stores were more of a threat than department stores to the small shopkeepers. G. D'Azambuja noted that many small shops were still to be found in the vicinity of department stores (although many that he cited were in foodstuffs). André Sayous, "Le mouvement de concentration dans le commerce de détail," in *La concentration des entreprises industrielles et commerciales*, ed. Arthur Fontaine (Paris: Félix Alcan, 1913), pp. 147, 152, 174-75; G. D'Azambuja, "Les grands magasins doivent-ils tuer les petits?" *La Science Sociale* (October 1901), p. 290; Saint-Martin, *Grands magasins*, pp. 19-20; J. Daugan, *Histoire et législation des patentes des grands magasins* (Rennes, 1902), p. 33; D'Avenel, "Le mécanisme," p. 367.

[37] Charles Gide, *Cours d'économie politique* (Paris: Librairie de la Société du Recueil, 1909), p. 182.

making his fortune the small merchant vegetates miserably when he is not ruined."[38] This theme of vegetation had been voiced earlier by Zola, who contrasted the demise of the small shopkeeper to the emergence of "modern activity." And, while others might debate the matter, the shopkeepers themselves had few doubts about where they stood. With increasing keenness they sensed that their livelihood, their community, and their traditions were threatened with extinction in the face of the department stores.

As early as 1843 complaints surfaced in the legislature, the deputy Fischel calling attention to "the growth of certain stores where, how horrible, the buyer can provide himself at once with stockings, handkerchiefs, shirts, shawls, woolen fabrics, and silk fabrics. That ruins the small shopkeeper."[39] These were desperate remarks, but few were yet prepared to treat them as such. The commercial tax rates, or the *patente*, of the following year revealed little interest in tampering with the new *magasins de nouveautés*. The *patente* had a fixed rate according to categories, but no store was to pay such a rate for more than one speciality, and the highest fixed rate was only 1,000 francs for stores employing more than twenty-four clerks. There was also a proportional rate, but this was set at a maximum of one-fifteenth of the rental value.[40]

Efforts to level the new stores were always to center on the *patente*, but for the next forty-five years proposals that seriously threatened the tax status of the *magasins de nouveautés*, and then the *grands magasins*, were easily suppressed. In 1850 a tax of 25 francs for each employee over five was added to the fixed rate, although the maximum remained 1,000 francs. The 1858 law merely raised the maximum to 2,000 francs. In 1872 parliament removed the maximum on the fixed rate and increased the proportional rate to one-tenth the rental value. Still, the effect on the very largest stores was minimal, and

[38] Joseph Bernard, *Du mouvement d'organisation de défense du petit commerce français* (Paris: A. Michalon, 1906), pp. 33-35.

[39] Daugan, *Histoire*, p. 52.

[40] *Ibid.*, pp. 54-57; R. Auscher, *La législation fiscale applicable aux grands magasins et maisons à succursales multiples* (Paris: 1923), p. 64.

the 1880 *patente* law confirmed that no store would be taxed for more than one speciality.[41]

All this began to change, however, with the creation of the League for the Defense of Work, Industry, and Commerce in 1888. Composed mostly of small shopkeepers, the league was in theory opposed to all "commercial monopolies," but it directed its attacks primarily at the giant stores: "there was the immediate danger, the immanent menace, the nearest disasters, the irreparable ruins."[42] Running like a thread through *La Revendication*, the league journal, was the belief that department stores represented a new feudalism, backed by enormous capital and building their prosperity upon the ruins of independent tradesmen and their families.

Issue after issue recounted the department stores' sins as the shopkeepers poured out their outrage, their frustrations, their self-pity, and their desperate desire to attain the public's sympathy. Bitterly they presented themselves as a forgotten people. They had been "good and loyal servants" to their customers, knowing them "from father to son." Yet while the public fretted over the tired feet of *demoiselles*[43] there were, they reminded, other women—wives and mothers of families—"who, since your mass emigration to several privileged stores, stand wilted in their shops that today are silent, deserted."[44]

Not that the league was itself unconcerned over the conditions of the *demoiselles*. To the contrary, *La Revendication* devoted a good deal of space to the difficulties of employees. In part this was because the small shopkeepers realized that the issue of commercial employees was another thorn that could be pressed into the side of the department store. But it also

[41] Daugan, *Histoire*, pp. 58-86; Auscher, *Législation*, p. 65; Etienne Juhel, *La patente des grands magasins* (Caen: 1907), p. 65.

[42] "Aux ligueurs," *La Revendication*, 20 September 1888.

[43] The countess Albert de Mun, the marquise de la Tour du Pin, the princesse de Beauveau, and a number of other similar ladies had organized a public campaign to oblige department stores to give *demoiselles* the right of sitting down when not waiting on customers. This eventually led to the "Seat Law" of 1900.

[44] "Femmes debout et femmes oubliées," *La Revendication*, 5 July 1888.

derived from the recognition that their own disastrous situation was being mirrored in the lives of the employees, that their own destruction could be seen in the dooming of so many clerks to permanent salaried positions.

Thus they cried out against this fate and all other conditions that seemed to contradict their own past and traditions. When the Louvre announced that wines and food goods would be provided on a limited basis, an action that further flaunted the departure from store specialization, *La Revendication* mockingly predicted that soon Paris would see advertisements vaunting:

PURE GUARANTEED MILK
BY THE
GRANDS MAGASINS DU LOUVRE

To our clients

Our baby milk will be taken from the natural source, and the stock of nurses offered to our lady clients will not for an instant permit them to suppose that this 'Property of the Louvre' has anything in common with the *Soldes et Occasions* [clearance and bargain sales] of which we give notice each week.

Besides, in spite of the devotion of our feminine personnel, we will not accept any of our employees for the articles of this special counter. The excessive work that we impose upon them, making them anemic rather quickly, obliges us to be faithful to our principles and to offer only

'Guaranteed Merchandise'[45]

More seriously the journal complained that the commercial employee, who formerly lived *en famille* with his employer, had become "no longer a man, but a number."[46]

[45] "Aux adversaires de la ligue," *La Revendication*, 16 May 1889.

[46] "Guerre aux bazars," *La Revendication*, 26 July 1888; Speech of M. Ratel at league reunion, *La Revendication*, 22 November 1891. The league also complained that factories and workshops were forced to cut wages so that orders for the new stores could be met.

At the same time the league lashed out at the pernicious effect that the stores could have on consumers. "These are not merchants that you are visiting; you are visiting artists, *fantaisistes*, idealists, psychologists, the inventors of tricks, the disciples of Dr. Charcot, the emulators of Robert Houdin." Under these conditions, as others had seen, the client was led down a treacherous path. To be in fashion she bought beyond her means, even though mass production and mass marketing had led to a decline in the quality of goods. She was likely to steal, and if not she was still regarded as a thief. Encouraged to buy with the option of returns, she thought nothing of purchasing merchandise with the intention of using it once for a desired effect and then returning it the following day. And, passing her days at the *grands magasins*, she lost track of her family concerns. This question of family was a favorite theme of the league, one that again enabled the shopkeepers to identify their own plight with that of others. Thus, as many of them saw their own family dreams ground up in the demise of their shops, so too did they insist that the department stores were ruining the family life of employees and the public. For the former the problem was long hours and meals away from home that made family life nearly impossible. For the consumers it was the monopolization of their lives by the stores—"a vice like alcoholism or drug addiction." Children were abandoned to grow up without the moral direction that only their mothers could provide. Husbands were driven to financial ruin as they speculated to support their wives' extravagances.[47]

As an organization the league became increasingly widespread and increasingly numerous. To the original committees that had formed in practically all Parisian arrondissements a section at Versailles was added in late 1888, and in the following year sections were formed at Rouen, Dijon, and

---

[47] "Les grands bazars et les journaux," *La Revendication*, 26 July 1888; "O, femmes!" *La Revendication*, 4 October 1888; 11 October 1888; "Tromperie," *La Revendication*, 23 May 1889; "Les grands bazars et la famille," *La Revendication*, 6 June 1889; Henry Vouters, *Le petit commerce contre les grands magasins et les coopératives de consommation* (Paris: Arthur Rousseau, 1910), pp. 59-60.

Nancy. At its 1895 congress representatives from over forty towns and cities were in attendance. Membership rolls grew with equal rapidity. If league statistics can be believed (and most likely they were inflated) there were 6,000 members in 1888, 11,000 in 1889, 70,000 by 1891, and 180,000 by 1896.[48] This was perhaps the high point, and by 1911 league membership had declined to approximately 9,000 members. However, the slack was taken up by a new organization that the league had helped to form in 1901, the Parti Commercial et Industriel de France, later known as the Fédération des Groupes Commerciaux et Industriels de France. In 1911 this organization claimed a membership of 70,000 to 80,000 persons.[49] Meanwhile alongside the league and the federation marched a host of powerful allies. Deputies like Delattre and Georges Berry took up their cause in the chamber.[50] Journalists and polemicists, ranging from Alexandre Weill to the anti-Semite Edouard Drumont, many of whom had their own ax to grind, carried into the national press the message of the league with all its unequivocalness and all its venom.

Consequently, the question of tax revision became a major political issue. If the league and its proponents had had their way, the department stores would have been crippled by vastly increased taxes in proportion to the number of their employees and by enormous taxes allocated according to the number of specialties assembled within a given store. In 1895, for example, Georges Berry offered an amendment to the *patente* law that would have resulted in a tax of more than 11,000,000 francs for the Bon Marché and the Louvre.[51] This was at a time when the Bon Marché's net profits were 9,368,779 francs, its distributable profits about 6,500,000.[52]

---

[48] See the following issues of *La Revendication*: 5 July 1888; 27 June 1889; 15 November 1891; 15 January 1896.

[49] Etienne Martin Saint-Léon, *Le petit commerce parisien* (Paris: Victor Lecoffre, 1911), pp. 108-12. The league was now called the Ligue Syndicale et Union Fédérative du Commerce et de l'Industrie.

[50] Berry's relations with the league were not always cordial. See, e.g., *La Revendication*, 6 June 1889.

[51] Daugan, *Histoire*, p. 163; Saint-Martin, *Grands magasins*, p. 131.

[52] B.M., AGO, 23 August 1895.

Wild schemes of this sort were never acceptable to the Chamber, which, as a group, was not prepared to suppress the big stores. But in their own way they served as a stalking horse for more practical plans for revision. Under pressure from the league and its advocates, the legislature voted increasingly higher taxes on employees and, beginning in 1893, taxes according to specialties.[53] In 1898 Berry managed to push through the Chamber an amendment that would have more than doubled the tax rate of the very largest stores, although this was later changed in the Senate.[54]

As it was, the commercial tax rate never got out of hand from the department stores' point of view. According to one set of figures, the Bon Marché only paid about ten percent of its profits in total taxes as late as 1913.[55] Nevertheless, the stores themselves reflected the keenness of the league's pressures. Assemblies at the Bon Marché during this period repeatedly registered anxieties over taxes, to the point where major decisions became influenced by the *patente* issue. As a result, construction proposals could be postponed until Chamber deliberations were conclusive or serious consideration could be given to absurd proposals, such as opening an agency in Abyssinia simply as a means of currying favor with the government.

In certain ways the problem of the small shopkeepers revealed conflicts that existed within the bourgeoisie themselves. The resentments of small shopkeepers towards concentration in the marketplace and their fear of competition all ran counter to the direction in which so much else of bourgeois society was moving. The small shopkeepers were the vestiges of an earlier bourgeoisie, one that had set limits on the capitalistic impulse within it. As the century progressed, they came to share less and less in common with the other side of their class, dynamic and expansive in character,

---

[53] The sole exception came in 1890, when an increase voted in 1889 that doubled taxes per employees in stores employing over 200 persons was then revised the following year in such a way that taxes on the two largest stores were reduced by about 6½ percent. Daugan, *Histoire*, p. 105.

[54] *Ibid.*, p. 186.   [55] Auscher, *Législation*, p. 128.

that had spawned the factories and the railroads and now the department stores. The one was backward-looking, fearful, and modest in its resources; the other forward-looking, confident, and generally affluent. The one saw itself as the victim of change and struck out against what it felt was a conspiracy of big capital, resorting to a vocabulary—"financial feudalism"—that was more in line with the end of the eighteenth century than with the coming of the twentieth. The other spoke of progress and material benefits and the immutable laws of development. It mustered its own set of polemicists to counter those of the league, denying the latter's charges, and placing the blame for the shopkeepers' misfortunes upon the shoulders of the shopkeepers themselves. If many small shops were going under or looked as if they ought to, this was because there were too many small shopkeepers and among these too many incompetents to run their affairs properly. At the very least, change had always resulted in its casualties. This was a sad thing, but it was the price one had to pay for progress. The loss of some shopkeepers was no greater tragedy than the disappearance of water carriers in the wake of indoor plumbing or that of the postmasters with the coming of the railroad.[56]

And yet, to see in the fate of the shopkeepers simply an issue between old versus new, lower bourgeoisie versus upper, would be to perceive only one side of things. The conflicts within bourgeois culture went deeper, and were far less clearcut. The small shopkeepers may have represented another bourgeois era, but they also bore within them values and traditions that the remainder of their class continued to cherish. They were independent, they preserved a close unity between family and business, and they retained an organic relationship with the people who served under them. They still maintained a sense of community. If they were egalitarian, they also had a sense of place and position. In many ways the small shopkeepers simply threw the doubts

[56] For an example of these writings, see: Edmond Demolins, *La question des grands magasins* (Paris: Firmin Didot, 1890); Michel, "Le commerce"; Emile Berr, "Les grands bazars," *Revue Bleue* (December 1889).

of people like Zola and Garrigues and Giffard and the psychiatrists into sharper relief. Both were troubled by the mass
bureaucratic consequences of department stores, both asked
what was to become of bourgeois life and culture in an impersonal, uniform, and overly materialistic age, the small shopkeepers simply raising this to a more specific and less am-
biguous level. Indeed one is struck by the degree to which
certain issues—employee relations, immorality, and decline
in standards—were repeated in the writings of both sets of
critics. What seemed to be at stake for everyone involved was
a whole way of life, a whole set of traditional or *gemeinschaftlich* elements that had persisted within a bourgeoisie reluctant to discard them. And if the uncertainties of one group
were always tempered by a fascination and an ultimate willingness to accept the new stores, it was nevertheless their
very ambivalence that permitted the laments of the others to
flourish and to spread into a national debate.

To bourgeois culture, then, in all its dimensions, the department stores posed serious problems, problems the stores
themselves could afford to ignore only at their peril. Their
presence had given way to fears and doubts and anxieties
and grievances, and these would have to be dispelled if the
future of the department store was to be a secure one. For an
enterprise like the Bon Marché, the largest and quintessential
grand magasin in France, the matter was especially acute, and
thus the Boucicauts and their successors once more were
obliged to turn their energies towards seeking accommodation—this time through selling the idea of the department
store itself.

A MODEL COMMUNITY

In combatting its critics, the Bon Marché was not afraid to
meet the polemicists headlong. It too talked of progress and
unavoidable casualties, although it placed greater emphasis
on the new system's benefits than on the old system's failings. Department stores, it pointed out, had lowered prices
and had democratized luxury. They had been built by men of

humble origins whose hard work, genius, and integrity had led to their success. They had stimulated new industries and regulated production. They were, on the whole, good for the nation.[57] Yet arguments of this sort could carry only so far, and in the main the Boucicauts and the directors never relied heavily on disputation alone. They seemed to sense that the league and its proponents could always be contained and that their principal efforts should be directed at the more ambivalent sentiments of the public they served. What was important was to overcome fears by revealing a department store world in which little of value would be seen to be lost.

This was another reason why creating an image of the Bon Marché as a national institution was such a basic part of the firm's public relations strategy. Service to the community had always been part of the Bon Marché's identification. Following the siege of Paris in 1870-1871, the Boucicauts had turned their store into a distribution center for food stuffs sent over from England. Several years later they had begun the practice of distributing milk to the poor of the quarter. They and their successors had always shown a largesse toward calls for subscriptions or requests for contributions. Twenty-two thousand francs had been subscribed in the name of the Bon Marché to the liberation loan of 1872. Fourteen thousand francs had been sent in 1875 for flood relief in the Midi. Thirty-six hundred francs had been contributed to welcoming ceremonies for visiting Russian sailors in 1893.[58] All this had been done, not to mention the public donations in Madame Boucicaut's will. But being an institution in store ideology had always meant far more. It had meant that the Bon Marché was as traditional a part of French culture as the Arc de Triomphe or even Notre Dame, and as integral a part of the bourgeois way of life as *lycées* or reception days. The Bon

[57] See, for example, B.M., *Note présentée par la maison du Bon Marché à messieurs les députés composant la commission nommée pour l'examen de la loi des patentes* (approx. 1891). Arguments of this sort could also be found in house pamphlets of the *Historique des magasins de Bon Marché* genre.

[58] The personnel were usually solicited (enjoined?) to participate in these offerings.

Marché was a bearer of French bourgeois values, a representative of the civilization from which it had sprung. This was
the message that the store carried forth in its *agendas*, its illustrated cards, and its world's fair pavillions.

Indeed nearly all of the imagery for selling consumption
was double-edged to sell the department store too. For
example, by enveloping their store in an aura of fantasy the
Boucicauts projected a world of magic and drama in the very
midst of their bureaucratic machine. Enchantment and bureaucracy were not incompatible by Bon Marché terms. The
one did not disappear with the coming of the other but simply altered its form in accordance with its surroundings. In
fact it was that part of the Bon Marché most symbolic of a
mass, rationalized order that was most wrapped in an ambiance of mystique.

This was the case of the *blanc*. An artificial exposition to
regulate the market and the most extensively planned event
of the store, the *blanc* was simultaneously the most breathtaking moment in the Bon Marché calendar.[59] It was also the
case in regard to deliveries, another operation of substantial
rationalization turned by the House into an exceptional occasion. There was an element of splendor and romance in the
Bon Marché wagons that filled the streets of Paris with their
carefully groomed horses, their coachmen in top hats and
great coats, and their garçons in livery. Even more, there was
an element of ritualization, a sense of pomp and ceremony in
the loading of the wagons and their outward processions—
or at least this was the image that the House intended to convey. The stables themselves were huge stately buildings with
decorated ceilings and hanging portico lamps. They were a
scheduled feature on the daily House tours. When it was
suggested that the store engage an outside delivery service
rather than maintain one of its own, the first point of opposition was that "the Bon Marché cavalry is part of the historical

---

[59] The Bon Marché went to such lengths to produce this effect as to wrap
the *blanc* in a mythology of its own, store history attributing the origins of the
sale to a legendary moment of Boucicaut inspiration prompted by a snow-
bound Paris.

tradition of the House; it is known and appreciated by Parisians and by foreigners who regard it with interest in the streets of Paris."[60]

Dress codes, livery for garçons, the accent on service, and evening concerts were all means of softening apprehensions over compromised standards in an era of mass production and mass distribution. The same might be said of the design of the House. Architecturally the Bon Marché was part of a nineteenth-century movement to create new kinds of structures for new kinds of purposes, a new city architecture for masses and for motion. Iron and glass had been used extensively, not to satisfy the architect's whimsy but because they were so functionally suitable to the needs of a *grand magasin*. In this respect the Bon Marché was as much an experiment in big-city design for an industrial age as were the first railroad stations or the new central markets. New technology, new forms, and new functions were all coalescing into an architecture very unlike what had existed in the past.

But as daring as Boucicaut and Eiffel had been in their exposure of iron, they had not been content to leave matters at that. Function alone was not yet suitable to determine form and design. Or rather function, as Boucicaut saw it, had a multiplicity of meanings, and thus stone was as necessary a medium as iron and glass, pediments as necessary as thin metal columns, palatial reading rooms as necessary as light open bays. This too made the Bon Marché very much a part of the architecture of its century, not simply in its eclecticism but in its deeply felt need that bourgeois buildings should represent more than the purpose for which they were intended. Like banks, railroad stations, and later hotels, each of which repeated the same monumental effects, the department store offered itself as something far more distinguished, far more traditional, and far more transcendent than the mass materialistic apparatus it had, in fact, become.

Quality and the department store were associated in still other ways. *Blanc* catalogues frequently carried the inscrip-

---

[60] B.M., *Conseils Généraux*, 12 June 1895.

tion that all its articles were hand-made. Ready-to-wear catalogues noted that "an extreme care is given to the needlework
of all ready-made objects at the Bon Marché, and whether a
lady chooses something already made, or whether she orders
something to be made, she will come across the same taste,
the same solidity, and the same advantages."

Propaganda of this sort did not neglect the children. One
card series was devoted to the level of craftsmanship to be
expected of Bon Marché goods. There were pictures of skilled
artisans working at their trades while a small insert showed
the Bon Marché department where these products were carried. On the reverse side the usual House picture was replaced with a history of the craft, ending with the suggestion
that the finest lace or the finest crystal could be found at the
Bon Marché. The Industrial Revolution, apparently, had
never been heard of.

Mottos were one more means of overcoming prejudices.
The Bon Marché fell back on the aphorism *"loyauté fait ma
force"* (honesty is my strength), not only because it sounded
nice, but because it was a direct reference to *concurrence dé-
loyale* (dishonest competition), two of the dirtiest words in the
French commercial language. In general the term related to
pre-revolutionary days when French trade was rigidly regulated so that one merchant would not profit at the expense of
another. Any illegal diversion of clientele was *concurrence dé-
loyale*, and although the guild system underlying it disappeared with the Revolution, aspects of the concept continued
well into the nineteenth century. Small shopkeepers, who
saw the two words as synonymous, were always quick to ac-
cuse the department stores of playing dirty. But there were
also many Frenchmen who simply continued to identify advertising with puffery and who consequently believed that
second-rate merchandise lay behind the imagery. So the
motto of honesty implied far more than just integrity (although this too was never minimized). Probity and correct-
ness reflected not only on practices, but on the goods themselves, and thus on the whole concept of quality within a
mass-marketing system.

Virtue also became a Bon Marché trademark. Especially sensitive to charges of immorality because of its large Catholic and provincial clientele, the Bon Marché did its best to appear as chaste as a convent. This is why the House was so strict with its employees, why it meddled in their personal lives, and why it allotted so much of its energy to overseeing their moral formation. Not surprisingly, the greatest care was devoted to protecting the virtue of the women, primarily through the medium of segregation. Women ate in separate dining rooms, most women salesclerks were concentrated in a few departments, and, aside from the library, live-in arrangements completely separated the two sexes. When in 1899 the offices were at last opened to female employees, it was decided that the women would be placed in a separate bureau.

For those persons not aware of these conditions, the store readily spread the message. Boasts of strict surveillance were made at the parliamentary inquest of 1883. The *agenda* of 1889 told of special care given young female employees and of how young men lodged by the store received "a care for their moral education as well as for their intellectual cultivation." Employee regulations, apparently available for public consumption, carried lists of live-in requirements and rules of decorum for waiting on customers. Concerts again became a House showcase, this time reflecting in the performers' cultivation the reign of respectability at the Bon Marché. As a result, the firm acquired the reputation as the most virtuous of the new stores, Zola noting that "today the people of the quarter raise their daughters to enter the Bon Marché."[61]

Imagery of this sort was particularly important because it was here that Bon Marché public relations found their most pervasive role. Above all, the selling of the department store was to depend on the uses of paternalism for external socialization ends. To a degree this was done to deflect the criticisms so sharply levelled against employee conditions in the

---

[61] The reference here was to the daughters of the petite bourgeoisie. Zola, NAF10278, p. 50

grands magasins.[62] One might even say that never was the intrusion of outside attacks on internal decision-making so evident as it was in regard to House programs. The pension plan for *ouvriers*, for instance, was largely a consequence of these assaults. As one director noted at the time of its adoption, "we will be happy to give a new proof of the interest that the great houses, so unjustly attacked, bear for their employees."[63]

But internal House bonds were also caught up in the far broader question of a changeover to a mass, bureaucratized society. In the end, the very idea of a greater Bon Marché household was so essential to public relations because it went to the heart of public uneasiness over the passing of traditions and of community values. This, more than the critiques over employee conditions, explains the emphasis placed on House programs. Paternalism, in the Bon Marché manner, identified the new commercial system with a way of life clearly in accordance with bourgeois ideals. In the end, too, it would not be unjust to suggest that much of the Boucicauts' paternalism was designed precisely with this effect in mind.

The means by which the Bon Marché focused public attention on its internal community were nearly unlimited. House tours passed through the employee living quarters. Regulations pamphlets carried details about paternalistic programs. At world's fairs, beginning as early as the Paris exposition of 1878, the Bon Marché entered social economy competitions. In turn, the medals the programs invariably won were announced in catalogues or on the backs of picture cards.

[62] It is to be remembered that this was also a period of intense agitation on the part of the employees' Chambre Syndicale, which was not above carrying its campaign to the public, primarily through posters that the middle-class eye could not necessarily avoid. In many ways the message of these posters resembled some of the arguments of the league. Consumers were reminded that their evening shopping lengthened the work day and separated families at mealtime. Claims that electric lighting concealed defects in merchandise made long hours a matter of consumer interest as well as of consumer complicity. See, for example, Préfecture de Police, Ba 153, "Manifeste A La Population Parisienne," 1 February 1888.

[63] B.M., AGO, 24 August 1891; 25 August 1892.

Principally, however, the public learned of household relationships through three media. One was the *agendas*—the Bon Marché publication most closely associated with the idea of a larger bourgeois community—and another was the special House pamphlets such as *A Visit to the Bon Marché* or *An Historical Account of the Bon Marché*.

Thirdly, there was the press, whose collaboration with the store has already been noted. Magazines like *L'Illustration* and *Le Monde Illustré* did not refrain from printing articles quite likely written by Bon Marché people, and occasionally favorable accounts were reprinted for House distribution.[64] Just how deeply this collaboration ran is difficult to determine. On the one hand, department stores were legitimate news, and many journalists favorably inclined towards the stores arrived at their conclusions through sentiments of their own. Yet the Bon Marché also had powerful means to influence publications. There was, of course, the power of advertisements. There was also the power of payoffs from House coffers. Direct evidence of this exists in the case of an article in an American journal.[65] Very possibly payoffs of this sort were also part of the 190,000 francs spent during 1891 and 1892 for "various work that had to be done and various persons employed for the defense of the Interests of the *grands magasins*."[66] Surveillance of the press was extensive. Following the death of Madame Boucicaut, the House prepared a twelve-page document classifying over 250 newspaper articles on the subject. In any case, the Bon Marché generally could rely on favorable reviews, even to the extent that its own image of employee relationships was directly echoed in press accounts.

[64] In 1891 5000 copies of a highly favorable article on the Bon Marché in *L'Illustration*, 10 August 1889, were prepared for distribution to persons taking the house tour. B.M., *Conseils Généraux*, 23 September 1891. Excerpts from this article were also published in the 1890 *agenda*. In 1892 it was similarly decided to distribute 2000 copies of Cucheval-Clarigny's *Etude sur le Bon Marché*. B.M., *Conseils Généraux*, 20 June 1892.

[65] In 1892 the council voted 200 francs "to pay an article on the house in the American journal 'Boot and Shoe Recorder.' " B.M., *Conseils Généraux*, 27 June 1892.

[66] *Ibid.*, 13 July 1891; 14 June 1892.

It simply became impossible to come into contact with Bon Marché news or with Bon Marché materials without learning about Bon Marché paternalism. Often this meant merely a straightforward presentation of House programs. *Agendas*, for example, printed pictures of music, fencing, and language lessons, of concerts and eating halls, and of live-in arrangements for the employees. Occasionally, as in 1889, they carried extracts from the statutes of the provident fund and statistics on participants, while information on the programs was a standard feature of the special house pamphlets.

On another level it meant the projection of a Boucicaut image that combined philanthropy with commercial genius and that portrayed the store's founders not only as creators of Paris' greatest emporium but also as creators of a great social institution. Thus the 1889 *agenda* carried a biography of Boucicaut (reprinted from the *Dictionnaire Larousse*), introducing him as the founder of "a great establishment at once philanthropic and commercial." The biography then proceeded, in all but a few lines, to recount his life as one of benevolent deeds towards his employees and his community. Alongside was a biography of Marguerite that concentrated entirely on the foundation of the *société* and the pension fund, and especially on the details of her testament. Together they were followed by a "Notice on the Bon Marché Store" that began:

"The Bon Marché is an *Oeuvre* whose entire existence, since its foundation, marks an epoch in the history of Paris and also in the social history of the century.

"It is one of the most beautiful creations of contemporary progress. And this creation, this marvel, is due to the genius of one man."

Further on the notice remarked:

"One cannot repeat it too much: M. Boucicaut has not simply founded a powerful and steadfast commercial house; he has founded a humanitarian work, a social institution."

Similarly, discussions of store history and paternalism in House pamphlets proclaimed that "the Bon Marché has thus become as famous for its social work as for its commercial development," or that Boucicaut "did not consider his employees as instruments but as associates for whom he ought to be a friend and benefactor," or that "the fate of *nouveautés* clerks has thus been happily transformed in every regard; if they wish to make their way in the House, they find themselves surrounded with respect [and] care, while their benefactor has secured for them a means of subsistence in their old age." Meanwhile *Dictionnaire Larousse* biographies were only one example of the tendency of the press to eulogize the Boucicauts and to make of them two of France's best known philanthropists. According to *L'Illustration* and *Le Monde Illustré*, the Boucicauts had founded a "model philanthropic institution."[67] Tributes to their paternalism were especially to be found following memorable House occasions, such as the creation of the retirement fund or the reading of Madame Boucicaut's will.

The picture that came to be drawn was one of a greater Bon Marché household—imagery that placed the firm squarely within bourgeois business traditions. As on the internal plane, the House always retained a personal element—the idea of a Maison Boucicaut—even well after the passing of the founders. There was never a semblance of corporate anonymity. The Boucicaut image could be found nearly everywhere, and in later years directors made a point of picturing themselves as Boucicaut associates, and as the heirs and continuators of their predecessors' ideas. The structure of ownership and its family character were made public knowledge.[68]

Even more so, *grande famille* rhetoric passed into the public record. Referring to Boucicaut's death, a *Notice Historique* remarked "he was taken from the affection of his House, one could say of his *grande famille*, the 26 December, 1877." On the occasion of the founding of the pension fund *Le Temps* wrote: "Madame Boucicaut has an adopted family: all the devoted agents who work with her for the renown and the for-

[67] "Les agrandissements," *Le Monde Illustré*, 9 October 1880; *L'Illustration*, 9 October 1880.

[68] See, for example, B.M., *Historique des magasins du Bon Marché* (approx. 1911), pp. 12-15.

tune of the Bon Marché."[69] After Madame Boucicaut's death, Cucheval-Clarigny noted "she passed away gently the 8 December 1887 . . . leaving to this Bon Marché personnel, whom she had made into her family, a brilliant token of her affection and her generosity."[70]

Family imagery became practically routine in coverage of the House. After one concert a *Gil Blas* review began by remarking "thanks to the generous initiative of Madame Boucicaut the four thousand Bon Marché employees, who form a tightly united *grande famille*, can enjoy distractions as pleasant as those of a more elevated rank." *Le Mot d'Ordre*'s review of the same concert reminded that "everyone knows the solicitude Madame Boucicaut has for her employees, but what many do not know is the tight solidarity that unites the members of this numberous family."[71] Later, covering *livre d'or* ceremonies, *L'Evénement* wrote of the "confident solidarity which reigns at the Bon Marché and makes of M. Fillot the head of a great, laborious family." A House banquet celebrating Fillot's fiftieth anniversary with the firm was referred to by *Le Figaro* as "this family feast."[72]

It would be a mistake, however, to see in such rhetoric a portrait of a Bon Marché household existing in spite of its rationalized setting. The relationship between the two presented to the public was a far more complex one that bore on the fullest implications of the store's public image. In effect,

[69] Reprinted in "Une donation du quatre millions, "*L'Univers Illustré*, 30 October 1886.

[70] Cucheval-Clarigny, *Etude*, pp. 22-23.

[71] "Une soirée au 'Bon Marché,' " *Gil Blas*, 29 November 1887; *Le Mot d'Ordre*, 29 November 1887. Two years earlier, the editor of *Gil Blas* had written to Karcher saying that unexpected late work had kept him from attending the concert. He then said that if the House were to send him an account, he would be happy to publish it. B.M., Letter of *Rédacteur en Chef* of *Gil Blas* to Karcher, 28 November 1885. The *Nouveau Monde*, which also referred to the Bon Marché family in their review of the November 1887 concert, sent a copy of their article to Karcher accompanied with a request to have the council approve advertising in their journal. B.M., Letter of *Le Nouveau Monde* to Karcher, 3 December 1887.

[72] *L'Evénement*, 8 May 1907; "Un cinquentaire," *Le Figaro*, 13 September 1911.

the real object of admiration was the Bon Marché itself, and all that the Boucicauts had accomplished, so that paternalism was never pictured as other than an especially bright feature in a more complete and integral work. For instance, no distinction was made between paternalism and an internal organization where salary and promotion were predicated on individual effort and talent. Each was viewed as part of the same commendable inspiration marking all of Boucicaut's actions in favor of his employees. Likewise, there was a tendency to regard as a whole paternalism and meritocracy, on the one hand, Boucicaut's merchandising innovations, on the other. All flowed quite naturally from a single Boucicaut conception where commercial genius and the founding of a social institution were inextricably mixed. Herein lay the significance of Bon Marché imagery: its ability to bring together in one comprehensive impression all the disjointed pieces of nineteenth-century French bourgeois culture. The Bon Marché was a machine, but it was also a family; it was change but it was also tradition; and there was no clearcut distinction between one sphere or the other.

Bon Marché paternalism in the public realm thus took on the same association as it did in the private one, the concept of household now inseparable from its new business setting. Indeed the very character of paternalism as the Boucicauts had structured it was central to the whole public message. More than the measure of House benevolence and traditionalism, Bon Marché paternalism became the measure of Bon Marché success. Vaunted for its solidary and participatory effects, paternalism was presented as the organizational glue that made the store work. Accounts of the House moved readily from a *grande famille* image to that of a beehive or an ant colony, as though the one were interchangeable with the other. They depicted a powerful organization that was enormously successful because each man performed his specialized task as best he could, linking his own destiny to that of the firm. House publications solemnly remarked "it was thus that Boucicaut stimulated the energy of all around him; and, seconded by the devotion and esteem of his assistants, he was able, by his commercial genius, to inaugurate with success an undertaking at once benevolent and magnificent." In like manner, Cucheval-Clarigny wrote: "M. Boucicaut rested the success of his House on a tight solidarity between *patron* and employee, and he was convinced that all the advantages secured the latter cemented this solidarity for the greater good of all."[73]

Thus the inner world of the Bon Marché was seen not only to be satisfying in itself, but to turn to the material benefit of employee, store, and bourgeois public alike. It was House solidarity in the Bon Marché fashion that brought prosperity to those who worked and who managed the machine, and a consumer's paradise to those who shopped in it. Household, efficiency, consumerism, wealth, and opportunity were all sequential links along one single chain. In Bon Marché imagery the family traditions of the French business community had not only survived, but had become transformed into the central ingredient of a mass bureaucratic market.[74]

And House solidarity brought one thing further, "a new conception," as the Bon Marché put it, "of the relations between capital and labor."[75] In the Bon Marché vision there was no place for class discord or conflict, no place for that nagging bourgeois nightmare that its century of change, with all its conglomerations of money and men, its factories and now its huge service bureaucracies, might be carrying within it the seeds of its collapse. The Bon Marché world was a harmonious blend of order, authority, cooperation, and social unity—or solidarity as the bourgeoisie interpreted the word at the end of the nineteenth century. The very repetitiveness with which the term appeared in Bon Marché writings, especially in its press coverage, was symptomatic of the power that such an image held over the collective bourgeois mind.

[73] B.M., *Historique de magasins du Bon Marché* (approx. 1911), p. 5; Cucheval-Clarigny, *L'Etude*, p. 18.

[74] This view is implicit in House pamphlets, in Cucheval-Clarigny, and, to a degree, in the *L'Illustration* article of 1889.

[75] B.M., *Au Bon Marché Nouveautés, Maison A. Boucicaut Paris: Anglo-French Exhibition London* (1908), p. 33.

Perhaps not every bourgeois felt comfortable with *La Nation*'s assertion that Madame Boucicaut had been a great experimenter in "the large and fecund theories of socialist doctrines." But undoubtedly few would have argued when the Bon Marché boasted: "Is this not truly socialism in the right meaning of the word, the best form in which can be clothed the association of capital and labor?" Or as Fillot expressed it in his 1912 speech warning against open share sales:

"When we must defend your interests that are constantly menaced, we do not fail to show all the advantages the House offers from the social point of view, and also to bring out that the diffusion of our shares among the personnel and the arrangements made to preserve this [situation] create an association where capital and labor agree and co-operate towards the same end. Very often we have had the impression that these arguments are fruitful."[76]

Ultimately, then, the Bon Marché turned employee socialization completely inside out, revealing the creation of organization men to be public virtues as well as private achievements.

So public relations, in Bon Marché hands, portrayed a department store world far from the menace that many envisioned. They demonstrated that change of this sort could come about without a decline in standards, without a direct threat to the morals and order of bourgeois society, without a suppression of those bourgeois values and relations that seemed, on the surface, to have little in common with a mass, industrialized age. In a way it was as if nothing had been changed, as if the Bon Marché were simply a part of a traditional scene. Even in pictures of the building—the consummate symbol of the power and energy of the new commercial system—a strong *gemeinschaftlich* element could be found in the foreground, where couples or families walked together, or where men on horseback stopped to shake hands with

---

[76] B.M., *Historique de magasins du Bon Marché* (approx. 1911), p. 36; *La Nation*, 27 December 1887; B.M., AGE, 12 July 1912.

passing acquaintances. Indeed if the underlying current of the new stores was one of increasing rationalization, on the surface the practice of affairs remained personal and communal. As early as 1875, Paul Leroy-Beaulieu noted that "these stores are not only places of sale, they also become places of gathering: women meet each other here as formerly men did at the barbershop." Later Dubuisson remarked: "It is necessary that she [the client] consider the *grand magasin* as a second home, larger, more beautiful, more luxurious than the other, where, as the case may be, she will be able to pass all the time that the concerns of her private life do not take from her, and where she will find about her only friendly faces. . . ."[77]

Thus it was that another Bon Marché community, this time of clientele and store, came into being. On the House side it was fostered by letters of invitation sent prior to sales, by invitations to join the greater Bon Marché household at its concerts and at its fencing competitions, and by an overriding concept of a "clientele fidèle" that had become another means of turning the store into a part of the daily pattern of living. The public response was to be seen in the letter of the woman who wrote the store in December 1887:

"I learned from the newspaper of Mme Boucicaut's death. I have been one of your own for such a long time that it is not possible for me to express to you the share I take in this sad event. Thank God, to what I can tell, the House will not perish. It will, I hope, be you who will continue the beautiful creation of M. Boucicaut to the equal profit of us, your clients. . . ."

It could also be seen in the remarks of Caslot that followed the destruction of a new building by fire thirty years later:

"We also have a tribute of thanks to address to our clients who, in this circumstance, have given us numerous testimonies by sympathy, certain ones even declaring that if they had been somewhat unfaithful to the House, they will

[77] Paul Leroy-Beaulieu, "Les grands magasins universels et les petits détaillants," *L'Economiste Français* (25 December 1875), p. 803; Dubuisson, *Voleuses*, p. 41.

be more than ever attached to it after the undeserved misfortune that has befallen it."[78]

And of still greater consequence was that all this pertained to a deeper side, a dimension beyond the proposal that a traditional way of life had not disappeared with the coming of the department store. At bottom the real goal of store public relations, as it had been of internal socialization, was to suggest a new concept of the bourgeois community, one that resided within, and was intrinsically a part of, a rationalized, mass, and dynamic context. In the end, if everything the Bon Marché represented was to be accepted, it was precisely because the Bon Marché itself was to be perceived as a model of a new world where the rational and the enchanting, the organizational and the familial, the efficient and the personal, and the concentrated and the integrated were all cut alike from the same fabric.

[78] B.M., AGO, 29 August 1916.

Conclusion

As ONE MIGHT EXPECT, time and events eventually took their toll of the system erected by the Boucicauts and followed so religiously by their successors. Already by the end of the prewar period the desire for greater share liquidity was a majority sentiment, and once Narcisse Fillot had departed from the directorship, carrying with him his immense personal and traditional authority, the special assembly gave its assent to open share sales.[1] Then the war came, bringing with it four years of duress and strains that led to a radicalization of commercial employees as well as of workers. So once again, as in 1869, the firm found itself caught up in a general protest movement; and in the fall of 1919 a strike occurred at the Bon Marché, the first since the creation of the new store fifty years previously. The strike lasted several weeks—at first it spread to four-fifths of the personnel—and in the end it turned violent before the last few thousand strikers capitulated with no immediate noticeable gains.[2]

Meanwhile other changes had occurred at the Bon Marché during the war years that were to have an even greater impact on the future of the store. One of these was the decision to expand into branch stores.[3] In July 1918 the special assem-

[1] Fillot retired in 1913. The decision for open share sales came at the AGE of 10 July 1914.

[2] Among the strikers' demands were salary increases according to the cost of living, an increase in pensions, the establishment of a "discipline council" to be composed partly of personnel, an eight-hour day, fifteen days of vacation with pay, promotion according to seniority, and promotion of auxiliaries to employee status after two months of service. For details of the strike and preceding events see Préfecture de Police, Ba 1389; Delon, *Employés*, pp. 79-83.

[3] In the last years before the war, the Bon Marché had become increasingly concerned over the growing competition for the provincial market from department store chains like the Société Paris France and the Société des

bly approved a request of the directors to establish a branch store at Vichy. The following year plans were laid to open a store at Algiers, with still other projects in gestation. In the meantime the Bon Marché was making plans to rebuild the new Sèvres-Bac building which had burned to the ground in 1916. The mood at the House was optimistic and ambitious, but this also created problems because ambitions required capital, indeed a good deal more than the firm had on hand in reserves or could hope to amortize during construction. For the first time since 1880 it was necessary to contemplate a new share issue. This in turn raised the question of changing the organization of the firm to a *société anonyme* or limited liability corporation.

The question was not a new one—it had been considered once before in 1910 during the revision of store statutes. Then, however, it had been simply a matter of administration. There had been some feeling that the enormous growth in operations and in sales volume since 1880 required an *anonyme* format where directors would be free to concentrate on day-to-day business, a Council of Administration placed above the directorate assuming responsibility for the general course of affairs. There had also been some feeling that the *anonyme* form would provide real surveillance over year-end accounts in contrast to the rubber-stamp role of the surveillance commission in a *société en commandite*, and that it would alleviate the problem of recruiting future directors who in the *commandite* form held positions of financial responsibility. But in 1910 the proposal remained a dead issue. Majority sentiment still preferred tight control over the totality of affairs by a single group of men. Above all, 1910 remained a time when tradition was the final arbiter, when men like Fillot feared that any tampering with the organization as it presently stood would be a leap into the dark.[4]

Ten years later, however, matters were different. Fillot's re-

---

Nouvelles Galeries. Moreover in 1912 the Printemps had opened its first branch store at Deauville.

[4] B.M., AGE, 11 March 1910.

tirement and the vote for open transfer had created an irreversible breach in the argument for tradition and for the status quo. Arguments for an *anonyme* were also far more telling, now that the firm was committed to expansion into branch stores and now that there was the pressing need for greater capitalization. By 1920 the forces for change were again ascendant, and in the summer of that year the final remnants of the familial form of ownership that Madame Boucicaut had set up in 1880 were abandoned, the Bon Marché converted into a *société anonyme*.[5]

Despite the deep changes that occurred in these years, and the fears of oldliners like Fillot over their consequences, there remained nonetheless a strong current of continuity at the Bon Marché. The war had brought a reaffirmation of the paternalistic tradition, the House deciding almost immediately to authorize grants to wives and children of mobilized personnel and to employees and workers temporarily laid off. Directors pledged one-half their monthly allocation and administrators 100 francs a month each to the Fillot Foundation. Later, money was transferred to this program from the pension fund (over 600 employees were to die in the war). Packages were sent to employees at the front and grants to families at home continued for all four years. In 1917 a new program was established for pregnant employees, granting 200 francs for a rest period before delivery and additional payments after birth to nurse the newborn at home. Still more grants to employees and families came with the ending of the war. Altogether, the House spent more than 10,000,000 francs in some form or other on its employees and workers because of the war experience.[6]

[5] *Ibid.*, 8 July 1920. A review of the financial reasons for this change can be found in these minutes.

[6] B.M., AGO, 4 September 1914; 29 August 1916; 28 August 1917; 28 August 1919; B.M., Printed Review of Programs, 1919. The rhetoric of paternalism during these years was as rich as ever. At the 4 September 1914 meeting, for example, Caslot (now head director) spoke of being "inspired by the traditions of paternal benevolence of M. and Mme. Boucicaut and our predecessors at the head of the House" and of how the assembly's decision had produced a "profound alleviation" of everyone's fears so that "today we can

The strike itself broke only partially with the patterns of the past. There was the incident of the gathering about Madame Boucicaut's statue and there was the incident the following day when 2,000 employees marched to the tomb of the founders. For its part the House responded predictably, reacting severely towards strike leaders and those identified with violence, welcoming back the remainder as children gone astray: "it was towards [the personnel] that the efforts of agitators were directed. . . . These events have not modified our solicitous sentiments for our collaborators, we have not wished that they become the victims of a wild moment they have since regretted."[7] The pension plan was reorganized to counter inflation through a twenty percent deduction from the profits—precisely the same principle that had guided Boucicaut forty-five years earlier when he created the provident fund.[8] Special provisions were made to facilitate employee participation in a new share issue, and in turn, 1,800 employees and workers did buy shares.

Even after the corporative firm had been adopted and outside managers brought in, the House continued to make an effort to preserve the ambiance of an internal store commu-

---

say that a single thought moves the hearts of all those who in some way are attached to the Bon Marché and that the House can count, more than ever, on the devotion of everyone." The decision at the August 1916 meeting was hailed as "a new proof of the manner by which solidarity between capital and labor is understood by the Bon Marché."

[7] B.M., AGO, 4 November 1920.

[8] At the special assembly where this reorganization was announced, a speaker quoted directly from Boucicaut's earlier remarks, noting as well that the personnel would now be reminded that "its fate is intimately tied to that of the shareholder, that the pension and capital figures we hope to constitute will rise more or less according to whether our profits rise or fall." The reorganization was as follows: All deductions were to go to the provident fund, although part of the amount would then be placed with the Caisse Nationale des Retraites pour la Vieillesse. These latter funds, along with contributions of half a franc a day by employees and one franc by seconds, department, office, and service heads (who were now participants in the programs) would be used to constitute an additional pension program alongside the older house program. Ouvriers were also to participate in this new program, as well as being admitted to the provident fund. B.M., AGE, 8 July 1920.

nity. When Albert Galicier—the first outsider—was admitted to the Council of Administration in the early 1920s, he made a contribution to the Fillot Foundation.[9] Another manager drawn from the outside, Frédéric Manaut, upon ascending to the presidency in 1930, assured the Council that he would "take inspiration in the performance of his duties from the unforgettable memory of Monsieur and Madame Boucicaut, the venerated founders of the House, and from the example of his [Manaut's] predecessors."[10] In 1931 Legion of Honor awards for three members of management were celebrated with a banquet to which representatives from all ranks of the Bon Marché were invited, an event that occasioned frequent references by Manaut to *"la grande famille du* Bon Marché."[11] Obviously, if the faces were new, the spirit was the same. The corporation may have accentuated the separation of ownership and control, but it did not collide with the old ethos among management of belonging to an institution larger than oneself, one with traditions, and one to which the manager was expected to feel a sense of loyalty while pursuing dynamic and rationalized business policies.[12] Nor had it overturned the old need of top management to play upon such sentiments in order to instill loyalty in their subordinates. In the face of the day-to-day problems of running their enterprises, the interests of corporative managers and the business leaders of the past were not all that far apart.

What had changed, then, by 1920, was not the underlying character of relationships at the Bon Marché, but the context in which they would continue to occur. After the experience of the First World War and the events of 1919, authority relations would never again be quite the same. After the structural reorganization in 1920, the situation of management would undergo a shift. But what would follow would evolve out of what had come before, not abandon it. Nineteen

[9] B.M., *Conseil d'Administration*, 8 December 1922.

[10] *Ibid.*, 22 July 1930.

[11] B.M., *Allocation prononcée par M. Frédéric Manaut*, May 1931.

[12] During the late 1920s the Bon Marché engaged in a self-conscious "rationalization" program.

twenty marked the end of the transitional phase, not the end of a separate era.

Still, the sense of a turning point was there in 1920, especially because of yet further changes. By the 1920s the Bon Marché no longer stood alone as the Parisian department store extraordinaire. There were new giants—especially the Printemps and the Galeries Lafayette—that were now as important as the House on the Left Bank. The Bon Marché was no longer the leader of the movement. In the 1920s the new Council discussed what the Galeries or the Samaritaine or the Printemps were doing, something that had never occurred in the minutes of prewar meetings. Meanwhile the very world of the department store was changing. There were now new challenges, new competitors, new difficulties. In the minds of some, the postwar period signaled an end to the golden years of earlier times.[13] The department store was an institution that had come to stay. For many people it was to become, even more than in the past, the very embodiment of their culture. But it was no longer on the cutting edge of society as it had been before the war.

So as France entered the postwar period, the Bon Marché too was entering a new stage in her history. What came after was in many ways shaped by what had come before, but in many ways it was also a very different history. The department store continued to be a force in society, but its principal contribution was essentially a part of its past. For these reasons it seems appropriate to end the story here.

Stories may end abruptly, but conclusions do not, and, at the risk of some repetition, there are still some words that remain to be said. This book began with the premise that the department store was a creation of bourgeois culture, both capturing and threatening many things that culture stood for. The size and the precision and the ingenuity with which the enterprise worked sprang directly from values and impulses within the burgeoisie, as did the consumer culture to which

[13] Pasdermadjian, *Grand magasin*.

the department store gave birth. Because everything about it was so implicit in bourgeois drives and ambitions, the department store became a fundamental part of the bourgeoisie's world. If few had envisioned that they were building a mass, bureaucratic society, when it arrived most recognized it as a creature of their own making.

Yet this was the rub. To recognize was one thing, to accept another. Throughout this narrative it has been my contention that bourgeois culture in France was divided within itself, not so much between upper and lower bourgeoisie or the forces of progress and stagnation as between two sets of values and attitudes, one that drove it to create what the other was bound to regret. If it was a culture that gave way to rationalized structures like the department store, it was also a culture that remained impregnated with strong relationships between family and business and one that believed in individual achievement. If it was a culture that carried within it a materialistic streak leading inexorably to a cult of consumption, it was also a culture whose sense of distinctions, self-restraints, and standards saw in much of this reason for fear and for horror.

The department store brought out bourgeois schizophrenia. There was a side to the bourgeois personality that was mirrored and fulfilled in the *grand magasin*; but there was also a side subverted by the bureaucratization of business and middle-class careers, and by the emergence of a mass consumer society. This was an essential dilemma that bourgeois culture had come to face by the end of the century. In an era where bourgeois gain appeared to be bourgeois loss, how could the culture commit itself to change without, in effect, relinquishing its past?

The significance of the Bon Marché and its history lay in its ability to resolve this dilemma by redefining traditions to fit new social contexts, thereby reconciling the divergent strains within bourgeois culture. Internally, a new idea of the firm integrated family values with bureaucratic realities. White-collar workers were fitted into bureaucratic work slots in ways that retained their loyalty to the firm and its goals and assured their identity with middle-class values. Managers were formed who did not contradict the family origins of entrepreneurial firms. A sense of an internal House community was associated with the workings of a dynamic and rationalized system. All this was accomplished through innovative uses of paternalistic traditions, uses that eased owners, and later managers, into new business roles that they would now have to occupy. The method was systematic but almost elegant in its simplicity. Household relationships were redesigned to build an organizational work force of managers and clerks. The new relationships in turn provided the basis for the reorientation of the family firm. One followed from another just as tradition became imbedded in change. Externally, the projection of an image where the old and the new were inextricably intertwined—again based largely on imaginative uses of Bon Marché paternalism—revealed that one set of values need not disappear with the triumph of the other.

The story of the Bon Marché is a fascinating one in its own right, but it is also one that transcends its history, bearing on the very manner by which the French bourgeoisie pulled themselves into the twentieth century. Part of a process of change that was less a watershed than an altering of course, the Bon Marché helped to set the pattern for the sort of society that was to evolve in the future. It was a society that was able to accommodate to change, but one that did so in accordance with its past, thus making it a far more complex one than historical or sociological stereotypes have tended to allow.

It was a society that leaned in many directions. It was bureaucratic but it was also familial. It was a mass society, but it was also one that incorporated a sense of community and hierarchy. There was no *gemeinschaftlich/gesellschaftlich* shift, the modern carrying within it a strong element of traditionalism. There was no disenchantment in the Weberian sense, the world of rationality creating its own world of magical entrancement.

It was a society in which the concept of one big family as the Boucicauts defined it remained, with more or less sophistication, management's ideal, whether the language be that of the past or of human relations or of a perspective still more contemporary. It was a society where a managerial revolution was to build upon the restructured relationships of the family firm, carrying the Boucicaut model (with adaptations) into the corporation, just as the directors, as an intermediate step, had brought it into the *commandite*. It was a society where bourgeois ambitions and identities of the past were transmuted to fit an organizational setting. It was a society where public relations continued to picture a world in which things changed and yet time held still. It was a society sold to consumerism.

In the final sense, the Bon Marché story is one of adaptation, and thus one that reveals a bourgeois France different from what historians have offered us in the past. We have been told that French businessmen were inherently conservative and that the French family firm was an institution unsuitable for an era of expansion and innovation. We have also been told, in analyses that have built upon this perspective, that the French bourgeoisie entered this century hesitantly and reluctantly, that they were imprisoned by their past, and that it was only after two decades of crisis and collapse—largely resulting from a failure to accommodate to change—that they found within themselves the means to come to terms with their present.

The arguments have been persuasive, but only so long as they have limited us to seeing one side of the picture. Once we draw back all the curtains, once we open up the world of the creative and the successful as well as the evasive and the obsolete, we stumble upon a bourgeoisie that was drawn to its new century, that was fascinated by the transformations occurring about it, and that was capable of committing itself to these changes precisely because it learned how to do so without undermining its traditions. The bourgeoisie that I have described in this history were often troubled by the modern, but just as often they were captivated by it too. They could talk of immorality and decline, but they could also not take their eyes off their newest creation, they could not keep from marvelling at the size of its operations and the machine-like way in which it worked, they could not avoid delighting in the benefits it brought, nor could they deny that this was part of themselves. They were businessmen who clung to family values, but they were also businessmen whose family firms contained the secret, not the obstacle, to change. They were people who inhabited a world where the old persisted side by side with the new, but they did so less as a result of stalemate than reconciliation.

They were, in sum, a bourgeoisie whose strengths outweighed their weaknesses, and whose flexibility was greater than their rigidity. They, and the Third Republic they built, deserve better than they have known.

Appendix

THE BON MARCHÉ ARCHIVES

MORE THAN ANY OTHER MAJOR STORE in Paris, the Bon Marché has made a conscientious effort to preserve the documents and mementos of its past—in itself a significant reminder of the importance of tradition at the firm. Unfortunately these efforts have not always succeeded in preventing the loss or misplacement of important source materials for the historian. One problem has been the failure of the "central archives" to gather all historical documents from various services, offices, and departments, although, in some cases, for reasons of space or administrative policy, this has been necessary and has not resulted in serious loss or damage. Another problem has been the continual state of spatial flux common to all department stores. Reallocation of space to meet new office or service or merchandise demands has meant the packing, movement, and unpacking of the documents, always a hazardous procedure at best. Not long before my arrival in 1972, the main body of documents formerly constituting what the House called its "museum" had been hastily thrown into several large bins and moved to an unoccupied room. They remained in this state of disorder (and perhaps with some consequent damage) until I had the opportunity to reclassify them. Upon my departure the documents were moved once again, although this time to the Interior Architecture Department, whose chief, M. Simonnot, was concerned with preserving the collection as best as possible. There has also been the problem of sheer carelessness. For example, during my stay a trunk containing concert documents was placed to be thrown out with the trash. Fortunately it was rescued by M. Simonnot.

As a result there are some serious gaps in the Bon Marché collection. There is, for instance, nearly a total lack of correspondence or of personal writings by the Boucicaut family. At present only a handful of unimportant letters by Aristide Boucicaut exist at the store. Whether documents of this sort were ever confided to a Bon Marché archivist is not certain, although checks among the descendants of the Boucicauts and the families of important figures such as Plassard and Fillot have failed to turn up more than a few Boucicaut documents in these quarters as well. Nor have any administrative records before 1888 remained. For the later period the first three years of council meetings are missing, as well as the council records from the period 1912-1920. Financial records from before the war have, I was told, been destroyed (although in this case it is possible that the House simply preferred not to make these available to me). As for publicity documents, there are gaps in certain series such as the agendas, and very likely a number of special House publications have been lost too. What else once existed, only to disappear over the years, can only be surmised.

Nevertheless, House archives do contain a valuable collection of documents, and these have provided the major source materials for my study. Within what may be called the "central archives" four particular sets of records stand out. First, there are institutional documents. These range from statutes of the *sociétés* or the various paternalistic programs, to copies of Madame Boucicaut's will, to historical documents such as Boucicaut's purchase of the store in 1863, to individual documents regarding store programs for employees (including statistics on the funds).

Secondly, there are personal documents. There is, for instance, a dossier containing most of the speeches by Fillot or by others on special house occasions. Fillot documents also include the 1906 *livre d'or* and other records relative to it. Then there are the Karcher letters to Madame Boucicaut (and some to Gouin), and Karcher has also left behind a chronology of what he considered to be the important events in store history from the earliest indications of the store's existence to 1888. Among other personal documents of particular interest are copies of several speeches by Boucicaut and Gouin concerning the provident fund, the 1878 letter of Boucicaut *fils* to the employees, poems or speeches relative to House gatherings, and certain employee documents, such as the 1888 letter of gratitude to the directors.

Thirdly, there are publicity documents. These include *agendas* for 1878, 1879, 1880, and most of the post-1885 period, three large albums of illustrated cards from 1896-1914, one carton of unclassified cards which are also primarily from this period, and one album of cards issued by the Bon Marché and by other stores in the pre-1896 period. There are also several House publications of the *Historique du Bon Marché* variety, large volumes prepared for international expositions, a scattered assortment of catalogues from the 1860s to the present day, a few fans and calendars from the 1850-1960 period, plus other diverse items of lesser importance.

The fourth set of documents comprehends various administrative records. There is an employee register from the 1872-1878 period that has recorded names and information on entering personnel. There are also two books from the early twentieth century on female sellers and five registers of *ouvriers* in the *ateliers de tapisserie* or auxiliaries for much of the 1870-1914 period. Other employee records include employee regulations from 1888 and the 1920s. In addition, there are such scattered administrative records as statistics for mail-order from the turn of the century, several books on salaries of the hierarchy in the latter part of the prewar period, and one accounting book from the early 1860s recording sales.

Finally, the "central archives" contain all sorts of diverse items. Among these one can find documents relative to funerals of the founders, documents and publications relative to House trips such as the celebration in honor of Boucicaut at Bellême in 1912, a dossier on aborted plans to establish a branch store in Abyssinia, scattered invoices from here and there, newspaper clippings or copies of articles about the Bon Marché (these proved quite useful), and various photographs of the founders and the store.

Outside the "central archives" I had access to three other sources of documents at the Bon Marché, all of which were

244   APPENDIX

extremely important. First, there were administrative records from the post-1887 period: records of AGOs and AGEs from 1888 to the present, of *Conseils Généraux* from 1891-1911, and of the Council of Administration from 1920-1934 (the House preferred that I did not review CAs from the more contemporary period). Secondly, there are thousands of employee dossiers preserved in the second-level basement of the store. Despite certain gaps (dossiers from the pre-1876 period in particular are not complete), these proved to be a bountiful find. Unfortunately, time limitations restricted me to a random sampling of several hundred dossiers. Thirdly, I had access to about a dozen boxes of catalogues issued from the 1860s to the 1940s that had been shipped to the Wissous warehouse of the store. By now these should be reunited with the "central archives."

There was, lastly, one other invaluable source for my study. This was the building itself—the original structure begun in 1869—and the great swarm of activity among employees, managers, and clientele that occurred during the three-quarters of a year that I passed at the House. No public archive could ever have provided a suitable substitute for this experience.

Bibliography

I. Archival Materials

A. Bon Marché Archives—see Appendix
B. Louvre Department Store Archives
   Ordres de Service 1875-1920
   Miscellaneous House publications
C. Bibliothèque Nationale, Paris
   Manuscrits Fonds Français:
   NAF10277, 10278—Emile Zola, Notes for *Au bonheur des dames*
   Estampes:
   Li mat. 30—Publicity documents
   Li mat. 30a—Publicity documents
   Recueils:
   4 WZ3264; 4 WZ3266; Fol. WZ211; Fol. WZ212—Bon Marché publicity documents
   4 WZ3230—Petit Saint-Thomas publicity documents
   8 WZ1716—A La Ménagerie publicity documents
D. Préfecture de Police, Paris
   Series Ba:
   Ba 152—Chambre Syndicale des Garçons de Magasins et Bureaux 1875-1885; Chambre Syndicale des Employés 1880-1883, 1899-1907; Chambre Syndicale Fédérale des Employés 1882
   Ba 153—Chambre Syndicale des Employés et Syndicat des Employés 1885-1904
   Ba 967—Boucicauts
   Ba 1389—Grèves de Nouveautés Employés
   Ba 1422—Employés de Commerce 1869-1895
   Ba 1431—Chambre Syndicale Magasin "garçons de"
E. Archives Nationales, Paris
   Series F12:
   F12 5095—Dossiers on M. and Mme. Boucicaut
   F12 5218—Dossier on Emile Morin
   F12 5253—Dossier on Ernest Ricois

Series 65AQ
    65AQ T20—Dossier on Bon Marché
    65AQ T151—Dossier on Printemps
F. Archives du Département de la Seine
    D 172—Publicity documents
    D 192—Publicity documents
    13 Eb/c—Publicity documents

II. Unpublished Materials

A. Theses

Lescure, A., "Naissance et développement des grands magasins parisiens de 1852 à 1882." Masters thesis, Faculté des Lettres et Sciences Humaines de Nanterre, 1970.

Pitts, Jesse R., "The Bourgeois Family and French Economic Retardation." Ph.D. dissertation, Harvard University, 1957.

B. Interviews

Cotillon, Mme. Paris, 1973
Gibault, François. Paris, 1974
Philippe, M. and Mme. Paris, 1974
Zédet, M. Paris, 1974

III. Newspapers and Magazines

A. Newspapers Consulted Regularly

Le Journal des Employés: 1 May to 1 November 1900
Le Ralliement des Employés: 1 June 1901 to 1 December 1909
La Revendication: 5 July 1888 to November 1896; January-November 1911

B. Newspapers and Magazines Consulted Intermittently for Advertisements, Articles, or Clippings

Le Citoyen	*Journal Vinicole*
L'Echo de Paris	*L'Illustration*
L'Eclair	*Le Monde Illustré*
L'Estafette	*Le Moniteur de l'Exposition de 1889*
L'Evénement	*Le Mot d'Ordre*
Le Figaro	*La Nation*
Galignani's Messenger	*Le National*
Le Gaulois	*New Orleans Times-Democrat*
Gil Blas	*Le Nouveau Monde*
Le Journal	*La Nouvelle France Chorale*

Les Nouvelles de Savoie
L'Orphéon
Le Panthéon de l'Industrie
Le Petit Economiste
La Petite République
Le Petit Journal
Le Petit Parisien
La Presse

Le Prolétariat
Le Rappel
La Réforme
Le Réveil de la Bourgogne
Le Siècle
Le Soir
L'Univers Illustré
La Vie Financière

IV. Books and Articles

Abegglen, James G. *The Japanese Factory*. Glencoe: The Free Press, 1958.

Ackerknecht, Erwin H. *A Short History of Psychiatry*. New York: Hafner, 1959.

Ambrière, Francis. *La vie secrète des grands magasins*. Paris: Les Oeuvres Français, 1938.

Annuaire-Almanach du commerce. 1845, 1852, 1863, 1875.

Appel, Joseph. *The Business Biography of John Wanamaker: Founder and Builder*. New York, 1930.

Arren, S. M. *La publicité lucrative et raisonnée*. Paris: Bibliothèque des Ouvrages Pratiques, 1909.

Artaud, A. *La question de l'employé en France*. Paris: Georges Roustan, 1909.

Auscher, R. *La législation fiscale applicable aux grands magasins et maisons à Succursales multiples*. Paris, 1923.

D'Avenel, Georges. *Le mécanisme de la vie moderne*, vol. 4. Paris: A. Colin, 1900-1905.

D'Avenel, Georges. "Le mécanisme de la vie moderne: les grands magasins." *Revue des Deux Mondes* (July 1894).

Avenel, Paul. *Les calicots*. Paris: Albert Delveau, 1866.

D'Azambuja, G. "Les grands magasins doivent-ils tuer les petits?" *La Science Sociale* (October 1901).

Baillarger, M. "Quelques observations pour servir à l'histoire de la médecine légale psychologique." *Annales Médico-Psychologiques* (April 1853).

Balzac, Honoré de. *La comédie humaine*, vol. 10: *Histoire de la grandeur et de la décadence de César Birotteau*. Paris: Furne, J. J. Dubochet, J. Hetzel, 1844.

Balzac, Honoré de. *La maison du chat-qui-pelote*. Paris: Garniers Frères, 1963.

Barnicoat, Constance. "French Women in Commerce." *The Eng-lishwoman* (May 1910).

Barral, Georges. "Une grande femme de bien." *Journal Barral* (January 1888).

Bendix, Reinhard. *Work and Authority in Industry*. New York: Harper and Row, 1963.

Berle, Adolph A., and Means, Gardiner C. *The Modern Corporation and Private Property*. New York: Macmillan, 1932.

Bernard, Joseph. *Du mouvement d'organisation de défense du petit commerce français*. Paris: A. Michalon, 1906.

Berr, Emile. "Les grands bazars." *Revue Bleue* (December 1889).

Besse, A. *L'employé de commerce et d'industrie*. Lyon: E. Nicola, 1901.

Beurdeley, P., and Drucker, G. "Les grands magasins et la liberté commerciale." *Les Annales Economiques* (5 May 1890).

Böhmert, Victor. *La participation aux bénéfices*. Paris: Chaix, 1888.

Boisgontier, Joseph. *Le syndicat des employés du commerce et de l'industrie*. Paris: Jouve, 1920.

Boismont, Brierre de. "Journaux italiens." *Annales Médico-Psychologiques* (July 1868).

Boissier, F., and Lachaux, G. "Contribution à l'étude de la kleptomanie." *Annales Médico-Psychologiques* (January 1894).

Boiteau, Paul. *Fortune publique et finances de la France*, vol. 1. Paris: Guillaumin, 1866.

Bollème, Geneviève. *Les almanachs populaires aux XVII et XVIII siècles*. Paris: Mouton, 1969.

"Au Bon Marché." *The Women's and Infants' Furnisher* (March 1906).

Bonneff, Léon and Maurice. *La classe ouvrière*. Paris: Publications de la "Guerre Sociale," 1911.

Bonnet, Pierre. *La commercialisation de la vie française du Premier Empire à nos jours*. Paris: Plon, 1929.

Boorstin, Daniel. *The Americans: The Democratic Experience*. New York: Random House, 1973.

Boudet, Jacques. *Le monde des affaires en France de 1830 à nos jours*. Paris: 1952.

Brandes, Stuart D. *American Welfare Capitalism 1880-1940*. Chicago: University of Chicago Press, 1976.

Brown, Sydney. *La peinture des métiers et des moeurs professionelles dans les romans de Zola*. Montpellier: 1928.

Buder, Stanley. *Pullman: An Experiment in Industrial Order and Community Planning 1880-1930*. New York: Oxford University Press, 1967.

Caldwell, T. B. "The Syndicat des Employés du Commerce et de l'Industrie (1888-1919): A Pioneer French Catholic Trade Union of White Collar Workers." *International Review of Social History* (1966).

Camp, Maxime du. *Paris, ses organes, ses fonctions et sa vie*, vol. 1, 2nd ed. Paris: Hachette, 1873.

Candille, M. "De la réalité au roman du Bon Marché de M. et Mme. Boucicaut au Bonheur des Dames de Zola." *Revue de l'Assistance Publique à Paris* (January-February 1953).

Caron, François. *Histoire de l'exploitation d'un grand réseau: la Compagnie du Chemin de Fer du Nord 1846-1937*. La Haye: Mouton, 1973.

Chambre de Commerce de Paris. *Statistique de l'industrie à Paris résultant de l'enquête faite par la Chambre de Commerce pour les années 1847-48*. Paris: Guillaumin, 1851.

Chambre de Commerce de Paris. *Statistique de l'industrie à Paris résultant de l'enquête faite par la Chambre de Commerce pour 1860*. Paris: 1864.

Champier, Victor. *Les anciens almanachs illustrés*. Paris: Deux Mondes, 1886.

Chandler, Alfred D., Jr., ed. *The Railroads*. New York: Harcourt, Brace and World, 1965.

Chandler, Alfred D., Jr., ed. *Strategy and Structure: Chapters in the History of the American Industrial Enterprise*. Cambridge: M.I.T. Press, 1962.

Chandler, Alfred D., Jr., ed. *The Visible Hand: The Managerial Revolution in American Business*. Cambridge: Harvard University Press, 1977.

Chevalier, Louis. *La formation de la population parisienne*. Paris: Presses Universitaires de France, 1950.

Clapham, J. H. *The Economic Development of France and Germany 1851-1914*. Cambridge: Cambridge University Press, 1936.

Cochran, Thomas C. "The Business Revolution." *American Historical Review* (December 1974).

Coornaert, Emile. *Les corporations en France avant 1784*. Paris: Les Editions Ouvrières, 1968.

Crossick, Geoffrey, ed. *The Lower Middle Class in Britain 1870-1914*. St. Martin's Press: New York, 1977.

Crouzet, François. "French Economic Growth in the Nineteenth Century Reconsidered." *History* (June 1974).

Cucheval-Clarigny and Flavien. *Etude sur le Bon Marché, Les Grandes Usines de Turgan*. Paris: Librairie des Dictionnaires, approx. 1890.

Dasquet, Marc. *Le Bon Marché*. Paris: Editions de Minuit, 1955.

Daugan, J. *Histoire et législation des patentes des grands magasins*. Rennes, 1902.

Daumard, Adeline. *La bourgeoisie parisienne de 1815 à 1848*. Paris: S.E.V.P.E.N., 1963.

Davis, Dorothy. *A History of Shopping*. London: Routledge and Kegan Paul, 1966.

Delloye, H.-L., ed. *Album revue de l'industrie parisienne*. Paris: Garnier Frères, 1844.

Delon, Pierre. *Les employés*. Paris: Editions Sociales, 1969.

Demolins, Edmond. *La question des grands magasins*. Paris: Firmin Didot, 1890.

Devinck, François-Jules. *Paris depuis un demi-siècle au point de vue commercial et industriel*. Paris: 1874

Devinck, François-Jules. *Pratique commerciale et recherches historiques sur la marche du commerce et de l'industrie*. Paris: Hachette, 1867.

Didier, Paul. *Les sociétés commerciales*. Paris: Presses Universitaires de France, 1965.

Dore, Ronald. *British Factory-Japanese Factory: The Origins of National Diversity in Industrial Relations*. Berkeley: University of California Press, 1973.

Dubuisson, Paul. *Les voleuses de grands magasins*. Paris: A. Storck, 1902.

Duclos, Léon. *Des transformations du commerce de détail en France au XIX ème siècle*. Paris: L. Boyer, 1902.

Dumuis, Solange, ed. *Le Printemps, cent ans de jeunesse*. Paris: 1965.

Dupouy, Roger. "De la kleptomanie." *Journal de Psychologie Normale et Pathologique*. 1905.

Durkheim, Emile. *The Elementary Forms of the Religious Life*. London: George Allen and Unwin, 1915.

Duveau, Georges. *La vie ouvrière en France sous le second empire*. Paris: Gallimard, 1946.

Emmet, Borris, and Jeuck, John. *Catalogues and Counters: A History of Sears, Roebuck and Company*. Chicago: University of Chicago Press, 1950.

Esquirol, E. *Des maladies mentales*. 2 vols. Paris: J.-B. Baillière, 1838.

Estang du Rusquec, Jean de l'. *De la réglementation du travail des employés de commerce*. Brest: 1912.

Feltaine, Edouard. *De la publicité commerciale*. Caen: 1903.

Ferry, John. *A History of the Department Store*. New York: Macmillan, 1960.

Fohlen, Claude. *L'industrie textile au temps du second empire*. Paris: Plon, 1965.

"Fortunes Made in Business: Aristide Boucicaut, the Bon Marché King." *London Society* (April 1879).

Foville, A. de. "Les causes générales des variations des prix au XIX siècle." *L'Economiste Français* (1 June 1878).

Franklin, Alfred. *La vie privée d'autrefois*, vol. 15. Paris: E. Plon Nourrit, 1894.

Fridenson, Patrick. *Histoire des usines Renault: la naissance de la grande entreprise 1898-1939*. Paris: Editions du Seuil, 1972.

Gailhard-Bancel, Maurice de. *Les anciennes corporations de métiers et la lutte contre la fraude dans le commerce et la petite industrie*. Paris: Bloud, 1912.

Gaillard, Jeanne. *Paris la ville, 1852-1870*. Paris: Editions Honoré Champion, 1977.

Galbraith, John Kenneth. *The New Industrial State*. Boston: Houghton Mifflin, 1967.

Galliot, Marcel. *La publicité à travers les âges*. Paris: Editions Hommes et Techniques, 1955.

Garrigues, Henri. *Les grands magasins de nouveautés et le petit commerce de détail*. Paris: Librairie Nouvelle de Droit et de Jurisprudence, 1898.

Gellately, Robert. *The Politics of Economic Despair: Shopkeepers and German Politics 1890-1914*. London: Sage Publications, 1974.

Gerschenkron, Alexander. "A rejoinder" and "Second Rejoinder." *Explorations in Entrepreneurial History* (May 1954).

Gerschenkron, Alexander. "Social Attitudes, Entrepreneurship, and Economic Development." *Explorations in Entrepreneurial History* (October 1953).

Gerschenkron, Alexander. "Some Further Notes on 'Social Attitudes, Entrepreneurship and Economic Development.' " *Explorations in Entrepreneurial History* (December 1954).

Gerth, H. H., and Mills, C. Wright, ed. *From Max Weber: Essays in Sociology*. New York: Oxford University Press, 1946; paperback, 1958.

Gibb, George Sweet and Knowlton, Evelyn. *History of Standard Oil of New Jersey*, vol. 2: *The Resurgent Years 1911-1927*. New York: Harper Brothers, 1956.

Gibbons, Herbert Adams. *John Wanamaker*. 2 vols. New York: Harper Brothers, 1926.

Gide, Charles. *Cours d'économie politique*. Paris: Librairie de la Société du Recueil J.-B. Sirey, 1909.

Giedion, Sigfried. *Space, Time and Architecture*. Cambridge: Harvard University Press, 1959.

Giffard, Pierre. *Paris sous la troisième république: les grands bazars*. Paris: Victor Havard, 1882.

Gilman, Nicholas Paine. *Profit Sharing Between Employer and Employee*. Boston: Houghton, Mifflin, 1889.

Girard, M. H. "Kleptomanie." *Gazette Médicale de Paris* (November 1845).

Grand-Carteret, John. *Les almanachs français*. Paris: J. Alisie, 1896.

Grand-Carteret, John. *Vieux papiers, vieilles images*. Paris: A. Storck, 1902.

Grand dictionnaire universel du XIX ème siècle, Deuxième supplément.

La grande encyclopédie inventaire raisonné des sciences des lettres et des arts. S.v. "Bon Marché (Magasins du)." Paris: 1886-1902.

Les grands magasins à Paris, à Berlin et en Amérique, leur organisation commerciale. Paris: Berger Levrault, 1913.

"Les grands magasins de Paris: Le Bon Marché." *Revue pour les Français* (25 May 1911).

Harriman, Margaret Case. *And the Price is Right*. Cleveland: The World Publishing Company, 1958.

Hatzfeld, Henri. *Du pauperisme à la sécurité sociale 1850-1940*. Paris: Armand Colin, 1971.

Honoré, M. F. *Les employés de commerce à Paris au point de vue social*. Paris: 1895.

Hower, Ralph. *History of Macy's of New York 1858-1919: Chapters in the Evolution of the Department Store*. Cambridge: Harvard University Press, 1964.

Hungerford, Edward. *The Romance of a Great Store*. New York: Robert M. McBride, 1922.

Janet, Pierre. "La kleptomanie et la dépression mentale." *Journal de Psychologie Normale et Pathologique* (1911).

Jarry, Paul. *Les magasins de nouveautés: histoire rétrospective et anecdotique*. Paris: André Barry, 1948.

"La journée d'une demoiselle de magasin." *Lectures Pour Tous* (1907).

Juhel, Etienne. *La patente des grands magasins*. Caen: 1907.

Juquelier, P. and Vinchon, Jean. "L'Histoire de la kleptomanie." *Revue de Psychiatrie et de Psychologie Expérimentale* (1914).

Kindleberger, Charles. *Economic Growth in France and Britain 1851-1950*. Cambridge: Harvard University Press, 1964.

Kuznets, Simon. "Notes on the Pattern of U.S. Economic Growth." In *The Reinterpretation of American Economic History*, ed. Robert Fogel. New York: Harper and Row, 1971.

Lacassagne, A. "Les vols à l'étalage et dans les grands magasins." *Revue de l'Hypnotisme et de la Psychologie Physiologique* (September 1896).

Lainé, André. *Les demoiselles de magasin à Paris*. Paris: Arthur Rousseau, 1911.

Lagarrigue, Louis. *Cent ans de transports en commun dans la région parisienne*. Paris: 1956.

Lambert, Richard S. *The Universal Provider*. London: George G. Harrap, 1938.

Landes, David. "French Business and the Businessman: A Social and Cultural Analysis." In *Modern France*, ed. Edward Mead Earle. Princeton: Princeton University Press, 1951.

Landes, David. "French Entrepreneurship and Industrial Growth in the Nineteenth Century." *Journal of Economic History* (May 1949).

Landes, David. "Religion and Enterprise: The Case of the French Textile Industry." In *Enterprise and Entrepreneurs in Nineteenth and Twentieth Century France*, ed. Edward C. Carter. Baltimore: The Johns Hopkins University Press, 1976.

Landes, David. *The Unbound Prometheus*. Cambridge: Cambridge University Press, 1969.

Lasègue, Charles. "Le vol aux étalages." *L'Union Médicale* (December 1879).

Laudet, Fernand. *La Samaritaine: le génie et la générosité de deux grands commerçants*. Paris: Dunod, 1933.

Laver, James. *Taste and Fashion from the French Revolution to the Present Day*. London: George G. Harrap, 1945.

Lavergne, A. de and Henry, L. Paul. *La richesse de la France: fortune et revenus privés*. Paris: Marcel Rivière, 1908.

Legrand du Saulle. *Les hystériques*. Paris: J.-B. Baillière, 1883.

Leroy-Beaulieu, Paul. "Les grands magasins universels et les petits détaillants." *L'Economiste Français* (December 1875).

Leroy-Beaulieu, Paul. *Précis d'économie politique*. Paris: Ch. Delagrave, 1888.

Leroy-Beaulieu, Paul. *Traité théorique et pratique d'économie politique*, vol. 1. Paris: Guillaumin, 1896.

Leroy-Beaulieu, Paul. *Le travail des femmes au XIX ème siècle*. Paris: Charpentier, 1873.

Letulle, M. "Voleuses honnêtes ébauche médico-légale." *Gazette Médicale de Paris* (October 1887).

Levasseur, E. *Histoire du commerce de la France*, vol. 2. Paris: Librairie Nouvelle de Droit et de Jurisprudence, 1904.

Lévy-Leboyer, Maurice. "La croissance économique en France au XIXe siècle. Résultats préliminaires." *Annales E.S.C.* (July-August 1968).

Lévy-Leboyer, Maurice. "Innovation and Business Strategies in Nineteenth and Twentieth Century France." In *Enterprise and Entrepreneurs in Nineteenth and Twentieth Century France*, ed. Edward C. Carter. Baltimore: The Johns Hopkins Press, 1976.

Lunier, L. Review of "Observations de folie instantanée chez des personnes inculpées de vol" by Boys de Loury. *Annales Médico-Psychologiques* (July 1848).

Lunier, Charles. "Des vols aux étalages." *Annales Médico-Psychologiques* (September 1880).

McBride, Theresa M. "A Woman's World: Department Stores and the Evolution of Women's Employment, 1870-1920." *French Historical Studies* (Fall 1978).

MacOrlan, Pierre. *Le Printemps*. Paris: Gallimard, 1930.

Magnan, V. *Recherches sur les centres nerveux*. Paris: G. Masson, 1893.

Marc, C.C.H. *De la folie considérée dans ses rapports avec les questions médico-judiciaires*. 2 vols. Paris: J.-B. Baillière, 1840.

Maroussem, P. du. "Les grands magasins tels qu'ils sont." *Revue d'Economie Politique* (1893).

Marsh, Robert M., and Mannari, Hiroshi. *Modernization and the Japanese Factory*. Princeton: Princeton University Press, 1976.

Martin Saint-Léon, Etienne. *Histoire des corporations de métiers*. Paris: 1922; reprinted. Geneva: Slatkine-Megariotis, 1976.

Martin Saint-Léon, Etienne. *Le petit commerce parisien*. Paris: Victor Lecoffre, 1911.

Mataja, V. "Les grands magasins et le petit commerce." *Revue d'Economie Politique* (May-June 1891).

Mercillon, H. *La rémuneration des employés*. Paris: Armand Colin, 1955.

Mermet, Emile. *La publicité en France, histoire et jurisprudence*. Paris: 1879.

Michel, G. "Le commerce en grands magasins." *Revue des Deux Mondes* (January 1892).

Mills, C. Wright. *White Collar: The American Middle Classes*. London: Oxford University Press, 1951.

Ministère de l'Intérieur. *Enquête de la commission extraparlementaire sur les associations ouvrières*, vol. 1. Paris: 1883.

Ministère du Commerce. *Annuaire statistique de la France*. Paris: 1882, 1890.

Miramas, André. "Une entreprise séculaire: le Louvre." *Transmondia* (1962).

Moride, Pierre. *Les maisons à succursales multiples en France et à l'étranger*. Paris: F. Alcan, 1913.

Nelson, Daniel. *Managers and Workers: Origins of the New Factory System in the United States, 1880-1920*. Madison: University of Wisconsin Press, 1975.

Nogaro, B., and Oualid, W. *L'évolution du commerce, du crédit et des transports depuis cent cinquante ans*. Paris: Félix Alcan, 1914.

Nystrom, Paul. *Economics of Retailing*. 2 vols., revised edition. New York: Roland Press, 1930.

Office du Travail. *Les Associations Professionelles ouvrières*, vols. 2, 4. Paris: 1901, 1904.

Office du Travail. *La Petite industrie (salaires et durée du travail)*: le vêtement à Paris. Paris: 1896.

Ozanne, Robert. *A Century of Labor-Management Relations at McCormick and International Harvester*. Madison: University of Wisconsin Press, 1967.

Palmade, Guy. *Capitalisme et capitalistes français au XIX ème siècle*. Paris: Armand Colin, 1961.

Parent-Lardeur, Françoise. *Les demoiselles de magasin*. Paris: Les Editions Ouvrières, 1970.

Paris comique, revue amusante. Paris: Chez Aubert, 1844.

Pasdermadjian, Hrant. *The Department Store: Its Origins, Evolution and Economics*. London: Newman Books, 1954.

Passama, Paul. *Formes nouvelles de concentration industrielle*. Paris: Bibliothèque d'Economie Politique et de Sociologie, 1910.

Perrot, Marguerite. *Le mode de vie des familles bourgeoises 1873-1953*. Paris: Armand Colin, 1961.

Perroux, François. "Prises de vues sur la croissance de l'économie française, 1780-1950." In *Income and Wealth*, vol. 5, ed. Simon Kuznets. London: Bowes and Bowes, 1955.

Pinkney, David. *Napoleon III and the Rebuilding of Paris*. Princeton: Princeton University Press, 1958.

Pitts, Jesse. "Continuity and Change in Bourgeois France." In *In Search of France*, ed. Stanley Hoffmann et al. New York: Harper and Row; Harper Torchbooks, 1965.

Porter, Glenn, and Livesay, Harold. *Merchants and Manufacturers: Studies in the Changing Structure of Nineteenth-Century Marketing*. Baltimore: The Johns Hopkins Press, 1971.

Renaudin, E. "Journaux allemands." *Annales Médico-Psychologiques* (April 1855).

Resseguie, Harry E. "Alexander Turney Stewart and the Development of the Department Store, 1823-1876." *Business History Review* (Autumn 1965).

Resseguie, Harry E. "The Decline and Fall of the Commercial Empire of A. T. Stewart." *Business History Review* (Autumn 1962).

Roy, Joseph-Antoine. *Histoire de la famille Schneider et du Creusot.* Paris: Marcel Rivière, 1962.

Rudolph, Lloyd I., and Hoeber, Susanne. *The Modernity of Tradition.* Chicago: University of Chicago Press, 1967.

Saint-Martin, André. *Les grands magasins.* Paris: Librairie Nouvelle de Droit et de Jurisprudence, 1900.

Saussure, Raymond de. "The Influence of the Concept of Monomania on French Medico-Legal Psychiatry (from 1825 to 1840)." *Journal of the History of Medicine* (1946).

Sayous, André. "Le mouvement de concentration dans le commerce de détail." In *La concentration des entreprises industrielles et commerciales,* ed. Arthur Fontaine. Paris: Félix Alcan, 1913.

Schuwer, Philippe. *Histoire de la publicité.* Lausanne: Editions Rencontre, 1965.

Simond, Charles. *Paris de 1800 à 1900,* vol. 2. Paris: Plon, 1900.

Stearns, Peter. *Paths to Authority: The Middle Class and the Industrial Labor Force in France, 1820-1848.* Urbana: University of Illinois Press, 1978.

Sutcliffe, Anthony. *The Autumn of Central Paris.* London: Edward Arnold, 1970.

Tönnies, Ferdinand. *Community and Society (Gemeinschaft und Gesellschaft).* New York: Harper and Row; Harper Torchbooks, 1963.

Tournouer, Henri. *Silhouettes Bellêmoises.* Alençon: 1907.

Trempé, Rolande. *Les mineurs de Carmaux, 1848-1914.* 2 vols. Paris: Les Editions Ouvrières, 1971.

Tudesq, André-Jean. *Les grands notables en France, 1840-1849.* Paris: Presses Universitaires de France, 1964.

Twyman, Robert. *History of Marshall Field and Co. 1852-1906.* Philadelphia: University of Pennsylvania Press, 1954.

Uzanne, Octave. *Les modes de Paris.* Paris: Société Française d'Editions d'Art, 1898.

Valmy-Baisse, J. *Les grands magasins.* Paris: Gallimard, 1927.

Vanier, Henriette. *La mode et ses métiers: frivolités et luttes des classes, 1830-1870.* Paris: Armand Colin, 1960.

Vial, Jean. *L'industrialisation de la sidérurgie française 1814-1864*. Paris: Mouton, 1967.

Vogel, Ezra F. *Japan as Number One: Lessons for America*. Cambridge: Harvard University Press, 1979.

Vouters, Henry. *Le petit commerce contre les grands magasins et les coopératives de consommation*. Paris: Arthur Rousseau, 1910.

Weber, Eugen. *Peasants into Frenchmen*. Stanford: Stanford University Press, 1976.

Weber, William. *Music and the Middle Class*. New York: Holmes and Meier, 1975.

Wendt, Lloyd, and Kogan, Herman. *Give the Lady What She Wants*. Chicago: Rand McNally, 1952.

D'Ydewalle, Charles. *Au Bon Marché: de la boutique au grand magasin*. Paris: Plon, 1965.

Zeldin, Theodore. *France 1848-1945*, vol. 1. Oxford: Clarendon Press, 1973.

Zola, Emile. *Au bonheur des dames*. Paris: Charpentier, 1883; Paris: Livre de Poche, 1971.

Index